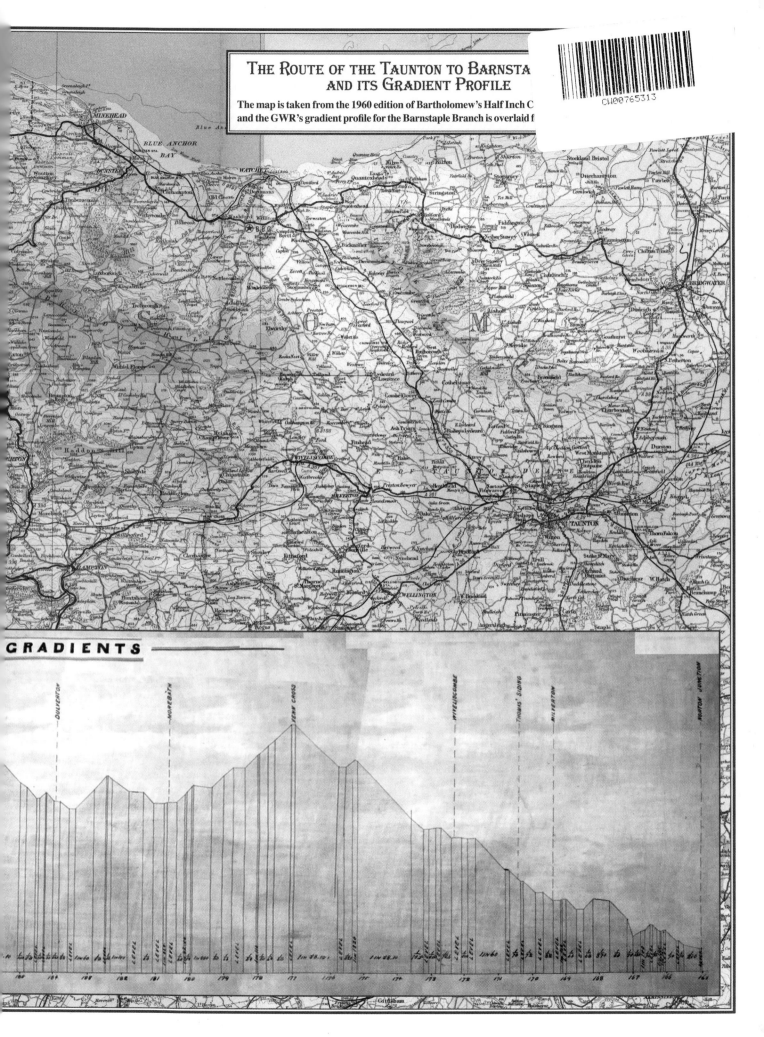

The Route of the Taunton to Barnsta[ple]
and its Gradient Profile

The map is taken from the 1960 edition of Bartholomew's Half Inch C[...]
and the GWR's gradient profile for the Barnstaple Branch is overlaid f[...]

GRADIENTS

THE
TAUNTON TO
BARNSTAPLE LINE

A HISTORY OF THE
DEVON & SOMERSET RAILWAY
VOLUME 2

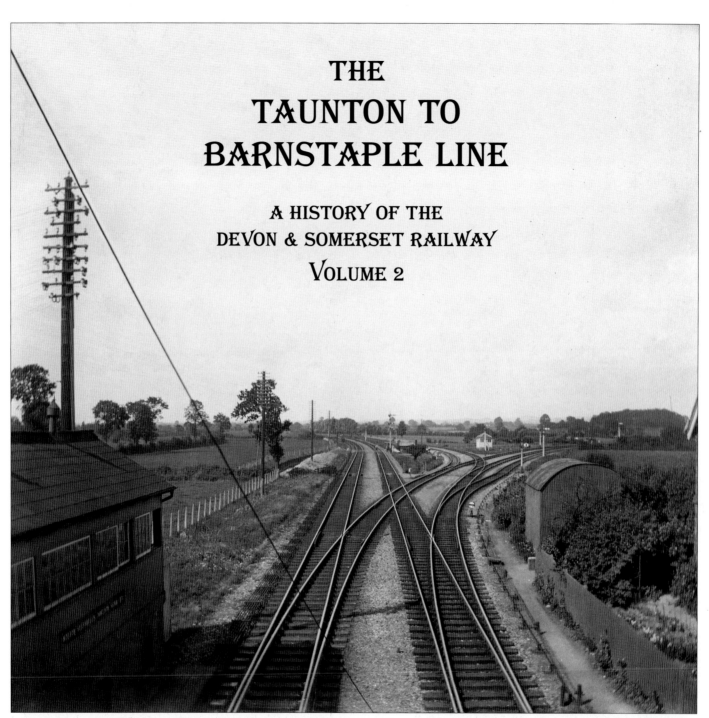

Norton Fitzwarren Junction circa 1931. On the left are the twin tracks of the main line to Exeter and beyond, whilst on the right the double line curving away north formed the start of the branch to Minehead, which became single a little further on. In between is the start of the Barnstaple Branch, which also became single track after a short distance at this date but that had been doubled all the way to Milverton by the end of the decade. The first Norton Fitzwarren Junction Signal Box, by this date reduced to ground frame status, stands between the Barnstaple and Minehead lines, with its 1891 replacement partially in view in the left foreground. A slightly different aspect of this scene can be found on page 409. *E. Wallis Collection, courtesy Kevin Robertson*

FRONT COVER: Dulverton station looking west towards Barnstaple in August 1963. *Neil Parkhouse collection*

BACKGROUND: The stonework is a close-up of the goods shed at Barnstaple Victoria Road. *Author*

REAR COVER: No. 7337 ambles away from Morebath Junction with an Up Barnstaple Junction to Taunton service on 9th June 1962. The signal box can just be seen to the right of the line, with the Exe Valley Branch heading off to the left. *Mark B. Warburton, courtesy Kevin Robertson*

A typical Taunton to Barnstaple line train of the 1950s and early 1960s, an ex-GWR '43XX' Class 'Mogul' at the head of a four-coach train, leaves Wiveliscombe bound for Taunton. The locomotive has just passed the Wiveliscombe Advanced Starting signal and note the GWR style milepost (172¼ miles from Paddington) on the right. St. Andrews church is prominent in the left background, whilst Wiveliscombe station is out of sight round the curve to the left. In the left foreground is part of Ashbeers Farm, with a McCormick International tractor parked in the field. *Michael J. Fox, courtesy Rail Archive Stephenson*

Published by LIGHTMOOR PRESS
© Lightmoor Press & Freddie Huxtable 2017
Designed by Neil Parkhouse

www.devonandsomersetrailway.co.uk

British Library Cataloguing-in-Publication Data. A catalogue record for this book is available from the British Library.

ISBN: 9781911038 31 3

LIGHTMOOR PRESS
Unit 144B, Lydney Trading Estate, Harbour Road, Lydney, Gloucestershire GL15 5EJ
www.lightmoor.co.uk
Lightmoor Press is an imprint of Black Dwarf Lightmoor Publications Ltd

Printed in Poland
www.lfbookservices.co.uk

THE TAUNTON TO BARNSTAPLE LINE

A HISTORY OF THE DEVON & SOMERSET RAILWAY

VOLUME 2:
THE ROUTE, STATIONS AND SIGNALLING

FREDDIE HUXTABLE

Ex-GWR Class '63XX' 2-6-0 No. 6340 starts away from Bishops Nympton & Molland station with the 10.10am summer Saturday's only service from Ilfracombe to Cardiff on 7th July 1962. These holiday trains were very much a feature of the line and the carriages would be joined at Taunton by the stock of a similar working from Minehead to Cardiff. From the late 1930s onwards, the Churchward 'Moguls' were the most commonly seen motive power on the old Devon & Somerset Railway and Taunton shed had a regular complement of between five and eight of these engines for working services over the route. No. 6340 was a 63B engine from April 1961 until withdrawal, which occurred within two weeks of this picture being taken. *Peter W. Gray*

Contents – Volume 2
The Route, Stations and Signalling

INTRODUCTION TO VOLUME 2

When I commenced writing the history of the Taunton to Barnstaple line (otherwise known as the Devon & Somerset Railway), little did I expect it to be two volumes or, indeed, the enthusiasm with which Volume 1 would be received when published. Thank you to all those who have acquired a copy. I am delighted that the hours of research has filled that gap in the history of the railways of Devon and Somerset, which was always the aim. However, whilst Volume 1 gave the background history of the line, its building and demise, it served mainly to whet the appetite and set the scene. Volume 2 was always intended to take matters on further and illustrate the D&SR in greater detail, essential for the railway enthusiast and modeller, as well as for those living locally who retain an interest in or deep affection for the old line.

However, I now have a confession. When discussing the production of Volume 2 with Neil Parkhouse of Lightmoor Press at the end of January 2017, it became clear to both of us that the amount of material and photographs justified a third volume. So whilst this second part of the series presents a detailed description of the railway, its stations and signalling, the operation of the line over the ninety-three years of its existence will be covered in Volume 3, along with the locomotives and rolling stock that were commonly used. This final volume will also include details of accidents that occurred on the line, events directly connected with it and personal recollections from those who worked on the route or who used it regularly.

I hope this does not disappoint too many devotees of the line, in that they will have a further wait for the full story to be told. Everything is written but it takes time to edit, typeset, design and print, as well as having to fit in with the Lightmoor schedule. It is also worth noting that this 42^1/$_4$ mile railway, which traversed a highly scenic part of the West Country and thus attracted the attention of a number of talented railway photographers, has previously had very little written about it, so the chance to cover it properly once and for all – in three volumes rather than two – was one not to be ignored.

I am also pleased to report that the first volume has inspired Geoffrey Bray and his friends Mike Kick and Sam Conolly to create a virtual journey down the line on computer. The project started as low key filming by drone along part of the route, coupled with the use of still photographs to illustrate a trip down the line (as in Chapters 6, 7 and 8 of this volume). Following discussions, this project has blossomed; the plan is now to produce a commercial black and white film with actors, to tell a story of the towns and key features, and some of the history of the line. It is hoped that will be on sale as a DVD, with the profits donated to charity. The chosen charity is Hope for Tomorrow, of which Geoffrey is a patron, and their website is www.hopefortomorrow.org.uk for those interested in knowing more.

I would like to point out that the use of 'Devon & Somerset Railway (or D&SR)' and 'Taunton to Barnstaple line' mean the same thing to me and are used interchangeably in the script. In reality, very few people in later years ever referred to it as the Devon & Somerset Railway but I quite like the original name, especially as it links my two favourite counties.

Every effort has been made to accurately record and reproduce my research. It is, I suspect, inevitable there will be some errors, minor I hope but they are solely my responsibility. However, I shall be grateful to anyone who points out any such errors or indeed is able to provide further information on the railway and its operations. If there is a second edition any need for revision or amendment will be taken into account. Any references to time in this book are based on the 12-hour clock throughout. BR adopted the Continental 24-hour clock in 1965, just one year before the line closed. Please note too that the chapter, appendices and page numbers all follow on from the first volume and will continue in to the third. This final volume will also then include a full index to all three.

For anyone who has comments, information or feedback they would like to pass on, I can be contacted direct via the website I have set up for the line: www.devonandsomersetrailway.co.uk

Freddie Huxtable
Ealing, London, 2017

The prime purpose of this second volume is to present a picture of the line and its stations as it existed in the 1950s and '60s, albeit with some earlier illustrations, and details of changes and worked carried out at the various locations over the years of the railway's existence. As such, whilst there is some variety in the motive power to be seen, the ex-GWR 'Mogul' 2-6-0s held sway over the route throughout the last decade or so of its life. Taunton shed had a number of these on their allocation, many of which were regular performers on the route, and we shall become intimately acquainted with several of the class through these pages. No. 7337 here clearly displays the Taunton 83B shedplate on its smokebox door, as it leaves Milverton with a four-coach Down train on 20th July 1963. Note the Intermediate Starting signal with its lattice metal post. *Peter W. Gray*

Acknowledgements

This now series of books would not have been possible without significant help from many people. Following publication of the first volume, a number of people came forward to provide further research information and materials. Thus, in this regard, I would like first of all to thank John Jenkins, Jonathan Lomas, Charlie Fennemore, Philip Cox, Geoffrey Bray and Mike Kick. Additionally, Blake Patterson, Richard Gibbs, Brian Conyard and Mike Roach have very kindly made further photographs available for Volumes 2 and 3.

Special thanks should also go to Ian Coleby, author of *The Minehead Branch 1848-1971* (Lightmoor Press 2006 & 2011) for his excellent work on the station track plans that appear throughout this volume, which I am sure the modellers amongst us will be delighted to see.

The list as now follows is as given in the first volume but I felt it only right, as some folk may only purchase this second part of the series, to repeat that *verbatim* here. Where possible and appropriate, I have also credited those mentioned in the body of the book.

So my thanks go to the railwaymen whose stories enthralled me – Jim Elson (signalman), Brindley Prust (driver), Dennis Bending (parcels), Harry Kirkland (fireman), Melvyn Baker (fireman), John Howard (signal & telegraph engineer) and Mrs Joyce Stone (widow of Eric Stone, signalman). Other authors, especially Ian Coleby, who gave me such great guidance and encouragement at the start, but also Sue Farrington, Richard Derry, Richard Antliff, Mike Christensen OBE (who did a sterling job reviewing and providing technical input on the signalling chapter), Amyas Crump and Kevin Robertson. My long-standing friend Thomas Hayes, who amongst other things explored the closed Dulverton station with me in the late 1960s and walked those parts of the line with me that could be traversed in the 2007-15 period. My long-standing friend Martin Bending, for promising to finish the book if I didn't and who provided useful guidance on railway matters and modelling. Special thanks are due to Lady Arran for agreeing to write the foreword, thereby creating that link between her family and the origins of the railway with my book. Credit is due to Karina Varma for designing the website (www.devonandsomersetrailway.co.uk) I am using to promote this and the following volume, as well as furthering knowledge of the line. Also to my mother, for her memories and Alison for her patience.

The photographers and those who have supplied pictures: Peter Gray, Peter Barnfield, John Spencer Gilks, the late Owen Mogg (Peter Triggs), the late Peter Treloar, Tim Stephens, Roy Denison, Gordon Bray, James G. Tawse, Stephen Derek, Hugh Davies, Roger Joanes, the late Michael J. Fox (Brian Stephenson), the late Ron Lumber (David Mitchell), Colin Caddy, David Burgess, Stephen Linney, Richard Antliff, David Burgess and John Alsop.

The modellers: Chris Nelder, Martin Bird, Mark Henshaw, Derek Garrett, Tony Hiscock, Douglas Grindlay, Jose Kimber, the Rev'd Canon Brian Arman, Maurice Sandell, Brian Morgan, Ian Harrison, Martin Tester and Norman Solomans.

Those who have helped generally, such as William Hancock, Wesley Wyatt, Graham Robertson, John B. Perkin, Ian Harrison, Mary Proffitt, Toni & Francois Jones, Rob Doidge, Derek Goodwin, Ken Morrish of the Grosvenor Church, Max Perry, Sylvia Manley, Stephen Jarvis, Mr & Mrs Anning (Venn Cross, goods shed), Mr & Mrs Wilson (Venn Cross booking office), Roddy Kane (Bathealton Tunnel) and Dr Sarah Blackburn (Dulverton goods shed), and also once again not forgetting my English teacher, Hilary Binding, who sadly died in December 2014 before seeing the publication of this work.

Those who have helped at a number of museums: Peter Treharne, at the West Somerset Railway Museum, Blue Anchor; Jenny Yendall, Alison Ricks, Andy Hedges and Phil Tonkin at the South Molton Museum; Ruth Spiers at the North Devon Museum, Barnstaple; North Devon Athenaeum, Barnstaple; Judith Elsdon and Patrick at Tiverton Museum; Elaine Arthurs at STEAM, the Museum of the Great Western Railway at Swindon; Laurence Waters of the Great Western Society at Didcot; Braunton Museum; Jan Ross OBE of the Dulverton Heritage Centre; and David Bird and others of the Railway Correspondence & Travel Society.

Significant research was carried out at the National Archives, Kew, the National Railway Museum, York, the Wiltshire Records Office at Chippenham, Somerset Archives & Local Studies at Taunton, at the Barnstaple Athenaeum and North Devon Records Office. The National Railway Museum proved invaluable for research and access, and the use of images from its photographic collection. Also Mr Warwick Burton of the Brunel University, Mowat Collection (3 Fairway, Clifton, York, YO30 5QA), the Lens of Sutton Association; Roger Carpenter; Robert Blencowe; Stephen Edge and David Holmes of the West Somerset Railway Association Journal; the Industrial Railway Society; and the Lynton & Barnstaple Railway and its associated magazine.

I am also indebted to the Signalling Record Society, the Great Western Study Group (and its Yahoo group members) and the Great Western Society, in particular Adrian Knowles.

Finally, I must specifically thank Lightmoor Press for taking on this project so enthusiastically and to Neil Parkhouse in particular for guiding a novice author professionally through the requirements of a publisher. He has further enhanced the book with some unique photographs from his own collection and given much assistance with additional information for many of the captions. I am grateful too to Ian Pope of Lightmoor Press, who compiled the introductory map overleaf.

Whilst every effort has been made to make the appropriate credits, it is not the intention to miss out anyone, so if it transpires there is an omission please let the author or publisher know so the matter can be put right in the future. Every effort has been made to identify and credit images wherever possible. Where there is no credit it will be the author's own, where it belongs to a collection this too is noted. Should an error have occurred this is entirely unintentional and if notified will be corrected in any subsequent edition.

Postscript: Shortly before this volume went to print, I received the very sad news that renowned West Country railway photographer Peter W. Gray had passed away. Peter's work is well known from the numerous railway books to which he has contributed and the many slide shows that he gave over the years. Indeed, he was kind enough to give my mother and I a personal slide show of the Taunton to Barnstaple line in the early days of my research – a wonderful 'journey' along the route from which he let me choose a generous selection of pictures for this series of books. By fortuitous coincidence, it transpires that several of the photographs that introduce this second volume were taken by Peter (along with many more within) and I can only say how sorry I am personally that he will not now see how much his art has enhanced this history of the Devon & Somerset Railway, a line he knew well.

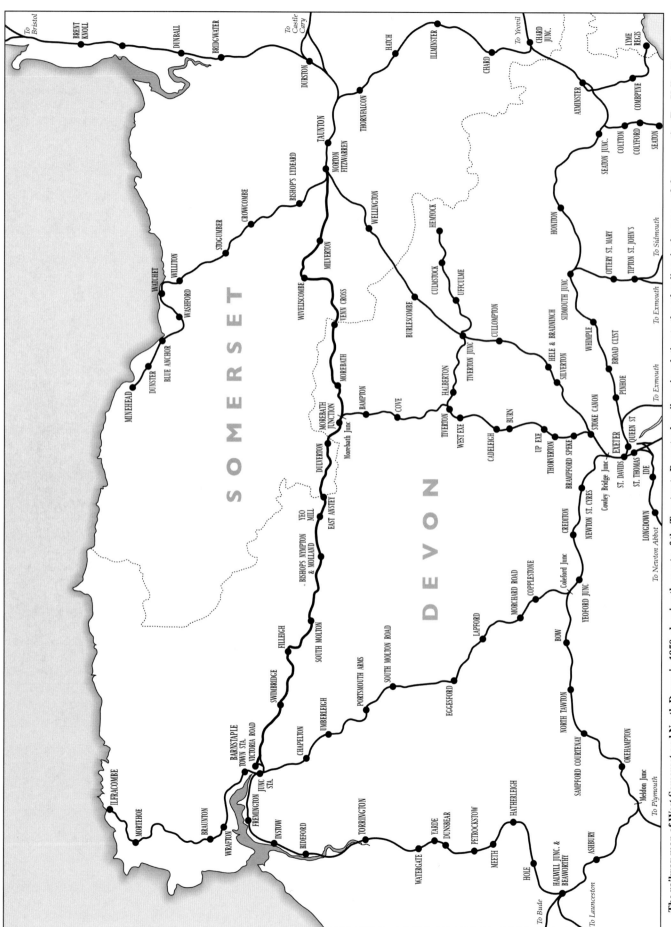

The railway map of West Somerset and North Devon in 1950, showing the route of the Taunton to Barnstaple railway in relation to the other lines in the area and the connecting Exe Valley Branch.

Chapter 6

A Description of the Line and its Stations Part 1: Taunton to Wiveliscombe

A view from the No. 3 bay platform at the west end of Taunton on 11th August 1962, with Class '43XX' 2-6-0 No. 7326 awaiting departure with a Barnstaple train. In the centre background, 'Hall' Class 4-6-0 No. 4917 *Crosswood Hall* approaches with a Newton Abbot to Bradford working. *Peter W. Gray*

We begin this volume with the first of three chapters that will describe the line by means of an imaginary journey circa 1956, before Barnstaple Victoria Road station was closed to passenger services in 1960. On arrival at each station, an outline of the key features is given, along with the development of that location. There will also be specific focus on certain buildings and structures at selected locations. The route and its surviving buildings as they are today are featured in Chapter 5 of Volume 1.

A line of this nature, passing through the varied countryside of West Somerset and North Devon, was inevitably going to have some significant engineering works in terms of bridges, viaducts and tunnels. It is therefore appropriate to also look closely at these features as we proceed on our journey, along with other interesting buildings and structures which the line possessed and where

information about them has been found. It is disappointing that more plans and related information have not been sourced but it is hoped that, if such items ever come to light, they can be incorporated in any future edition. These secondary structures, too, are given due consideration in turn as our journey reaches them. An indication of the construction methods and materials used on the line is made in passing in Volume 1. However, for a more detailed account of tunnel, bridge and building construction reference should be made to Appendix 3 of Volume 1, which summarises the specifications attached to the initial contractors contract between the Devon & Somerset Railway (D&SR) and Messrs William and John Pickering. Although this contract was eventually rescinded before Reed took over as contractor, it provides an insight into the requirements and quality of work expected.

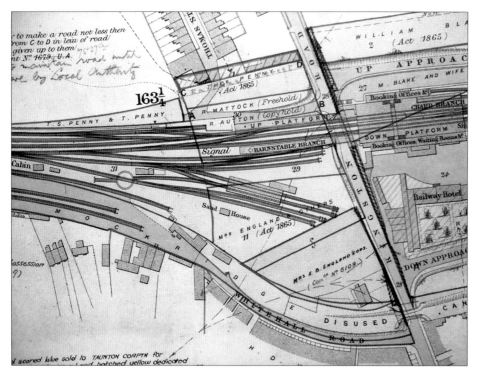

There were four tunnels on the line – Bathealton, Nightcott, Venn Cross and Castle Hill or Filleigh. The deep 22 yard-long bridge on the Dulverton side of East Anstey is not regarded as a tunnel, based on the British Railways (BR) *Regional Appendix 1960* rules and regulations, although early engineers' reports refer to five tunnels on the line with that at Anstey being the additional one. There were two substantial viaducts, Tone and Filleigh, which were located close to the two main tunnels, Bathealton and Castle Hill respectively. Both viaducts were built to a similar design.

When the line was built throughout to Barnstaple it was constructed at almost a bare minimum in terms of cost and facilities, with just three crossing places and a temporary station at Barnstaple. In 1876,

the number of crossing places was doubled, with loops being added at Morebath, East Anstey and Bishops Nympton & Molland. Milverton subsequently was also provided with a loop in 1880. The remaining stations also eventually followed suit, with Swimbridge in 1904 and Venn Cross in 1905 but Filleigh had to wait for its loop until 1937.

In reviewing the track plans with particular reference to the various goods yards at the smaller stations, a similar pattern emerges. A simple layout was originally provided, often a headshunt reached by a facing point off the running line and two lines that 'kicked-back' from this, one into a goods shed and the other a mileage siding. Most goods yards were on the Down side, with Wiveliscombe, Filleigh and Swimbridge being exceptions to this. Dulverton had a yard on both sides in later years but on the Up side only when the line opened.

Readers should note that Chapter 9 on Signalling complements the developments mentioned in this section, as does Chapter 3 of Volume 1.

TAUNTON

Taunton was a large station and is not an integral part of the railway to Barnstaple, merely the starting point. The intention therefore is not to cover it in detail here but merely to set the scene. Further information on the station and its history can be found in a variety of other publications.

Taunton station was built by the Bristol & Exeter Railway (B&ER) and opened on 1st July 1842. The original Brunel one-sided station was replaced in August 1868 by a more conventional layout, with an overall roof. D&SR trains used the main station platforms until a designated

ABOVE: A portion of a GWR 2-chain survey of circa 1887, showing the west end of Taunton station as rebuilt by the broad gauge Bristol & Exeter Railway in 1868, along with the 'Barnstable [sic] Branch' bay added (also by the B&ER) in 1871. The GWR absorbed the B&ER in 1876, so this would have been the first detailed survey of their new acquisition. Note that there was no separate bay for Minehead Branch trains at this date. *Courtesy National Archives*

RIGHT: On 30th May 1964, '63XX' Class 'Mogul' No. 7337 stands at Taunton's Platform No. 8 with the 2.24pm from Barnstaple. In the left, background BR 'Standard' Class '3' 2-6-2T No. 82001 is preparing to leave with the 4.20pm to Barnstaple. *Tim Stephens*

RIGHT: 'Mogul' No. 6363 waits for departure from the Down bay platform with the 5.47pm Barnstaple-bound train on Saturday 29th August 1964. *Tim Stephens*

BOTTOM LEFT: The station board at Taunton shows what an important interchange station it was in the period up to the early 1960s. The photograph was taken on 1st September 1962, before closure of the Chard Branch on 10th September 1962. *Stephen P. Derek*

BOTTOM RIGHT: Another of the ubiquitous 'Moguls', No 6327, backs onto its coaches in the Barnstaple bay platform to form the 1.30pm departure to Barnstaple Junction at Taunton on 15th April 1963. The Minehead Branch platform is to the right of the train. *Stephen P. Derek*

bay platform was built by the GWR on the Down side at the west end (see diagram opposite). The 1932 rebuilding work saw the virtual reconstruction of the station and the opening, on 4th February 1932, of the quadrupled lines to and from Norton Fitzwarren, providing Down Main, Down Relief, Up Main and Up Relief lines. This work had taken about two years and was undertaken by the GWR in conjunction with the Development (Loans Guarantees & Grants) Act 1929. From this point in time, D&SR trains then normally used the relief lines between Taunton and Norton Fitzwarren.

Operationally, Barnstaple trains that terminated at Taunton would normally arrive at Platform No. 8 (the bay on the Up or north-west side of the station). After the passengers had disembarked, the coaching stock would be released by the west end station pilot (understood often to be No. 5812 in the 1940s) and taken to the carriage sidings or placed in the Barnstaple bay platform (No. 3) for a later departure. This was next to the Down Main line platform on the south-west side of the station. It was a single line sandwiched between the Down platform on one side and the Minehead Branch bay platform on the other. The arriving locomotive, having been released, would then go to the shed for light maintenance, to replenish

its coal and water, and for turning, especially if it was to work back down the branch later in the day.

A fresh locomotive (usually a Churchward 'Mogul' 2-6-0 in the 1950s and early 1960s) would come off the shed and back onto its rolling stock in the departure bay. The stock usually consisted of a two-coach non-corridor B-set and a Hawksworth Brake Third coach or some similar hotch-potch of carriages, as this was, after all, a utilitarian service not a luxury one.

Our journey takes the passenger westwards from Taunton to Barnstaple, which is in the 'Down' direction in railway parlance. On the Great Western Railway, 'Up' was always the general direction towards London and this remained the same throughout the British Railways era. We are on the 10.15am departure from Taunton.

After the locomotive had coupled up to its carriages, the driver would make his final checks and with the departure time approaching and the 'road' clear, the bay platform Starting signal would be pulled 'off'. Once the train had got the signal and the guard had waved his green flag, with watches showing 10.15am, the driver would sound two long whistles, followed by a pause and then two further long whistles. As the brakes were released, the train would slowly weave

LEFT: No. 6337 waits to depart with a Barnstaple train in 1960. *Peter Barnfield*

BELOW LEFT: Classmate No. 6363 about to leave with the 5.55pm to Barnstaple Junction on 22nd June 1963. No. 7901 *Dodington Hall* and a 'Hymek' are on shed on the right. *Stephen P. Derek*

BOTTOM: 'Manor' Class 4-6-0 No. 7809 *Childrey Manor* on a Down local, most likely to Exeter, runs towards the Forty Steps footbridge west of Taunton station on 9th September 1953.
The late Owen Mogg, courtesy Peter Triggs

its way out of the bay platform, past Taunton West Signal Box on the right hand side and on to the Down Relief line. The forty-five mile, almost two-hour journey had begun.

First passing carriage sidings on the left and under 'Forty Steps' (the footbridge across the mass of lines to the west of Taunton), the Taunton goods avoiding line would come in from the left hand side. The train would then pass under a substantial iron girder bridge carrying the A3027 Staplegrove to Taunton road.

The train would gather speed as it headed towards Silk Mills Level Crossing and its first stop at Norton Fitzwarren.

The first leg of this journey of some 2 miles and 1 chain, was conducted almost on the level, as the line was close to the River Tone, which flowed eastwards towards Taunton. Fairwater freight yard would then be passed on the left-hand side; freight trains for the

RIGHT: With the customary three coach composition that sufficed for most of the weekday services on the Barnstaple line, No. 6327 coasts into Norton Fitzwarren on 29th September 1962. In the left background are some of the Nissen huts just before Blinkhorn military supply depot. No. 6327 has just passed under the impressive signal gantry on the approach to Norton Fitzwarren.
The late Owen Mogg, courtesy Peter Triggs

BELOW: No. 6364 drifts into the Norton Fitzwarren Down Relief platform with a Barnstaple-bound train on 7th April 1959. *Roger Joanes*

Barnstaple Branch would leave from here towards the end of the line's life. Passing over Silk Mills Level Crossing and as the train approached Norton Fitzwarren station, a number of dull-black corrugated iron Nissen army huts would have been seen on the right hand side of the line. Just after this was Blinkhorn military supply depot, which was established during the Second World War and taken over by the American forces (at which time the depot was known as 'G50'); it was the main depot for stores in the west of England. During the war years it was rail connected and had a dozen or so sidings within

the War Department premises.

Having passed this military depot the train would then begin to slow for the first stop. On arrival at Norton Fitzwarren station on time at 10.19am, the locomotive would come to a stand at the Down Relief platform alongside the 131-lever, timber-constructed Norton Fitzwarren Signal Box. There would be no need for a token at this point, as the line was double track as far as Milverton and had been since line improvements in 1937. The stop here would be brief; just one minute.

Mixed broad and standard gauge track at Norton Fitzwarren Junction in 1892. This view is shortly before the removal of all broad gauge rails on the main line west of here. Note the mixed gauge track still in place on the Minehead Branch, which had otherwise been converted to standard gauge in 1882, a year after the D&SR line; the third rail remained *in situ* for the first few hundred yards as a refuge siding for broad gauge trains. The broad gauge express is possibly the Up North Mail and is hauled by an unidentified 'Iron Duke' Class 4-2-2. In the right background can be seen the original Barnstaple Branch cabin, which it is thought was named Norton Fitzwarren Branch Ground Frame at this date. It was replaced with the rebuilding of the junction in 1937. Norton Fitzwarren Junction Signal Box can also just be seen in the left foreground. *Courtesy National Railway Museum*

NORTON FITZWARREN

Although Norton Fitzwarren station was not strictly part of the Taunton to Barnstaple line and thus is outside of the scope of this book, it is appropriate to mention some key features and dates. A more detailed summary of the station is contained in other publications.

The station was originally built by the B&ER and opened in 1873, the year in which the Taunton to Barnstaple line opened throughout. Prior to that and for the first two years of the D&SR (when it was open just to Wiveliscombe), there was a junction here for the West Somerset Railway (WSR), that had opened to Watchet in 1862; at this date it was known as Watchet Junction. When the B&ER was absorbed by the GWR in 1876, its main line and stations, including Norton Fitzwarren, became GWR property. In

The B&ER-built Norton Fitzwarren station circa 1905, looking west towards the junction, just visible through the footbridge. Note the Down arm of the bracket signal, on a tall post raising up high enough to be visible over the bridge. *Courtesy Lens of Sutton Association*

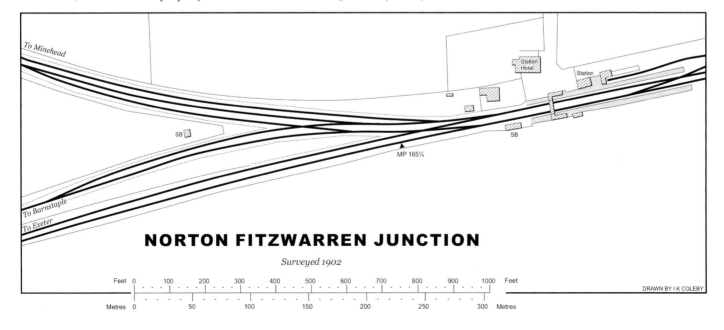

To Minehead

To Barnstaple
To Exeter

SB

MP 165¼

Station
Hotel

Station

SB

NORTON FITZWARREN JUNCTION

Surveyed 1902

Feet 0   100   200   300   400   500   600   700   800   900   1000   Feet

Metres 0   50   100   150   200   250   300   Metres

DRAWN BY I K COLEBY

A circa 1963 view of an unidentified 'Mogul' departing from Norton Fitzwarren on the Up Relief line. This may well be a through train from Ilfracombe and includes a couple of chocolate & cream liveried coaches. *The late Owen Mogg courtesy Peter Triggs*

1864, the population of Norton Fitzwarren was recorded as 634 by the Parliamentary Select Committee on the L&SWR (North Devon Extension) Bill.

The B&ER built it as a two-platform station, situated on either side of the Up and Down Main lines. Just to the west of the station in the early period, a simple double track junction served both the Minehead and Barnstaple branches, curving away sharply to the right. It will be seen by reference to the 1893 2-chain survey of the junction (*Vol. 1 page 101*), that the line to Barnstaple then branched

left off the West Somerset Railway and ran as double track for a short distance. It became a single line just before milepost 165½ and the 1 in 70 climb up Allerford Bank.

As part of the Taunton station and related area improvements, the track and station layout were substantially remodelled in the early 1930s. Two new island platforms were built to the east or Taunton end of the existing station. Opened on 2nd December 1931, the two outer sides of the new platforms faced on to the Up and Down Relief lines and thus served branch passenger trains to and from the

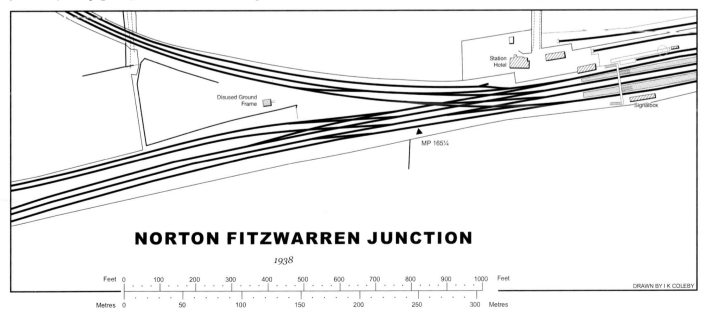

Disused Ground Frame

Station Hotel

Signalbox

MP 165¼

NORTON FITZWARREN JUNCTION

1938

Feet 0 100 200 300 400 500 600 700 800 900 1000 Feet

Metres 0 50 100 150 200 250 300 Metres

DRAWN BY I K COLEBY

The impressive series of junctions at Norton Fitzwarren, as seen from the station footbridge on 30th May 1964, with No. 7337 coming off the Barnstaple Branch on to the Up Relief line at the head of the 2.24pm Barnstaple Junction to Taunton service. This more complex junction dated from the 1930s, when the GWR four-tracked the line between Taunton and Norton Fitzwarren. Through the arms of the bracket signal, a runaway line can be seen heading off to the left from the Down Relief line. Moving across then from left to right, the lines are the Down and Up Main, the twin lines of the first section of the Barnstaple Branch, the Minehead Branch and finally, with some loaded open wagons standing on it, a siding. *R.A. Lumber courtesy Dave Mitchell*

Minehead and Barnstaple lines. With four lines running through the station, this necessitated a much more complex junction at the west end of the station, rebuilding work being completed by 7th February 1937. Following this, the Barnstaple line then had its own designated junction on a gentler curve between the main lines and the Minehead Branch. The new layout also made it possible for Down trains to run on either the Down Relief or the Down Main line to gain access to either branch. Correspondingly, Up trains coming off either branch could access either the Up Relief or Up Main platform, thus giving some flexibility to running. This is well illustrated in the photograph of the junction opposite, as well as by the signal box diagram in Chapter 9 (pages 408-09).

Although Norton Fitzwarren was never really a station for interchange traffic (as all trains ran through to Taunton), it remained in use until 30th October 1961, when it closed to passenger traffic.

Our journey continues. Once the road was clear, the driver would sound two whistle blasts and the train would pull out of the Down Relief platform. It would immediately branch to the right off the Down Relief line, to join the Down Main for just a few yards and would then branch right again, to snake its way across both the Up Main and Up Relief lines by way of a pair of parallel diamond crossings, to start along the branch proper at milepost 165^1/$_4$. Access to the Minehead Branch, which also went off to the right of the main line at this point, was via a junction slightly ahead of that for the Barnstaple Branch, curving away sharply to the north-west.

The twin tracks of the Barnstaple Branch ran parallel to the main line for around a quarter of a mile, before diverging away as they

ABOVE: Class '63XX' No. 6390 was a few yards further forward from sister engine No. 7337 in the previous photograph, when seen here departing Norton Fitzwarren on 19th August 1961, with the 4.35pm Taunton to Barnstaple service. The pony wheels at the front of the locomotive are passing over the point that branched to the right for the Minehead Branch.
Michael J. Fox,
courtesy Rail Archive Stephenson

LEFT: A classic 1950s view of the junction at Norton Fitzwarren, looking west from the station footbridge. The Down Relief line is on the left and the main lines lie straight ahead, whilst the Barnstaple and Minehead branches swerve off to the right – in the middle distance and the right respectively. This view, with the sun reflecting off the rails, makes it easy for the observer to identify and follow the various lines.
The late Owen Mogg courtesy Peter Triggs

RIGHT: Taunton shed's No. 7337 again, at the start of the climb up Allerford Bank with the 4.39pm Taunton to Barnstaple service on 8th June 1961. The main line can just be seen in the right background and note milepost 165³/₄ on the left.
Michael J. Fox,
courtesy Rail Archive Stephenson

BELOW: Whilst the ex-GWR '43XX' Class 'Moguls' became synonymous with the branch throughout the 1950s and '60s, No. 7337 was clearly one of the most popular. The engine is seen here again accelerating away from the main line up the 1 in 70 grade and approaching Allerford bridge on 3rd June 1963 with a train for Barnstaple.
The late Owen Mogg courtesy Peter Triggs

rose at 1 in 70 up an embankment towards and over the Allerford Road bridge, just under 1¹/₂ miles away from the Norton Fitzwarren Junction. The Blackdown Hills were to the left, rising above Wellington about 7 miles away. Wellington Monument, a simple stone needle, was visible on the top of those hills on a clear day.

Beyond this point, the line passed through the green pastures of the wide Tone Vale in Taunton Deane. The only speed restriction on this first stretch was the maximum of 60 miles per hour which applied to the line as a whole. After passing over the bridge leading from Hill Farrance to Pontispool Farm (Pontypool Farm on the 2-chain survey), the line gently weaved left and right on curves of 37 and 40 chains radius for about 1¹/₂ miles, through the parishes of Hill Farrance and Heathfield on the north side of the line and Oake on the south side. It then passed under Pig and Whistle Bridge, which carried the road from Oake to Milverton and, after also passing through the arch of Blagroves Road bridge (at milepost 168¹/₄), the line entered the parish of Milverton. Beyond that point, the tracks then curved more noticeably to the right on a 29 chains radius, as the backs of the houses of the nearby village of Preston Bowyer could be viewed out of the right-hand side of the train. Preston Bowyer

ABOVE: No. 7333 near Oake with the 4.25pm Taunton to Barnstaple Junction service on 20th July 1963. *Peter W. Gray*

BELOW: Classmate No. 7326 east of Milverton with the 12.25pm Ilfracombe to Taunton train, also on 20th July 1963. Note the quality of the permanent way – the neat ballast, lack of weeds and the general tidiness of the track side. *Peter W. Gray*

RIGHT: An unidentified 'Mogul' on the sylvan approach to Milverton in the 1960s. *Tim Stephens*

BELOW: No. 7333 again, bursts through Station Road bridge and in to Milverton station with the 5.55pm Taunton to Barnstaple train on Saturday 13th July 1963. It appears as if the fireman has just put coal on the fire in readiness for the 7 mile climb to the summit at Venn Cross. *Michael L. Roach*

was a small collection of farms and houses but had no station to serve its inhabitants.

At milepost 169, the line started to curve back to the left and at this point the train would have faced a speed restriction of 55 miles per hour. Mid-way round this bend of 26 chains radius, the line passed under a road bridge, with Preston Mills then appearing immediately on the left-hand side, once through the arch. Looking ahead but still to the left, Milverton was then visible in the near distance, with St. Michael's church being its most prominent feature, on the low hillside on which the village stood. After Preston Mills, the line straightened for a quarter of a mile, running alongside the mill leat, before turning on a gentle right-hand curve of 29 chains radius under the A361 road bridge and running in to Milverton station, $4^{1}/_{4}$ miles from Norton Fitzwarren and 6 miles 39 chains from Taunton. Arrival at 10.27am was slightly early. The inclines on this stretch of the line between Norton Fitzwarren and Milverton were modest: there were four short stretches at 1 in 70 (the longest being 24 chains), 23 and 44 chains at 1 in 66 and 13 chains at 1 in 75.

LEFT: A view of Milverton from an old postcard, looking west from Station Road bridge at the Taunton end of the station circa 1930. At the far end of the Down platform, note that the Starting signal had a goods arm lower down the post, controlling access to the goods yard. *John Alsop collection*

The ubiquitous No. 7337 again, passing through Milverton station with the 11.05am Ilfracombe to Wolverhampton (Saturdays only) service on 20th July 1963. Note the fireman is leaning out of the cab ready to hand over the token for the single line section from Wiveliscombe. This train ran through from Barnstaple Junction, with calls at only South Molton, Dulverton and Wiveliscombe *en route* to Taunton, where the four carriages seen here will be joined by coaches from the 12.45pm ex-Minehead service. Note that the second siding in the goods yard had been lifted by this date, with just a short length of rail left in place on which was positioned a rail-mounted, 4-wheeled a crane. *Peter W. Gray*

This cropped enlarged view from a 1920s postcard view of Milverton shows the platform facing wall of the goods shed apparently with wooden battens fixed all of the way along it, running from platform level to the roof line. This was not original and was presumably done to aid fixing the noticeboards to the wall; they do not appear in any of the later views. Note also that the lattice-post Intermediate Starting signal was at this date positioned 'wrong side' of the line, at the end of the Up platform. *John Alsop collection*

Milverton (6 miles 39 chains from Taunton)

Opened to Passengers .... 8th June 1871
Opened to Goods .... 8th June 1871
Closed to Passengers .... 3rd October 1966
Closed to Goods .... 30th September 1963

Milverton station was sited just a short walk of about half a mile to the north of the village, which had a population of circa 1,895 people at the time the line was under construction and as recorded in the 1864 Parliamentary Select Committee.

When the line first opened to Wiveliscombe in 1871, Milverton was the only intermediate stop. It was built originally as a single platform station on the south side of the line but, in 1880, a crossing loop was installed and the Up platform, along with a small shelter, was built on the north side. The Up platform was built to a longer length (149 feet more) than the Down platform, which remained unaltered. The Up refuge siding, trailing back from the west end of the Up loop, was also added at this time; it had a capacity of nineteen wagons.

The original road overbridge at the Taunton end was stone-built and wide enough to accommodate two lines (*see Vol. 1, page 58*) but, as the picture on page 253 shows, it was later rebuilt with a wrought iron span. It has not been ascertained exactly when this bridge was reconstructed but it may well have been in 1880 and it had certainly

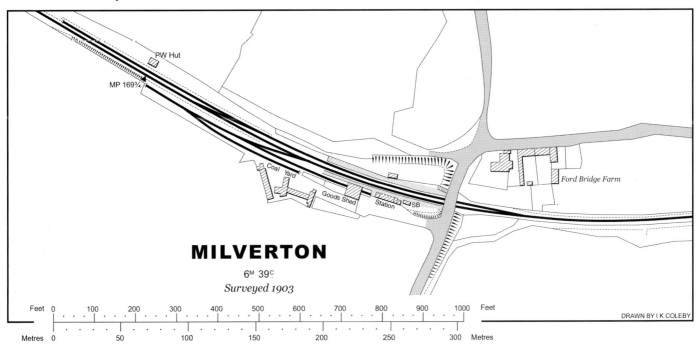

MILVERTON

6ᴹ 39ᶜ

Surveyed 1903

Feet 0 100 200 300 400 500 600 700 800 900 1000 Feet

Metres 0 50 100 150 200 250 300 Metres

DRAWN BY I K COLEBY

Both the Starting and Advanced Starting signals are clear for No. 7304 as it passes Milverton with the Down working of the Wolverhampton Low Level to Ilfracombe summer Saturdays only train on 20th July 1963. Note the crane on its isolated length of rail on the right. *Peter W. Gray*

been done by circa 1900, as several of the early postcard views of the station show the new span.

The crossing loop was originally of 450 feet in length but was extended westwards in 1925 and again in 1936, by a few yards on each occasion. In February 1937, the single line section to Norton Fitzwarren was doubled to cope with the increase in train services and, in particular, the extra holiday trains that ran on summer Saturdays.

The platforms were both constructed of stone, the Down side having a simple, single-storey B&ER 'H' style brick-built station building, located towards the middle of the platform, the central waiting room area of which was open to the elements on the platform side. The Down platform was 247 feet in length, whilst that on the Up side was 396 feet.

The first signal box built for the opening of the line was of timber construction. It was located on the Down side platform (the only platform at that time) at the Taunton end (*see Vol. 1, pages 56-58*). The brick-built goods shed, which was of a standard design used by the D&SR, was sited at the west end of the station and was 40 feet in length. The simple goods yard was located behind it. The goods shed was originally built with an arched doorway but this was later restructured, with a flat lintel support above the rail access doorway. In 1903, it was replaced by a larger brick-built signal box just slightly west of the old cabin on the Down platform. This new box was a GWR type '7B' (as designated by the Signalling Railway Society) and is covered in more detail in Chapter 9.

The Up platform had a simple B&ER designed timber shelter, with decorative barge boards and a slated gable roof. There was no footbridge and passengers

Clearly another stalwart of the line in the early 1960s, No. 7304 arrives with a two-coach Taunton-bound 'stopper' in 1961. *E.T. Gill, courtesy Rob Blencowe*

A 'Mogul' we have not seen to date, No. 6372 calls at Milverton with the 8.12am Barnstaple to Taunton train on 24th March 1962. *Michael J. Fox*

therefore had to cross the line by means of the barrow crossing at the east end of the station platforms, just beneath the road overbridge and under the watchful eye of the signalman.

The goods yard was accessed from the west end of the Down line running into a headshunt with a capacity for seven wagons, which then enabled a reversal back into the goods shed road, that had a capacity for six wagons outside the shed and two inside. The goods shed road also contained the cattle pens and a small 45 foot loading dock adjacent to the shed on the west side. There was one other general purpose siding alongside the goods shed road, with a capacity for five wagons, which had vehicular access and was thus used for unloading coal, fertiliser and other merchandise. A wagon mounted crane was made available in the yard as required. In later years, this was located just to the west of the goods shed, on its own short set of rails, which were actually the remains of the otherwise lifted second siding. The goods shed had a 30-cwt platform-mounted, steel-built, manually operated crane inside. Its turning radius was 12 feet, its lift height was 12 feet at platform level and 15 feet 1 inch at rail level. This crane was installed

in August 1929 at a cost of £96, being £68 for the crane, £18 for the foundations and £10 for fixing. It was fabricated by Herbert Morris Ltd of Loughborough and was sold to Messrs Netherway Bros in Newport in October 1964, after goods services ceased. Notes on the crane register indicate that it may have been made redundant as

No. 6372 again, coasts to a stop with a Taunton-bound train on 15th June 1963. *Edwin Wilmshurst*

early as 11th September 1947, so perhaps it was at this time the rail mounted crane was introduced.

The goods yard was on the Down side of the line and, from a practical point of view, the detaching, attaching and shunting of wagons normally took place from Down goods trains. There was a gradient of 1 in 100 falling towards Milverton from Norton Fitzwarren but the station layout was then on the level.

At its peak, the staff here at Milverton comprised a station master, two signalmen (on shifts) and a lad porter. Traffic summaries for the station for the years 1903, 1913 and 1923-1938 are given in the accompanying tables.

Goods inwards comprised coal, fertilisers and livestock, whilst the outward traffic, certainly in later years, was primarily sugar beet. A siding to serve the limeworks of William Thomas & Company existed

ABOVE: Milverton station looking east to Station Road bridge and through it towards Taunton on 15th June 1963. In the foreground, a metal, round post WR signal had replaced the wooden-posted Down Starting and goods arm seen in the earlier views. The goods shed rail entrances at both ends were rebuilt from the original arches (*see Vol. 1, page 57*) with square doors and iron lintels supporting the brickwork. Note the 45mph maximum speed sign on the right. *Edwin Wilmshurst*

LEFT: The main station building pictured on the last day of services, 1st October 1966. Note that entry to the building could only be made from the platform. Also, on the noticeboard at this end, British Railways new arrows logo makes an appearance and manages instantly to look out of place on the old B&ER style building. *Michael L. Roach*

A close-up of the 4-wheeled, rail-mounted, hand-operated crane in the goods yard, which was effectively marooned on its own section of track with the lifting of the rest of the siding. Sadly, as the picture is taken from a colour slide and is thus not as sharp as a black & white negative, little of the identification detail can be made out, but it was built by the GWR at Swindon and dated from circa 1890. *Alan Jarvis*

MILVERTON.

Station is on an Incline of 1 in 66 falling towards Norton Fitzwarren.

No vehicle must be detached and allowed to remain on the Main Line.

When an engine of a Freight train performing work is detached from the train, the brake of the guard's van must be securely applied, and sufficient wagon brakes put down and sprags used to prevent the train moving. Any wagons shunted on to the train must be immediately coupled up.

Guards of Freight trains must fully apply the hand brake before leaving their vans.

A sufficient number of sprags must be kept, 10 yards apart, between the Main Lines, and to the rear of the Up and Down Home Signals.

A view of the road approach to the station in June 1965. Note that there was no entrance in to the station building from this side but there was a window in the rear wall of the signal box, presumably so the signalman could keep an eye on any comings and goings. There was also a gate across the entrance to the goods yard, although goods services had been withdrawn nearly two years prior to this date. *John Alsop*

A second view of Milverton in June 1965, looking south-west from Station Road just a few yards to the north of the overbridge. The view is similar, albeit from a slightly more elevated position, to that showing the station under construction in Vol. 1 (pages 56-57). The village of Milverton is here now hidden by the trees that grew on the far side of the entrance road, behind the signal box. The tower of St. Michael's church – common to both photographs – can here just be seen on the horizon through a gap in the trees on the left. A roundabout now occupies the immediate foreground. *John Alsop*

between 1872 and 1884, which was situated on the north side of the line, about a quarter of a mile to the west of the station (*for further details see Vol. 1 Chap. 3*).

The track layout was rationalised before closure in May 1964, with the Down goods sidings and connections being recovered, signalling amended and levers bolted. The double track section to Norton Fitzwarren remained in use until closure in 1966 and the signal box remained operational.

At Milverton, the fireman would have to collect from the signalman the first of many tokens on the Down trip, before the train could proceed westwards on the single line section ahead. There would be time for little else, a stop of one or two minutes being the norm at all intermediate stations, unless the Down train had to wait for an Up service to pass. On the occasion of our trip, the train departed late at 10.29am as there had been parcels to load.

Over the stretch from Milverton to Wiveliscombe the line continued to climb. There were no downgrades and only five short level sections. As a consequence, all Down trains were constrained to a maximum of 45mph, this restriction applying right through to Wiveliscombe and as far as the Tone Viaduct at Waterrow.

As the line left Milverton, past

MILVERTON – PASSENGER, PARCELS & STAFF STATISTICS 1903-1957					
Year	Payroll cost £ (& staff no's)	Total Receipts £ (incl. goods)	Tickets issued (season tickets)	Passenger receipts £	Parcels etc receipts £	Total £ (incl. Parcels)
1903	202 (3)	3,045	14,661 (na)	1,090	212	1,302
1913	235 (3)	3,309	13,222 (na)	1,140	183	1,323
1923	587 (4)	5,972	13,502 (62)	1,393	837	2,230
1924	519 (4)	5,412	13,560 (60)	1,366	834	2,200
1925	511 (4)	5,842	13,634 (94)	1,336	649	1,985
1926	572 (4)	5,929	11,362 (66)	1,214	633	1,847
1927	588 (4)	6,184	10,890 (55)	1,125	436	1,561
1928	582 (4)	5,133	9,992 (74)	1,023	420	1,443
1929	586 (4)	5,016	10,037 (74)	983	392	1,375
1930	608 (4)	4,478	8,226 (74)	861	282	1,143
1931	603 (4)	3,454	8,079 (87)	800	173	973
1932	582 (3)	3,087	8,295 (92)	783	132	915
1933	507 (3)	3,067	7,464 (86)	701	152	853
1934	514 (3)	2,891	7,017 (90)	700	167	867
1935	548 (3)	3,111	6,610 (77)	660	113	773
1936	527 (3)	2,491	5,817 (77)	623	105	728
1937	605 (3)	2,383	5,823 (80)	631	86	717
1938	537 (3)	2,016	4,637 (68)	503	115	618
1940	627 (3)	A	4,560 (45)	725	76	801
1945	1,134 (3)	A	9,445 (182)	2,233	559	2,792
1950	(4)	B	2,826 (16)	931	140	1,071
1955	(3)	B	1,899 (136)	550	308	858
1957	(3)	B	7,462 (231)	1,141	208	1,349
A – goods receipts not disclosed; B – Goods zoned at Taunton						

Year	Coal/Coke charged/ forwarded (tons)	Other minerals (tons)	General merchandise forwarded (tons)	Coal/Coke charged/ received (tons)	Other minerals received (tons)	General merchandise received (tons)	Coal/Coke not charged forwarded/ received (tons)	Total goods tonnage	Total receipts (excl. not charged) £	Livestock wagons forwarded/ received	Total carted tonnage (incl. total goods tonnage)
1903	11	100	1,077	366	1,612	1,620	1,594	6,387	1,743	140	402
1913	31	9	1,231	388	1,669	1,542	1,471	6,341	1,986	104	455
1923	4	0	1,705	313	1,191	1,709	1,269	6,191	3,742	94	458
1924	16	0	1,154	444	988	1,967	1,446	6,015	3,212	117	408
1925	0	97	1,693	351	2,652	1,931	1,383	8,107	3,857	160	430
1926	26	632	1,266	216	4,342	1,758	937	9,177	4,032	141	404
1927	10	957	1,312	248	5,475	1,821	1,456	11,279	4,623	105	417
1928	41	205	1,514	284	2,940	1,534	1,201	7,719	3,690	146	356
1929	0	844	1,541	201	585	1,208	1,342	5,721	3,641	147	321
1930	5	835	1,577	48	933	1,012	1,347	5,757	3,335	103	314
1931	13	132	1,243	135	384	967	1,356	4,230	2,481	98	287
1932	5	432	1,161	144	174	707	1,180	3,803	2,172	66	243
1933	5	916	1,121	120	99	645	1,135	4,044	2,214	53	247
1934	24	634	1,079	60	81	700	1,124	3,702	2,024	34	372
1935	5	854	1,155	85	51	781	1,174	4,105	2,338	84	615
1936	9	193	1,117	35	79	623	822	2,878	1,763	76	551
1937	17	363	1,112	26	88	435	832	2,873	1,666	62	528
1938	5	531	750	18	102	411	686	2,503	1,398	29	592
1940	24	850	1,038	56	99	454	791	3,312	Not provided	17	Not provided
1945	17	720	1,215	0	32	523	809	3,316	Not provided	43	Not provided
1950	Zoned at Taunton										
1955	Zoned at Taunton										
1957	Zoned at Taunton										

MILVERTON – GOODS TRAFFIC 1903-1957

milepost 169³/₄, it swung gently north-west on a 29 chains radius right-hand curve. Within a quarter of a mile, on the north or right-hand side of the line, we pass the site of the long-closed lime kilns that used to belong to Thomas & Co. but no evidence of them remains.

The line then started cutting into the gently rolling, hilly agricultural land near Croford and, for around a mile, it formed a flat 'S' shape, before curving left-handed at 20 chains radius out of a cutting from milepost 171 and onto an embankment. It then ran over the Croford road bridge, just over a quarter of a mile further on. An old quarry could be seen to the right-hand side of the line just after that bridge. Beyond this, the line then curved left on a 25 chain radius curve as it cut into the fields again, with a low embankment supporting the

No. 7306 coasts downhill towards Milverton with the 10.12am Ilfracombe to Cardiff on Saturday 25th July 1964. *Peter W. Gray*

No. 6327 passes over Croford bridge on the approaches to Wiveliscombe with 1.57pm Taunton to Ilfracombe service on 20th July 1963. *Peter W. Gray*

line on the left-hand side.

Just beyond this point the line approached and ran parallel to the main Taunton to Barnstaple road (A361) on an embankment for about a quarter of a mile, after which it turned to the right on a

25 chains radius curve as it went into a short cutting, which hid the railway from the road.

The line then diverged away from the main road as it continued on its right-hand curve of 25 chains radius. It straightened at milepost

Southern 'N' Class 2-6-0 No. 31406 photographed on Saturday 25th July 1964 about half-way between Wiveliscombe and Milverton, alongside the A361 Taunton to Barnstaple road, with the 9.25am Ilfracombe to Taunton train. *Peter W. Gray*

171³/₄ for half a mile, running round the rear of some houses. After heading beneath the stone-built Castle road bridge, which carried a lane leading to King's Castle, a neolithic hill fort about half a mile to the east of the town and looking down on the railway from the north, the line then began a sweeping left hand curve of 28 chains radius at milepost 172, passing behind Ashbeers Farm and onto an embankment. It passed over the A361 road bridge and into Wiveliscombe station, just 2³/₄ miles from Milverton and 9¹/₃ miles from Taunton. St. Andrew's church could be seen to the right of the line, with some of the town's houses located close by.

The line's course on the approach to Wiveliscombe, through the station itself and beyond for about one mile was built on a 22 chain radius curve, which almost created a horse shoe-shape (*see the 2-chain survey on pages 104-105, Vol. 1*). It turned the line through approximately 110 degrees, so from heading west-north-west as it approached the town, it departed in a south-south-easterly direction.

It would be at Wiveliscombe that passengers would have observed the hills starting to close in on the line, those straight ahead giving the perception of a barrier to the westbound train. Indeed the course of the line avoided those hills ahead by diverging to their left for the first mile and then cutting in behind them as it drove westwards. This course was dictated by the need to serve Wiveliscombe after leaving Milverton but it also meant that, at the point where the line turned west again, near Hamworthy, it had travelled just over 4 miles but was still only around 2 miles from Milverton.

The town of Wiveliscombe was not far from its station, merely a short walk to the main street. Arriving at 10.35am, there may have been a replenishment of water for the locomotive but, in addition, the fireman would have needed to steel himself, making sure that the fire in the grate was well prepared for the next section – almost 5 miles of virtually uninterrupted rising gradients.

Top: Looking back towards Croford bridge, a Down train heads towards Wiveliscombe behind No. 6363, with a mixed consist of Bullied and Mk 1 coaches in tow, forming the 11.25am Taunton to Barnstaple Junction service on 25th July 1964.

Middle: Further illustrating the countryside near Wiveliscombe, No. 7303 accelerates away from the town with the 12.20pm Ilfracombe to Taunton train on 25th July 1964. In the background is the Wiveliscombe Down Distant signal and the Castle road bridge.

Bottom: Classmate No. 7304 works the six-coach 9.20am Ilfracombe to Taunton train on 20th July 1963.
All Peter W. Gray

No. 7337 nears Wiveliscombe with the 11.15am Ilfracombe to
Wolverhampton service, comprising six coaches. *Peter W. Gray*

A fine panoramic view of No. 6345 leaving Wiveliscombe and passing Ashbeers Farm with the 7.55am Ilfracombe to Taunton on 25th July 1964. The station
is in the centre distance, the goods shed the most prominent of its buildings, the embankment sweeping round to reach it. The train is about to pass the
Wiveliscombe Advanced Starting signal, which was a long way from the signal box – its cream painted timber sides making it stand out to the right of the
goods shed. The signal was on the right-hand or 'wrong' side of the line, to facilitate the driver's view of it. It was required to protect the section and allow
for shunting from the goods yard, situated at this end of the station, onto the running line, as there was no headshunt. *Peter W. Gray*

Wiveliscombe (9 miles 31 chains)

Opened to Passengers ....8th June 1871
Opened to Goods ....8th June 1871
Closed to Passengers ....3rd October 1966
Closed to Goods .... 6th July 1964

Wiveliscombe station was situated just east of the main part of the town and it is interesting to note that it was probably the closest to the town or village it served of any station on the line, with the possible exception of Swimbridge. Before the line was authorised in 1864, Wiveliscombe had a population of 2,735 (Parliamentary Select Committee).

The station was the terminus from 8th June 1871, when the section of line from Taunton opened, until 31st October 1873. The railway right the way through to Barnstaple was then brought in to operation the following day. During the period it acted as the temporary terminus, the station had a 42 foot turntable located at the eastern end, which was subsequently moved to Barnstaple once the line opened throughout. The run round became a passing loop once the line

Above: Some modest custom here at Wiveliscombe, as No. 7337 pauses with the 11.15am departure from Taunton on Saturday 30th May 1964. *Tim Stephens*

Below: A deserted Wiveliscombe station, looking towards Taunton on 15th June 1963. It was still well looked after at this date, with the platforms swept, the flower and herbaceous borders lovingly tended and evidence of neglect having yet to set in. The ground signal controlled entry in to the horse dock on the Up side at this end of the station. *Edwin Wilmshurst*

Wiveliscombe viewed from the foot of the Down platform in the summer of 1964. The short horse dock siding was taken out in May 1964 and the rails from this, cut in to short sections, have been stacked between the running lines to await collection. The ground signal had also been removed. The single storey brick building on the left, behind the nameboard, was the base of the original signal box, whilst the brickwork of the station building was, uniquely for the line, given a coat of white-wash in the later years (but presumably not during the 1939-45 war). In a turnaround of what had happened with the goods shed at Milverton, the rail entrance at this end had originally been square but had been rebuilt as arched, at an unknown date post-1907 (circa 1907 views in Volume 1 show it as still square). Oddly, however, the other end retained its original square entrance. On the right is the Down side water column, with the leather hose hanging over a drain in front and the brazier to keep it from freezing in winter just behind. Note the highly ornate gas lamps on the right. *Tim Stephens*

DRAWN BY I K COLEBY

TAUNTON ROAD

Station Road

Cattle Pens

MP 172½

Goods Shed

Station

SB

Town Mill

A general view of the station in May 1965. *Peter Barnfield*

WIVELISCOMBE

9ᴹ 31ᶜ

Surveyed 1902

Feet	0	100	200	300	400	500	600	700	800	900	1000	Feet

Metres	0		50		100		150		200		250		300		Metres

was opened to Barnstaple, the station being the first of the three original passing places encountered heading west along the single track route when it opened in 1873.

The line through the station was level but there was a 1 in 60 climb from the Milverton direction, which eased to a 1 in 500 downwards gradient just before the station throat. There was then a 1 in 72 gradual incline leaving the station, which led to a 1 in 58 climb beyond to the west.

The single-storey station buildings, located on the Up platform, were constructed of red brick and in B&ER 'H-style'; they thus were similar to Milverton albeit on the opposite side of the line, but were otherwise unlike those at any of the other stations on the D&SR. The main building had a large bay window on the platform side and an open waiting area in the middle, protected by a roof, along with a booking hall and toilets. The roof gables at each end of the main building were unequal, that at the Taunton end being higher. In later

years, the outside of the main buildings were white-washed, further distinguishing them from other stations on the line.

The original platforms were constructed of stone. The first signal box was also stone-built and located on the Up platform at the west (Barnstaple) end of the station. However, this was replaced in 1906, although only the upper portion of the box was demolished. The replacement was a timber box (GWR type 27C) on a brick base, located off the end of the Up platform just beyond the goods shed. However, when the platforms were extended in 1907, the signal box remained in its location and, in consequence, became platform mounted, as the extension was built around it. The timber base of the box to platform level was maintained until closure.

The Down side platform had only a simple waiting shelter constructed of wood with a gabled slated roof; it was not as ornate as the one at Milverton. Alongside this shelter was one of two attractive cast-iron gas lampposts, which were most likely originally oil lamps.

RIGHT: Wiveliscombe station throat from the east end in 1966. Notice the token exchange apparatus for Down trains on the left. An air of decay was by now setting in, with weeds on the platforms and untended flower borders, whilst the closed goods yard on the right was also becoming overgrown and was partially lifted.
G.H. Tilt, courtesy Mike Christensen

BELOW: A view from the end of the Up platform, looking towards Taunton in the early 1960s, with the water column partly obscuring the Up Starting signal. Note the gas lamp, the 172$\frac{1}{2}$ milepost in the flower bed and the token exchange apparatus for Up trains visible on the far side of the bridge spanning the A361 road to Taunton, now redesignated as the B3227. The bridge no longer exists, its site now hidden beneath a roundabout.
The Lens of Sutton of Sutton Association

BOTTOM: Looking from the rear of the goods yard towards Taunton. The nearest wooden open wagon had most likely delivered a load of coke and now with the coal wagons await return. All have there side doors hanging open to facilitate unloading. *The Lens of Sutton Association*

There was no footbridge, so passengers had to cross the line by way of the barrow crossing at the west end of the station. There were two water cranes, one each at the end of the Up and Down platforms. The main water supply tank was mounted on a brick base and was fed from an artesian well. It supplied the station and the two water cranes, and was located near the horse dock, on the Up side of the line at the west end of the station. Wiveliscombe was the first of the three intermediate stations with a water crane in the Down direction.

The goods shed was on the Up side, at the Taunton end of the station, adjacent to the platform and constructed of red brick. It was 60 feet in length, could accommodate three wagons and had a platform-mounted 2-ton crane. The jib crane register indicates that a 30-cwt crane was installed in August 1929 (like Milverton, for the same cost and from the same manufacturer). Again of steel construction, the manually operated crane had a 12 foot radius but a lift height of 11 feet 10 inches at platform level and 15 feet at rail level. It was also sold to Netherway Bros after goods services ceased, on 6th July 1964. Latterly, a corrugated metal provender store was added adjacent to the goods shed on the station side, by the access road side of the line.

The goods yard was also at the Taunton end on the Up side of the station and ran behind the goods shed and signal box. When first built, there were four sidings – the goods shed road, plus two further sidings, with a kick-back siding off the furthest of these.

RIGHT: Looking towards Taunton along the sweep of the Up platform. The white-washed brickwork of main buildings is clear in this view, as some of it was beginning to weather away. Note the varied collection of platform barrows in the foreground. *Peter Barnfield*

BELOW: A close-up of the main buildings on the Up platform in May 1965. The ticket office was housed in the left-hand end and the ticket office window faced in the open waiting area. The differing ends to the building, higher on the right and thus with a more steeply pitched roof, are clearly shown in this view. The nearest noticeboard carries a poster for tours in Southern Ireland. *Peter Barnfield*

Following improvements in 1907, the sidings were lengthened and an outer mileage siding added, giving three long sidings fanning out behind the shed; the kick-back siding was removed. Shunting had to be carried out on the running line, hence the need for an Advanced Starting signal. The goods shed road could hold six wagons to the east of the shed, adjacent to a 76 foot loading bank which also accommodated the cattle pens. The west side of the shed (where the provender store was located) had a 45 foot loading bank with a capacity for two wagons. The siding running alongside the loading dock adjacent to the shed could hold six wagons. This bank, 80 feet

in length, did not have a hard core surface and had a carriage shoot at its end. The next siding ran parallel to the previously described siding and could contain eight wagons, with arrangements for an end-loading dock and a short bank alongside. The outer mileage siding could accommodate sixteen wagons.

Goods delivered included coal, fertiliser and animal feedstuffs, along with general merchandise. The local coal merchants were Messrs Goodlands. In the outwards direction, agricultural products and beer from the Hancock Brewery were despatched.

The horse dock and siding at the Barnstaple end, off the Up

RIGHT: A close-up of the modest wooden waiting shelter on the Down platform at Wiveliscombe in May 1965. The noticeboards hold a second tours in Southern Ireland poster, on the right, whilst the one on the left was about tying parcels securely. *Peter Barnfield*

BELOW: Another angle of the Down side shelter, from the end carriage of a four-coach Up train about to depart on 30th May 1964. Note the brick-built shed at the rail entrance to the goods yard, just beyond the Starting signal; it does not feature on the 1930 plan opposite and the brickwork looks quite new, so it was probably a post-war addition. *Tim Stephens*

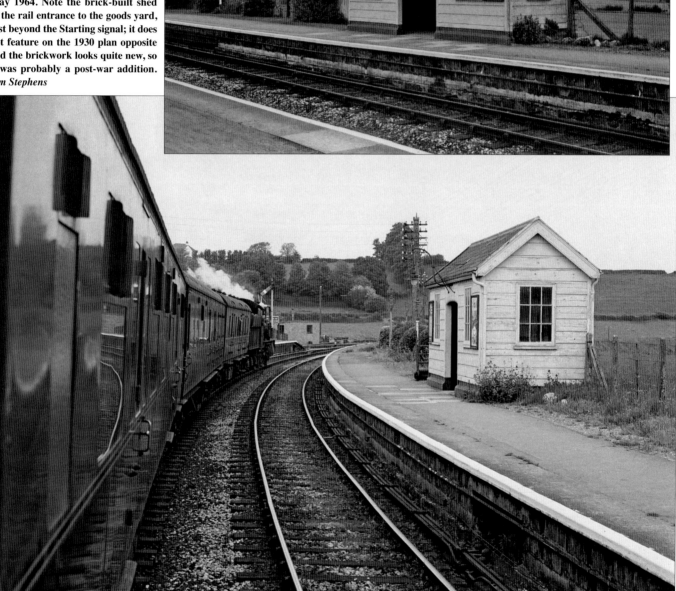

platform, were built in 1904, for use mainly for horses from the Hancock and Farringdon families to go hunting. It could hold three wagons alongside a 70 foot loading bank.

Cattle were driven down to the station yard and kept in pens before being marked and then loaded into wagons for transshipment. The local market (held the second Tuesday of every month) increased in prominence with the arrival of the railway. The accompanying tables detail the traffic dealt with in the years 1903 and 1913, and then the period from 1923 to 1938 but selected market trading figures for

heads of livestock loaded at Wiveliscombe are given below:

Year	Sheep	Cattle	
1900	50,000	9,000	(approximate figures)
1929	12,097	2,635	
1945-46	16,545	3,510	
1961	0	427	
1963	0	424	

In 1907, the station platforms were extended eastwards towards Taunton resulting in a 470 foot Up platform and a Down platform

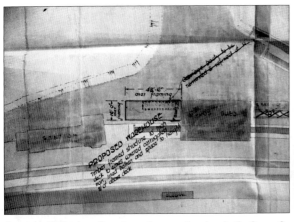

ABOVE: A 1930s plan of a proposed provender store in the form of a timber-framed, corrugated iron clad warehouse by the goods shed. *Courtesy National Archives*

ABOVE: Looking in the Down direction, towards Barnstaple from near the east end of the Up platform. No. 6345 is arriving with a Taunton-bound train on 8th February 1964. *Peter W. Gray*

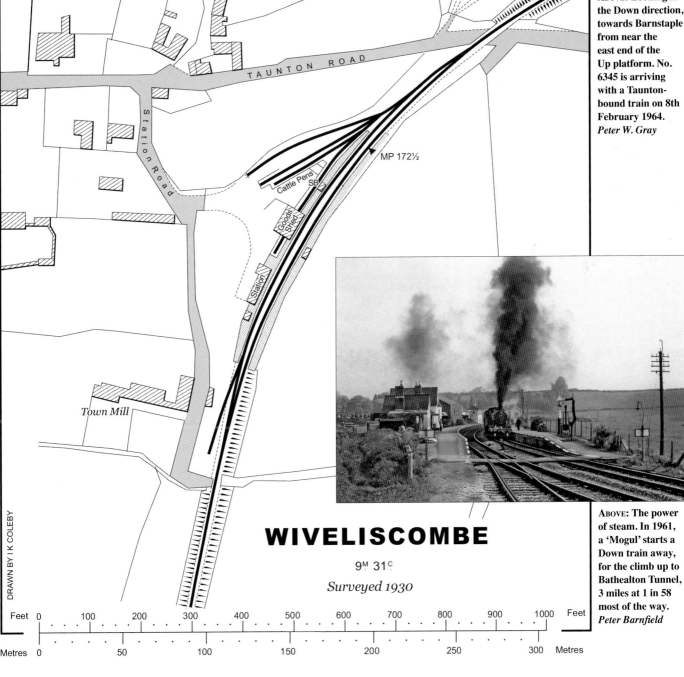

TAUNTON ROAD

Station Road

Cattle Pens

SB

MP 172½

Goods Shed

Station

Town Mill

DRAWN BY I K COLEBY

WIVELISCOMBE

9ᴹ 31ᶜ

Surveyed 1930

| Feet | 0 | 100 | 200 | 300 | 400 | 500 | 600 | 700 | 800 | 900 | 1000 | Feet |

| Metres | 0 | 50 | 100 | 150 | 200 | 250 | 300 | Metres |

ABOVE: The power of steam. In 1961, a 'Mogul' starts a Down train away, for the climb up to Bathealton Tunnel, 3 miles at 1 in 58 most of the way. *Peter Barnfield*

A view inside the open waiting area on the Up platform in May 1965. Detail studies such as this are extremely useful for modellers, as well as serving to give a real flavour of a station's ambience. Note the glass fronted notice board and GWR leaflet rack beneath it, as well as the GWR cast-iron 'TICKETS', 'IN' and 'OUT' signs, and the balustrade in front of the ticket office window. Wooden benches with cast GWR supports, a gas lamp hanging from the ceiling and the photographer's bicycle all contribute to the scene. *Peter Barnfield*

of 496 feet, which enabled eight coach trains to be accommodated. The crossing loops were 600 feet long and were extended on three separate occasions: in 1906, 1911 (to the west only) and 1939. For this later extension, the embankment had to be widened and the bridge at the end of Mill Lane extended (as evidenced by different brickwork), to enable a further 4 chains (88 yards) of track to be added. Also catch and trap points were incorporated to enable trains to enter the station from both directions simultaneously, provided each train came to, or nearly came to, a stand at the relevant Home signal. The loop lengths were stated in the *1947 Appendix to the Service Time Table* as 756 feet (both Up and Down) following the 1937 extension.

The first station master in 1873 was John Goddard, followed in 1883 by George Morgan, who remained in office until 1910. He was succeeded by William Allen (until 1919), then William George Tucker (until at least 1927). In 1929, the station was staffed by a station master, goods clerk,

WIVELISCOMBE – PASSENGER, PARCELS & STAFF STATISTICS 1903-1958						
Year	Payroll cost £ (& staff no's)	Total Receipts £	Tickets issued (season tickets)	Passenger receipts £	Parcels etc receipts £	Total £ (incl. Parcels)
1903	296 (6)	7,618	20,613 (n/a)	1,988	712	2,700
1913	317 (5)	7,903	17,894 (n/a)	1,923	892	2,815
1923	876 (6)	12,303	19,616 (117)	2,889	1,000	3,889
1924	856 (6)	12,090	18,382 (125)	2,858	584	3,442
1925	875 (6)	12,342	17,828 (111)	2,687	579	3,266
1926	807 (6)	11,685	15,531 (83)	2,341	745	3,086
1927	827 (6)	11,794	16,125 (85)	2,715	688	3,403
1928	733 (6)	12,338	14,331 (98)	2,288	846	3,134
1929	830 (6)	11,697	15,018 (124)	2,242	615	2,857
1930	840 (6)	10,861	13,292 (146)	2,080	569	2,649
1931	884 (7)	10,636	12,796 (130)	1,869	496	2,365
1932	943 (7)	9,319	12,948 (129)	1,768	521	2,289
1933	1,000 (7)	9,853	11,886 (130)	1,593	521	2,114
1934	1,024 (7)	9,565	11,816 (104)	1,621	455	2,076
1935	1,156 (8)	8,703	11,368 (109)	1,622	219	1,841
1936	1,193 (8)	8,408	10,760 (95)	1,487	199	1,686
1937	1,225 (8)	8,245	10,911 (146)	1,622	195	1,817
1938	1,180 (7)	8,187	10,299 (176)	1,608	202	1,810
1940	1,356 (7)	A	8,584 (114)	1,640	472	2,112
1945	2,233 (7)	A	14,973 (204)	4,265	1,303	5,568
1950	(7)	B	6,007 (101)	2,193	848	3,041
1955	(8)	A	9,013 (307)	2,867	282	3,149
1958	*(10)	A	16,611 (648)	3,832	300	4,132

A – goods receipts not disclosed; B – Goods zoned at Taunton from 2nd June 1947
* Milverton and Venn Cross included with effect from 1 August 1958; staff numbers increased to (14)

Steam escapes from the heating pipes of the rear carriage of the 11.15am Taunton to Barnstaple Junction train on 8th February 1964, as it heads away from Wiveliscombe behind No. 6326. A long climb to Venn Cross lay ahead for the locomotive and the footplate crew. The passengers who alighted here now use the barrow crossing to the Up platform and exit from the station, as no footbridge was ever provided here. The horse dock platform on the right still had its short siding intact at this date but it was soon to be removed, as the picture overleaf shows. *Peter W. Gray*

porter, goods porter and two signalmen (on shifts). By the mid 1930s, the goods porter had been replaced by a porter-signalman and a goods carter added to the staff. This latter appointment probably coincided with the 'Country Lorry Service' introduced by the GWR to serve Wiveliscombe and the surrounding area in 1934. Other staff members in later years were W. Webber (station booking office), D. Yeandle (ganger supervisor) and Messrs Alby Hobbs and Payne (platelayers). The signalmen latterly were Ron Searle, Edgar Webber, Harold Elliott, Harold Screech and A. Timperley.

Passenger tickets issued in 1903 were 20,613 but had fallen to 11,886 in 1933, where they steadied until the increase brought by the Second

World War, up to 14,973 in 1945. They dropped back substantially to just over 6,000 in 1950 but then climbed again through the 1950s almost to pre-war levels. The apparent peak in 1958, however, also included the figures for Milverton and Venn Cross. Total goods tonnage was at 14,322 in 1903 and apart from a peak in 1925 of 15,704 tons, steadied at around 10,000 tons during the 1930s until a dip to 7,693 tons in 1938. The war years not surprisingly saw a substantial increase, to 13,858 tons in 1945. Livestock transportation peaked at 531 wagons in 1930. As the photographs show, Wiveliscombe was well kept right up until the early 1960s, with flower beds, climbing roses and shrubs, often a signature of the country station.

Year	Coal/Coke charged/ forwarded (tons)	Other minerals (tons)	General merchandise forwarded (tons)	Coal/Coke charged/ received (tons)	Other minerals received (tons)	General merchandise received (tons)	Coal/Coke not charged forwarded/ received (tons)	Total goods tonnage	Total receipts (excl. not charged) £	Livestock wagons forwarded/ received	Total carted tonnage (incl. total goods tonnage)
1903	7	587	2,035	854	3,658	4,435	2,746	14,322	4,918	302	1,749
1913	39	13	1,733	2,546	1,846	4,657	2,454	13,288	5,088	346	1,980
1923	11	163	2,233	1,080	1,748	3,774	2,352	11,361	8,414	356	1,603
1924	9	28	2,447	997	2,696	4,548	2,415	13,140	8,648	433	1,797
1925	5	118	2,543	888	4,998	4,588	2,564	15,704	9,076	378	1,923
1926	19	130	2,755	803	3,145	4,087	1,728	12,667	8,599	483	1,657
1927	10	293	1,541	947	2,416	4,469	2,327	12,003	8,391	473	1,777
1928	11	249	2,663	885	2,774	4,373	2,521	13,476	9,204	486	2,025
1929	31	196	1,953	818	1,927	4,708	2,744	12,377	8,840	495	2,262
1930	23	216	1,338	796	887	4,782	2,891	10,933	8,212	531	2,133
1931	0	77	958	792	2,284	5,582	2,795	12,488	8,271	462	2,068
1932	10	46	840	661	512	4,999	2,794	9,862	7,030	440	1,868
1933	9	92	1,078	940	1,707	5,298	2,514	11,638	7,739	398	3,000
1934	0	173	963	581	285	5,647	2,791	10,440	7,489	308	3,189
1935	10	60	893	828	330	5,596	3,007	10,724	6,862	266	3,752
1936	11	49	647	684	291	5,457	2,873	10,012	6,722	215	4,727
1937	17	15	1,014	725	231	4,397	2,483	8,882	6,428	200	4,190
1938	0	114	1,038	851	154	3,610	1,926	7,693	6,377	182	3,622
1940	9	70	1,588	1,925	268	2,870	2,032	8,762	Not recorded	373	Not recorded
1945	41	257	5,018	20	478	4,317	3,727	13,858	Not recorded	495	Not recorded
1950	Zoned at Taunton from 2nd June 1947										

WIVELISCOMBE – GOODS TRAFFIC 1903-1950

No. 7337 coasts down the bank in to Wiveliscombe station with the 2.24pm train from Barnstaple Junction to Taunton on 30th May 1964. The siding serving the horse loading dock on the right had just been taken out, hence half of the boarded crossing had also been temporarily removed. The view also provides good detail of the brick tower housing the pumping apparatus for filling the water tank which sat on top of it. *Tim Stephens*

No. 7333 is about to leave the Down loop as it heads away from the station and rejoin the single line on the way to Bathealton Tunnel, with the 9.55am Taunton to Barnstaple train on 24th March 1962. *Michael J. Fox, courtesy Rail Archive Stephenson*

RIGHT: No. 7326 heads up the bank away from Wiveliscombe with the 11.45am Taunton to Barnstaple Junction service on 18th August 1962.
Peter W. Gray

BELOW: From the other side of the line and a few yards further on, No. 6372 starts the relatively gentle initial stages of the climb with the 2.17pm train from Taunton to Ilfracombe service 18th August 1962. Having got their trains started out of the station, neither locomotive in these pictures as having to work hard at this point. Note that the Down Home signal is visible in the top right distance, graphically illustrating the sweeping horse-shoe curve that the line took through Wiveliscombe.
Peter W. Gray

LEFT: A distant view of a 'Mogul' trailing a white cotton wool plume of smoke as it blends with the beautiful countryside west of Wiveliscombe on 22nd August 1964, with the 7.00am train from Taunton to Ilfracombe. *Tim Stephens*

BELOW: Leaving a rather dirtier smudge in the sky, another ex-GWR 2-6-0 heads west from Wiveliscombe with a six-coach train for Ilfracombe on 5th September 1964. The stone arch bridging a lane between Bathealton and Wiveliscombe still survives but the embankment is now completely shrouded by trees. *Michael J. Fox, courtesy Rail Archive Stephenson*

Chapter 7

A Description of the Line and its Stations Part 2: Wiveliscombe to South Molton

Negotiating the sort of exquisite countryside that would typify most of the rest of the route across west Somerset and north Devon, an unidentified 'Mogul' climbs towards Bathealton with a Taunton to Ilfracombe train on 22nd August 1964. *Tim Stephens*

At 10.37am, one minute late, the train was ready to depart from Wiveliscombe. There was initially a brief 1 in 72 climb out of the station as the railway passed through fields of grazing cattle and sheep, before being on the level for a short distance on a low embankment. As the line came off the continuing left-hand bend that it had followed for one mile, it straightened, entered a cutting and went under a road bridge. It then continued straight for a quarter of a mile, through the cutting and out onto an embankment, before passing over the Bathealton to Wiveliscombe road bridge. For the next half a mile, the route curved through a ninety degree turn to the west, on a radius of 30 chains and on a rising embankment through

green pasture land. Here the climb began in earnest, at 1 in 58 for just under 2 miles.

Once off the curve, the line passed over the stone bridge beneath which ran the Chipstable to Bathealton road. Looking right and left at this point and for the next mile, the railway passed by scattered copses; on the left-hand side, near milepost $174^3/4$, the buildings of the appropriately named Woodlands Farm could be seen. Still rising but in a cutting and with the route straight at this point, the final efforts would be made by the fireman before the line curved to the left, on a 20 chains radius, which then brought into view the east portal of Bathealton Tunnel.

Bathealton Tunnel

Although built to broad gauge width, Bathealton Tunnel presented something of an ominous sight for the driver and fireman, as for some reason it appeared low and tight. It may have been an illusion caused by the proximity and steepness of the sides of the cutting but the smoke and fumes retained by the tunnel were no illusion for the footplate crew. It is understood that the footplatemen would often dampen their handkerchiefs and tie them across their face cowboy-style to avoid inhalation of the smoke, dust and sulphuric fumes generated by the locomotive, one of the least pleasant attributes of being on the footplate.

Bathealton Tunnel was the longest on the line at 447 yards and was a dead-straight bore. The eastern portal was 175 miles and $14^1/_2$ chains from London and the approaching gradient continued to rise at 1 in 58 into the tunnel from the east. The chain survey map in Volume 1 gives a plan of the tunnel, detailing the shafts and mounds created by the excavations, and these mounds are still visible today. The historical background and progress in building the tunnel is also given in Chapter 3 of the first volume.

Once in the tunnel, its length would have seemed like an eternity until the summit was reached deep inside. Emerging into the light again and with some relief from the smoke, the footplate crew would obtain short respite. There was a falling gradient at 1 in 63 for about half a mile from the west end of the tunnel and down through a cutting, with the line then emerging onto the four-span Tone Viaduct.

Top: A westbound train on the final stages of the climb up to the eastern portal of Bathealton Tunnel in February 1958, with No. 6364 working hard despite its relatively light three-coach load. The tunnel looks to be a tight fit for the approaching train, although it was originally built to broad gauge specifications. *James G. Tawse*

Above: The west portal of Bathealton Tunnel, looking back towards Taunton in March 1949. This view makes an interesting comparison with the contractor's photograph showing the tunnel and cutting under construction seventy-eight years earlier in Vol. 1, page 62. *R.J. Sellick, courtesy National Railway Museum*

Right: No 7320 emerges from the eastern portal of the tunnel hauling the 6.48am Barnstaple Junction to Taunton service on Saturday 22nd August 1964. The train will coast down the 1 in 58 gradient to Wiveliscombe – about two miles – giving the fireman some respite. *Tim Stephens*

Tone Viaduct

The Tone Viaduct, so named after the river than ran underneath it, was also referred to as Waterrow Viaduct, as it was near that hamlet, and sometimes as Venn Cross Viaduct. It was located half a mile to the west of Bathealton Tunnel and 176 miles from Paddington. It ran in a straight line across the valley, was 162 yards long and rose to a maximum height of 101 feet. The continuous iron girder construction was supported by three stone-built piers which tapered towards the top and there were stone built abutments at either end. Underneath the rail level was a walkway for maintenance workers. Approximately 4,000 cubic tons of masonry and 260 tons of iron were used in the viaduct's construction in the early 1870s.

Trains were required to cut their speed to 25mph to cross the structure. Passing over it, passengers were able to view the fields and wooded valley stretching north towards Waterrow in the near distance and

The Tone Viaduct from the valley floor and largely lost amongst the trees in the 1960s. *Tim Stephens*

ABOVE: A 'Mogul' heads west between Bathealton Tunnel and the Tone Viaduct in the early morning of 22nd August 1964, with the Saturday's only 7.00am Taunton to Ilfracombe service. *Tim Stephens*

Huish Champflower beyond. Just below the viaduct was a cottage and scattered buildings, whilst to the south the valley was again heavily wooded.

In the *1900 Working Time Table* for the line, the speed over the viaduct was stated '*not to exceed 15 miles per hour*'. However, this was increased later in the line's life to 25mph. There were also restrictions for coupled locomotives travelling together over the viaduct. Two 'Mogul' 2-6-0s, for example, would have to uncouple and pass over the viaduct separately to avoid extra stress on the structure, which was deemed unable to cope with the concentrated weight of two approximately 60-ton locomotives and their 40-ton tenders passing over it. However, such double-headed operations were rare in practice. It is believed (but not confirmed from any official sources seen) that some

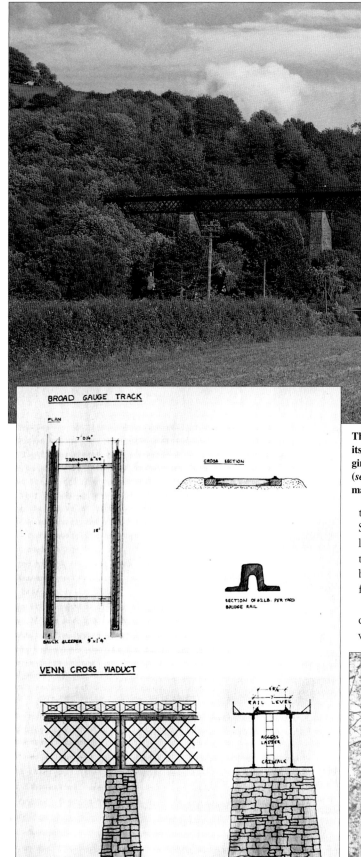

This view rather creates the illusion that the Tone Viaduct was lower than its 100 feet but does show the continuous girder construction well. The iron girders had originally slotted in to masonry extensions at the top of each pier (*see Vol. 1, page 67*) but these had been removed, leaving the joins exposed (for maintenance?) at an unknown date. *Michael J. Fox, Rail Archive Stephenson*

tests were carried out with a 'Hall' Class 4-6-0 on the viaduct after the Second World War but it was not found possible to increase the weight limit over it. The *North Devon Railway Report* of the early 1960s noted the heavy maintenance costs of the structure and with the similar but larger Castle Hill Viaduct, and they were to be one of the key factors in the closure of the line.

Coming off the west end of the viaduct, the line went into a short cutting. To the left of the railway at that point was an old quarry, which was used in the building of the line as a source of stone for the viaduct

Diagrammatic details of the viaduct, produced for reducing the gauge in 1881 (*see Vol. 1 pages 87-89*). Note that the stone pier extensions are not shown; had they already been removed? *Courtesy Martin Tester*

A detail view taken in April 2011, which clearly shows the ornate stone parapet supports at the top of one of the abutments. *Author*

Above: No. 6375 crosses the viaduct with the 11.25am Taunton to Barnstaple Junction train on 22nd August 1964. Note the three Southern Region coaches at the front, being returned to Barnstaple whilst also providing extra capacity on this summer Saturday working. *Tim Stephens*

Left: No. 6340 negotiates the short curving cutting on the approach to the eastern portal of Venn Cross Tunnel, with a westbound service on 14th July 1962. One of the buildings of Wey Farm can just be made out peeping over the ridge above the line of fence posts, whilst the escarpment of Hagley Plain rises up to the skyline in the centre distance. *John Spencer Gilks*

piers. The next phase of the journey was the $1^{1}/_{4}$ mile climb up to Venn Cross, which was at a gruelling 1 in 58 gradient again. However, as a slight consolation, this part of the route was largely straight and there was a speed restriction of 55mph for both Up and Down trains.

On this section the line cut through a landscape of scenic rolling woodlands and farmland. Coming off an embankment on a gentle right-hand curve of 38 chains radius, it then went into a short cutting on a left-hand bend of the same radius, just beyond which was the eastern entrance to Venn Cross Tunnel. This was 243 yards in length and again was straight but the gradient was still evident right through the bore.

Venn Cross Tunnel

The 243 yards long Venn Cross Tunnel was located at the eastern end of Venn Cross station and was, like Bathealton, dead straight. The western portal opened up a few yards short of the platforms, so westbound trains burst out of the tunnel and straight in to the station. It took the railway line under the A361 Taunton to Barnstaple main road (now downgraded as the B2227). The eastern end of the tunnel was 177 miles and $6^{1}/_{4}$ chains from London.

Only when out of the tunnel but still climbing at 1 in 60, would the summit of this first section of the line be reached, at 666 feet above sea level. Venn Cross station was almost on the level, the grade just falling towards Wiveliscombe. However, when the train drew to a halt at the platform alongside the signal box, the locomotive crew would have seen the obvious 1 in 60 downgrade to Morebath ahead. It was now 10.46am – the service was back on schedule. As the train came out of the tunnel it was still in Somerset but by the time it pulled up at the platform and stopped by the signal box, it had crossed in to Devon, the county boundary being between the goods shed and the signal box. Venn Cross was at milepost $177^1/_4$ and 12 miles from Norton Fitzwarren, so just over 14 miles from Taunton.

RIGHT: Our first glimpse of something other than a 'Mogul' on the line in the time period covered by most of these views is this snapshot of an unidentified Collett Class '22XX' 0-6-0 about to enter the tunnel with an eastbound train at an unknown date. *Courtesy Tiverton Museum*

An enlargement from a view which appeared in Vol. 1, page 158, looking eastwards straight through Venn Cross Tunnel on 29th August 1964. The steepness of the climb through the bore is clearly shown. Both platforms had been lengthened by additions at the Barnstaple end in the late 1930s, to allow the closure of a slightly shorter section of both at this end of the station, hence the dismantled platform edge. *Tim Stephens*

VENN CROSS (14 MILES 13 CHAINS)

Opened to Passengers .... 1st November 1873
Opened to Goods .... 11th November 1873
Closed to Goods .... 30th September 1963
Closed to Passengers .... 3rd October 1966

Venn Cross station was isolated, there being no village of that name. It served several local dwellings, and nearby hamlets and villages such as Clayhanger (274 population in 1864), Raddington (121) and farms around Waterrow, all in an area of around two miles radius from the station. Located in a cutting, just beyond the western end of the tunnel, the station was originally built as a single platform on the south side of the single line that passed through it. However, due to the constraints of the site at rail level, the one-storey station building and station master's house were located at the top of the cutting and alongside the main road. They were reached from the platform by a pathway that started its climb by the signal box.

The simple goods yard comprised a headshunt and goods shed siding located at the west end of the platform. However, access to the sidings was by a complex set of pointwork.

The stone-built goods shed was of the same standard design as for the rest of the line (with the exception of Barnstaple Victoria Road shed) but was 40-foot in length and was located on the Down side adjacent to the platform. It had a capacity for two wagons and contained a 30-cwt crane. There was a loading bank of 24 feet length adjacent

No. 7320 emerges from the tunnel, still climbing as it enters the station with a Down train on 5th September 1964, just a few days before steam ceased on the line. Note the catch point in the foreground and the sign on the left for goods trains, emphasising the safety measures taken at this location where a 1 in 60 gradient applied in each direction making shunting difficult and care was needed. *Michael J. Fox, courtesy Rail Archive Stephenson*

A view looking east through Venn Cross station on 15th June 1963, with the summit of this section of the line clearly visible at the end of the platforms. The Somerset/Devon county boundary passed beneath the photographer's feet at this point. *Edwin Wilmshurst*

The crew of No. 6327 exchange tokens with the Venn Cross signalman as they coast to a halt with the 10.50am Barnstaple Junction to Taunton train on 3rd June 1963. Note the trap point at the end of the Up platform and the catch point on the Down line opposite. With a 1 in 58 down hill gradient towards Taunton starting at the end of the platforms, these were essential safety features. *Peter W. Gray*

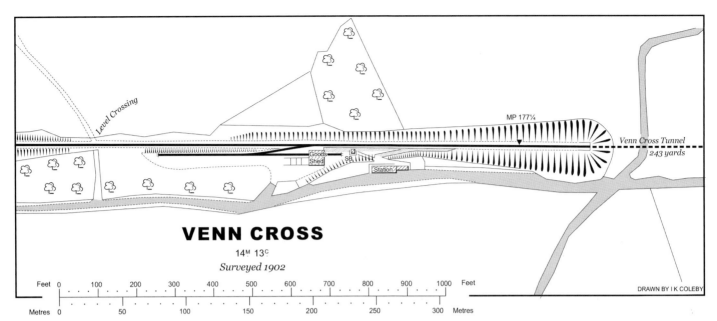

VENN CROSS

14ᴹ 13ᶜ

Surveyed 1902

to the shed and next to this were the cattle pens, with a capacity for two wagons. The cattle pen platform was located just ahead of the crossing into the yard. The headshunt, needed for access to the goods shed, could hold ten wagons clear of the pointwork leading to it. This siding also allowed roadside access to wagons positioned there and would appear to have doubled up as a milage siding when required.

A new signal box (a GWR type 7B) was opened in April 1905, on the Down platform just east of the goods shed; it replaced the original small cabin installed here in 1893.

The loop and the Up platform were added in 1905, which also necessitated a new track layout to enter the existing goods yard, and the Down platform was raised in height. Also added was the goods refuge line at the west end of the Up loop, to accommodate twenty-eight wagons plus the engine and brake van in the set-back siding.

The Up platform had a small brick-built waiting shelter with a canopy extending at the front and contained the gentlemen's toilets. It was positioned towards the Taunton end, facing the point at which the steps down from the road and station building came out on the Down platform. The platform lengths were equal at 350 feet each and the loop was 735 feet.

A rare early 20th century photograph of the Venn Cross station staff and a couple of the local permanent way gang. The view also shows the new Up loop, platform and waiting shelter, which were added in 1905. Everything looks clean and fresh, whilst the embankment behind is still bare, so the picture is likely to date from that year.
Courtesy of Mr & Mrs Wilson of Venn Cross

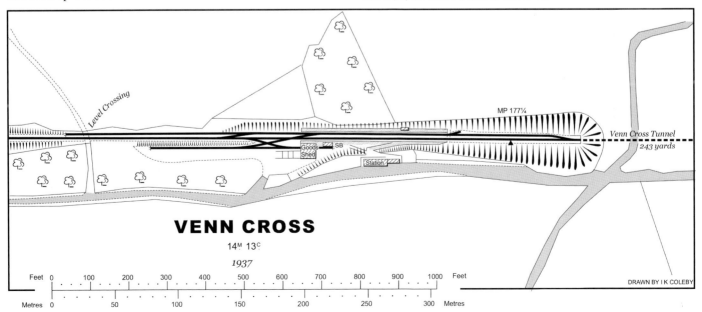

VENN CROSS

14ᴹ 13ᶜ

1937

Demonstrating the impressive work of which this class of sturdy mixed traffic locomotives were capable, No. 7337 pulls out of Venn Cross with an unusual and heavy load comprising ten coaches on Saturday 18th August 1962. The train was actually a combination of the 10.10am working from Ilfracombe to Cardiff along with the 11.15am from Ilfracombe to Wolverhampton and was presumably a result of the locomotive of the former train failing somewhere near Barnstaple Junction. *Peter W. Gray*

In 1937, the platforms were lengthened to 365 feet and the loop to 750 feet clear. There was no footbridge, passengers having to cross the line by way of the barrow crossing at the west end of the station. In 1947, the loop lengths were stated in the *Appendix to the Service Time Table* as 825 feet (both Up and Down).

As mentioned a little earlier, the station uniquely fell in to both Devon and Somerset. The county boundary ran from north to south across the platforms and railway lines at the west end of the station, just by the signal box, leaving the western end of the platform and the goods shed in Devon and the remainder of the station in Somerset. Its high location towards Exmoor also exposed it to the extremes of weather in winter and the cutting was prone to blockages with heavy snow falls.

There was a 1 in 60 drop down towards Morebath, which was apparent at the west end of the station, and similarly eastwards through the tunnel. Operationally, any Up goods train had to propel its load back into the refuge siding and pin down brakes before making the cut to shunt or collect wagons. The complex pointwork into the yard, dating from the remodelling in 1905, meant that the shunting of wagons from Up trains took place across the Down loop directly into the headshunt. If wagons arriving from the Up direction were to be placed in the shed road, they would most likely be worked back manually or roped from the headshunt. Wagons dropped off Down trains could be propelled back across the trailing point directly in to the goods shed road. The *Appendix*

to the Service Time Table 1947 stated that every freight train having to attach or detach wagons at Venn Cross must be provided with a 20-ton brake van at the rear, because of the falling gradients both ways.

Goods inwards comprised mostly fertiliser and cattle food. There was little coal traffic but higher figures for minerals in the 1924-1930 period was as a result of inward deliveries of stone ballast. Sugar beet and rabbits were despatched seasonally but there seems to have been little in the way of other agricultural traffic such as livestock. The Wiveliscombe motor lorry also collected and distributed goods locally.

For most of its life, Venn Cross was under the control of a station master. However, the position was dispensed with from 1st August

VENN CROSS – PASSENGER, PARCELS & STAFF STATISTICS 1903-1958						
Year	Payroll cost £ (& staff no's)	Total Receipts £	Tickets issued (season tickets)	Passenger receipts £	Parcels etc receipts £	Total £ (incl. Parcels)
1903	96 (2)	1,513	3,107 (n/a)	230	264	494
1913	158 (3)	1,250	3,135 (n/a)	255	210	465
1923	486 (3)	1,751	3,314 (6)	418	191	609
1924	487 (3)	1,990	3,228 (5)	410	127	537
1925	505 (3)	1,895	2,794 (7)	347	106	453
1926	507 (3)	1,920	2,193 (8)	291	149	440
1927	508 (3)	2,189	2,214 (9)	306	162	468
1928	501 (3)	2,118	1,827 (11)	232	111	343
1929	515 (3)	1,973	2,345 (15)	272	106	378
1930	517 (3)	2,322	2,007 (16)	256	114	370
1931	517 (3)	1,935	1,709 (9)	215	91	306
1932	505 (3)	1,703	1,590 (5)	188	85	273
1933	525 (3)	1,577	1,405 (10)	199	83	282
1934	566 (3)	1,306	1,463 (8)	175	107	282
1935	552 (3)	1,484	1,410 (12)	178	125	303
1936	547 (3)	1,735	1,341 (12)	173	163	336
1937	573 (3)	1,301	1,257 (6)	153	108	261
1938	581 (3)	1,278	1,106 (11)	157	73	230
1940	672 (3)	A	2,154 (18)	368	385	753
1945	864 (3)	A	3,572 (37)	710	436	1,146
1950	(3)	A	1,617 (50)	429	1,128	1,557
1955	(3)	A	1,573 (108)	365	87	452
1958	(3)	A	1,245 (174)	302	20	322
A – Goods receipts not reported						

More locomotive variety, in the shape of BR 'Standard' Class '3MT' No. 82008, departing Venn Cross on 7th September 1963 with a Saturdays only Wolverhampton to Ilfracombe train, which on this occasion consisted of four coaches and a parcels van (immediately behind the engine). No. 82008 was reallocated from Neyland to Taunton shed in October 1961, where it remained until withdrawal early in 1964. *Ron Lumber, courtesy Dave Mitchell*

VENN CROSS – GOODS TRAFFIC 1903-1950

Year	Coal/Coke charged/ forwarded (tons)	Other minerals (tons)	General merchandise forwarded (tons)	Coal/Coke charged/ received (tons)	Other minerals received (tons)	General merchandise received (tons)	Coal/Coke not charged forwarded/ received (tons)	Total goods tonnage	Total receipts (excl. not charged) £	Livestock wagons forwarded/ received	Total carted tonnage (incl. total goods tonnage)
1903	0	17	340	17	843	1,431	126	2,774	1,019	50	256
1913	0	7	154	41	697	976	109	1,984	785	54	178
1923	0	0	187	5	413	948	42	1,595	1,142	64	112
1924	0	15	112	34	1,832	1,013	55	3,061	1,453	61	113
1925	0	37	120	9	1,022	1,077	111	2,376	1,442	114	122
1926	0	40	200	21	787	1,186	88	2,322	1,480	94	116
1927	0	25	283	65	1,237	1,301	227	3,138	1,721	125	153
1928	0	29	373	39	584	1,286	158	2,469	1,780	128	190
1929	0	80	232	57	379	1,231	326	2,305	1,595	142	196
1930	0	13	191	76	2,125	1,377	209	3,991	1,952	90	196
1931	0	0	185	156	559	1,372	210	2,482	1,629	82	182
1932	0	40	138	238	372	1,268	211	2,267	1,430	52	262
1933	0	97	143	74	877	1,125	256	2,572	1,295	43	898
1934	0	73	124	29	170	1,211	136	1,743	1,024	36	1,094
1935	0	61	165	8	72	1,286	11	1,603	1,181	42	1,242
1936	0	8	349	13	73	1,321	4	1,768	1,399	27	1,332
1937	0	0	320	0	29	902	4	1,255	1,040	20	962
1938	0	0	271	0	123	730	5	1,129	1,048	22	815
1940	0	0	120	0	45	542	0	707	Not provided	14	Not provided
1945	0	0	51	0	189	228	6	474	Not provided	11	Not provided
1950	Zoned at Taunton from 2nd June 1947										

No. 7333 trundles past the west end of the goods yard as it arrives at Venn Cross with a two-coach train forming the 11.19am from Barnstaple Junction to Taunton on 21st July 1961. There is a view of the crossover pointwork that provided access to the goods yard in the right foreground, whilst the open wagon standing on the headshunt appears to have delivered a load of ballast for the local pw gang. Note also how the running line drops down towards Morebath, whilst the goods headshunt remained on the level. *Michael J. Fox, courtesy Rail Archive Stephenson*

RIGHT: A Barnstaple Junction-bound train about to depart from Venn Cross behind the usual 'Mogul' motive power in June 1961. Note the Whitaker token exchange apparatus in the foreground, along with the complex pointwork in the goods yard. The GWR had an aversion to facing points on running lines, hence access was via a trailing point from the Up loop for eastbound trains and a trailing point from the Down loop for those heading west.
Peter Barnfield

BOTTOM: No. 7333 coasts in to Morebath with a Down train in June 1962. The bridge carrying the Bampton to Skilgate road over the line can just be seen behind the rear coach and the gradient down from Venn Cross is also evident.
Peter Barnfield

VENN CROSS.

Station is on the Summit of Inclines of 1 in 60 in both directions, and in the Station the line falls slightly towards Wiveliscombe.

No vehicle must be detached and allowed to remain on the Main Line.

Wagons to be put off Down Freight trains into the Mileage Siding must be formed on the van. After the train has come to a stand on the Down Loop Line inside the catchpoint at the Taunton end of the Loop, and before the engine is detached, the brakes on the two leading wagons must be securely applied. The engine to run round the train to detach traffic at the rear. Before the wagons are cut off, brakes must be securely applied on the two rear wagons of the train left on the Loop. Sprags to be placed in the wheels of the four wagons which have been braked. The Guard will be held responsible for carrying out these instructions.

Wagons from the Mileage Siding to go forward by a Down train must be formed on the van.

An Up Freight train having to put off or pick up wagons must be placed in the Refuge Siding. Any wagons shunted on to the train in the Refuge Siding must be immediately coupled up.

The Guard and the Signalman must come to a clear understanding before making any shunting movement.

Guards of Freight trains must effectively apply the hand-brake before leaving their vans.

Six sprags must be kept, 10 yards apart, between the Loop Lines.

The provisions of Rule 39(a) do not apply to the operation of the Down Home Signal so far as Down Freight and Down Passenger trains, booked to stop at Venn Cross, are concerned.

1958, when the station was brought under the control of the Wiveliscombe station master and the staff thereafter comprised two signalmen (on shift) and a porter. Its isolated location meant that the station was never busy, as the tables of statistics show. Tickets issued in 1903 amounted to just 3,107 and this paltry figure had more than halved by 1933 to 1,405. A war-time rise saw the station reach its zenith with a figure of 3,572 in 1945 but this had halved again by 1950 and dropped to 1,245 in 1958.

The falling gradients leaving Venn Cross going west would range between 1 in 58 and 1 in 110 but there was a short rising gradient at 1 in 880 just to the east of Morebath. On pulling away from Venn Cross station at 10.47am, the crew could let the train run down the wooded Batherm Valley, at which point the line was surrounded by open fields but it passed through several short and shallow cuttings near Berry Farm and Petton village, as well as under access bridges near those locations. This run was virtually straight and through agricultural land for 3^1/$_2$ miles, with mild undulations near Hayne Barton. It then passed under the Bampton to Skilgate road bridge, just a quarter of a mile from the isolated Morebath station, which was reached just ahead of milepost 181.

MOREBATH (17 MILES 61 CHAINS)

Opened to Passengers ....1st November 1873
Opened to Goods ....11th November 1873
Closed to Goods ....3rd June 1963
Closed to Passengers ....3rd October 1966

Curiously, Morebath station was nearer the village of Shillingford, about half-a-mile away to the south, than Morebath village, which lay nearly two miles away to the north-west, whilst the small town of Bampton was three miles to the south-west. Prior to the opening of the Exe Valley line in 1884 – which was routed through Bampton

ABOVE: Moments after taking the previous picture and watched by the fireman who had been able to take a breather on the downgrade from Venn Cross, the photographer swung round to capture this view of No. 7333 entering the station, which also shows the pointwork at the entrance to the goods yard. The small shed on the left, mounted on a wooden platform, was the provender store. *Peter Barnfield*

LEFT: Looking west from the Up platform circa 1906, before the extension of the loop and platforms at this end. As will be seen from the later views, the extensions changed the character of the west end of the station quite noticeably.
Courtesy The Lens of Sutton Association

and on which it thus got its own station – the station was named Morebath & Bampton, which also better explained its location in between these two local centres of population. Morebath had a population of about 430 people in 1864 (Parliamentary Select Committee), whilst Bampton had a population of 1,971 at the same date.

The original stone-built platform and station buildings were located on the Down side. Initially, the station was served by a single line but a passing loop was added in 1876, along with a new stone-built Up platform and timber waiting shelter. The platforms were each of 245 feet in length at this date, with a loop length of 450 feet. When the loop was lengthened in 1937, the west end of the platforms were also extended but these additions were of timber construction, as they had to pass over a road bridge and on to an embankment. In 1947, the loop lengths were stated in

ABOVE: Another early 20th century view of the station, contemporary with the previous picture but looking towards Taunton from the west end. As was generally the case with these local postcard views, the staff have come out to pose for the photographer.
Courtesy The Lens of Sutton Association

LEFT: A similar but later view eastwards through the platforms, showing more detail of the west end of the goods shed. Note that this has the arched rail entrance that all the line's goods sheds were originally built with but, as we shall see, the entrance the other end was rebuilt at an unknown date. The pine trees flanking the rear of the Up platform, a feature of so many GWR stations, were later to be removed, possibly when the platforms were extended. The simple wooden shelter seen in these views was all that was ever provided on the Up side.
John Alsop collection

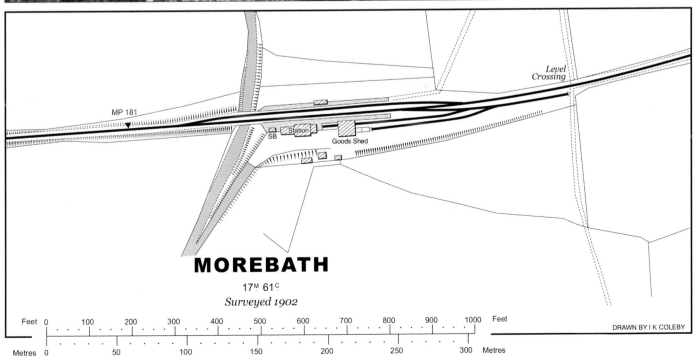

MP 181

Level Crossing

SB | Station

Goods Shed

MOREBATH

17ᴹ 61ᶜ

Surveyed 1902

| Feet | 0 | 100 | 200 | 300 | 400 | 500 | 600 | 700 | 800 | 900 | 1000 | Feet |

| Metres | 0 | 50 | 100 | 150 | 200 | 250 | 300 | Metres |

DRAWN BY I K COLEBY

the *Appendix to the Service Timet Table* as 742 feet (both Up and Down).

The main station building, situated on the Down side, was a single storey structure, originally built entirely of stone. It had a central section, with the apex of the roof at right angles to the line and two wings either side with lower roofs running parallel to the line. The one to the west of this central section housed the waiting room and was almost certainly originally built with an open front, in the same style as Milverton and Wiveliscombe. At an unknown date in the 19th century but perhaps in 1876 when the new Up platform was built, the front of the waiting area was bricked in. This was probably done as protection against the prevailing weather and the pine trees behind the Up platform may well

have been planted for the same reason, although possibly at a later date. The buildings contained the booking office, waiting room and ladies' toilet, whilst the gentlemen's toilet was at the east end. The Up platform was spartan; a simple open-fronted wooden shelter, located centrally on it and painted white with a backward sloping roof, was all that was ever provided to protect east-bound travellers. Following the improvements, passengers had to cross the line by the barrow crossing at the east end of the station, there being no footbridge. Prior to this, the barrow crossing had been located at the west end.

The signal box was originally located just beyond the west end of the Down platform but before the bridge that supported the line as it passed over the Shillingford to Skilgate road. The original box was replaced in June 1937 as part of the overall line improvements and although the new cabin was sited in the same location, because of the extension of platforms at the same time, it was platform mounted. The second box was a GWR type 12A and was one of the first on the line to be closed, on 2nd March 1963, when the loop was taken out of use and the station reduced in status to an unstaffed halt.

The simple goods yard was located at the east end of the station and behind the Down platform. There was a set-back siding which could hold six wagons, a road holding nine wagons that ran in front of the goods shed and a further siding parallel to this road with a ten-wagon capacity and road access. The stone-built goods shed was located alongside the Down platform and was of similar stone construction to the other such buildings on the line. It was 40 feet in length with a capacity for two wagons and housed a 2-ton, platform-mounted crane. Again one of the rail entrance arches to the shed, that at the east end, was rebuilt with a supporting lintel at some stage. Beyond the shed was a 32 foot loading bank with a capacity for a single wagon. Adjacent to the goods shed on the Taunton side were the cattle pens. There was also a small provender store (a half-shed structure like the original one at Dulverton), which was located alongside the back siding on its own wooden platform. The Down pick-up goods would shunt the yard when required. Reference to the Morebath Signal Box train register for the period April 1959 to March 1960, shows no evidence of any Up goods trains stopping to drop off or collect wagons.

Goods traffic here, both inwards and outwards, was always light and even in the recorded peaks of 1913 and 1930, only amounted to around 40 tons a week being handled. Most of the time it averaged only around 30 tons and in 1945, the final year it was recorded prior to Morebath goods being zoned with Tiverton in 1947, the total amounted to just 4 tons a week. The main inward traffic would have

Above: Looking west from the Down platform in the early 1960s, showing the 8 foot wide wooden platform extensions carried out in 1937. *Courtesy The Lens of Sutton Association*

Below: The main station buildings on the Down platform in May 1965, by which time Morebath was an unstaffed halt. Note the yellow brick front to the waiting room; clearly this was not original, as the rest of the building was built of stone, so it is likely that the waiting area was originally open like those at Milverton and Wiveliscombe. However, the early 1900s views show this already bricked in, so it is likely to have been a 19th century modification. *Peter Barnfield*

BELOW: **Morebath station forecourt in June 1965, showing the stone construction of the buildings this side. It would appear that when the front of the waiting area was bricked in, a window was added in the rear wall which also had a yellow brick surround. Note too the end of a wall tie high up on the goods shed, again lending credence to the theory that problems were experienced with the construction of these buildings, hence some of the arches having to be rebuilt.** *John Alsop*

MOREBATH.

No vehicle must be detached and allowed to remain on the Main Line.

When an engine of a Down Goods train performing work is detached from the train, the brake of the Guard's Van must be securely applied, and sufficient wagon brakes put down and sprags used to prevent the train moving. Any wagons shunted on to the train must be immediately coupled up.

An Up Goods train having to perform shunting must be drawn into the Up Loop and secured in accordance with the instructions for Down trains. If the train cannot be drawn into the Up Loop, it must remain outside the Home Signal, but before the engine is detached, the brake of the Guard's Van must be securely applied, and sufficient wagon brakes put down and sprags used to prevent the train moving. Any wagons shunted on to the train must be immediately coupled up.

Guards of trains must effectively apply the hand-brake before leaving their vans.

A sufficient number of sprags must be kept, 10 yards apart, between the Loop Lines, and to the rear of the Up Home Signal.

been agricultural in nature, animal feed and fertiliser for instance, plus stone ballast, whilst there was a small amount of outwards livestock.

The Morebath station staff latterly comprised two signalmen (on shift) and a porter-signalman, the post of station master having been withdrawn circa 1959, after which the responsibility fell to the Dulverton incumbent.

Passenger receipts were always low, being little different to those at Venn Cross. Tickets issued in 1903 amounted to 3,208 but this had plummeted to 1,184 in 1933. There was the usual climb back up during the war years, to 2,898 in 1945, but the figures then dropped off again, down to 1,315 in 1955 and a miserly 871 in 1958 – less than 3 a week!

Returning to our journey, we head east away from Morebath at 10.53am. The line was initially on the level, after which it climbed at 1 in 66 for about 26 chains, levelling again before a 1 in 100 climb to Morebath Junction. The route passed through a short cutting near Keens and was then straight for about a mile. As the railway passed under the B3190 road bridge from Bampton to Morebath village, the line curved to the right, just beyond which the double track section of

the junction began. Extended in 1937, the loop at the junction was long enough for two trains to pass when required. A short speed restriction of 40mph began here, running through the junction to the occupation crossing at 182 miles and 50 chains, just beyond Morebath Junction Halt.

MOREBATH – PASSENGER, PARCELS & STAFF STATISTICS 1903-1958

Year	Payroll cost £ (& staff no's)	Total Receipts £	Tickets issued (season tickets)		Passenger receipts £	Parcels etc receipts £	Total £ (incl. Parcels)
1903	129 (2)	1,176	3,208	(n/a)	377	130	507
1913	191 (3)	1,524	3,264	(n/a)	531	103	634
1923	450 (3)	2,327	3,050	(7)	762	225	987
1924	451 (3)	2,335	3,033	(5)	770	220	990
1925	496 (3)	2,482	2,784	(1)	719	198	917
1926	433 (3)	2,288	2,252	(0)	576	288	864
1927	450 (3)	2,273	2,278	(0)	555	333	888
1928	476 (3)	2,353	1,954	(0)	414	428	842
1929	479 (3)	2,197	1,838	(0)	351	368	719
1930	483 (3)	2,941	1,664	(4)	379	495	874
1931	414 (3)	2,485	1,381	(1)	291	539	830
1932	372 (3)	1,903	1,185	(0)	258	288	546
1933	409 (3)	1,397	1,184	(5)	264	191	455
1934	379 (3)	1,650	1,193	(4)	274	219	493
1935	384 (3)	1,664	1,210	(6)	264	145	409
1936	368 (3)	1,747	1,190	(1)	303	141	444
1937	439 (3)	1,414	1,234	(1)	315	100	415
1938	426 (3)	1,471	1,259	(6)	323	59	382
1940	528 (3)	A	1,473	(11)	447	188	635
1945	756 (3)	A	2,898	(6)	869	132	1,001
1950	(3)	A	2,011	(30)	767	170	937
1955	(3)	A	1,315	(30)	464	99	563
1958	(3)	A	871	(28)	332	47	379
A – Goods receipts not provided							

MOREBATH – GOODS TRAFFIC 1903-1950										
Year	Coal/Coke charged/ forwarded (tons)	Other minerals (tons)	General merchandise forwarded (tons)	Coal/Coke charged/ received (tons)	Other minerals received (tons)	General merchandise received (tons)	Coal/Coke not charged forwarded/ received (tons)	Total goods tonnage	Total receipts (excl. not charged £	Livestock wagons forwarded/ received	Total carted tonnage (incl. total goods tonnage
1903	0	299	465	180	148	557	104	1,753	671	52	96
1913	0	8	288	14	560	974	251	2,095	890	87	144
1923	0	0	227	28	226	876	116	1,473	1,340	77	117
1924	10	0	154	16	282	837	135	1,434	1,345	85	135
1925	0	20	379	26	183	886	127	1,621	1,565	75	152
1926	0	62	227	8	152	996	67	1,512	1,424	82	140
1927	0	43	194	10	177	963	198	1,585	1,385	49	157
1928	0	0	229	0	205	855	132	1,421	1,511	83	220
1929	0	33	275	10	312	868	126	1,624	1,478	80	277
1930	0	0	683	0	223	978	130	2,014	2,067	93	262
1931	0	2	229	8	185	1,008	92	1,524	1,655	91	245
1932	0	0	308	5	135	1,018	84	1,550	1,357	90	185
1933	0	0	128	10	101	717	97	1,053	942	48	237
1934	0	0	169	0	130	974	57	1,330	1,157	62	386
1935	0	0	105	0	62	942	80	1,189	1,255	133	596
1936	0	0	262	0	84	750	70	1,166	1,303	109	427
1937	0	0	139	0	79	456	54	728	999	112	496
1938	0	0	114	0	89	352	66	621	1,089	101	442
1940	0	0	864	0	31	264	53	1,212	Not provided	24	Not provided
1945	0	0	40	0	0	182	0	222	Not provided	50	Not provided
1950	Zoned at Tiverton from 1st August 1947										

LEFT: Ex-Southern Railway 'N' Class No. 31843 of Exmouth Junction shed with the 4.10pm Barnstaple Junction to Taunton train on 25th April 1964. The location is thought to be Keens Bridge, which carried a lane between Morebath and Shillingford over the line. Situated around a mile east of Morebath Junction, this stone-built arched bridge is still extant today. The 4.10pm was a regular turn for Southern Region locomotives. No 31843 was withdrawn from service a little over four months after this picture was taken, part of a mass withdrawal of the 'N' Class 2-6-0s from Exmouth Junction in September 1964. The signal wire is believed to be going out to the Morebath Down Distant, located adjacent to Keens Plantation. *Michael L. Roach*

BELOW: No. 7337 accelerates away rapidly from an automatic token exchange at Morebath Junction, with a Taunton-bound train in June 1963. *Peter Barnfield*

MOREBATH JUNCTION

However, on our trip today there is a signal check, the 9.50am Exe Valley service from Exeter having been slightly delayed. Due to arrive at Dulverton at 10.53am, it should have cleared the junction and left the halt at 10.49am but was a few minutes late and is now just ahead of us.

Beyond milepost 182¼, the Exe Valley line can be seen joining from the left on a gentle curve. At the junction itself and on the right-hand side of the line was the signal box. Tokens would be exchanged here (either with the automatic apparatus or by hand with the signalman standing by the line near his box).

The line traversed fairly flat terrain around Morebath, as this view east back towards the station shows. No. 7337 ambles towards Morebath Junction with a westbound train on 31st January 1964. By the early 1960s, the view along the valley here had been spoilt by a line of electricity pylons that ran parallel to the track at this point and which remain today. *Peter W. Gray*

No. 7337, hurrying eastwards with a two-coach train for Taunton, comes off the Morebath Junction Up loop line in June 1962. *Peter Barnfield*

ABOVE: No. 6345 leaves the Up loop at Morebath Junction with a Taunton-bound train on 31st January 1964. *Peter W. Gray*

BELOW: Looking south-west from the fields behind Morebath Junction Signal Box, as the 8.20am Barnstaple Victoria Road to Taunton service heads east with No. 6398 in charge on 26th February 1960. *John Spencer Gilks*

ABOVE: No. 7304 has a favourable signal as it heads for Morebath with an Up train on 30th August 1961. *Michael J. Fox, courtesy Rail Archive Stephenson*

BELOW: With the photographer standing on the Up loop to the Exe Valley line, No. 7326 negotiates the junction with a four coach train bound for Taunton. Morebath Junction Halt is just visible behind the train and note the Exe Valley catch points sign. The locomotive had lost the '7' from its smokebox door numberplate. *Michael J. Fox, courtesy Rail Archive Stephenson*

ABOVE: A view of the junction from the fields south of the line, as a Barnstaple-bound train passes in front of the signal box on 30th August 1961. Note the array of token exchange posts. *Michael J. Fox, courtesy Rail Archive Stephenson*

BELOW: Class '14XX' 0-4-2T propels an auto working from Dulverton to Exeter via Tiverton through the junction and on to the Exe Valley line. As the sign on the left indicates, there was a 15mph speed restriction across the junction for branch trains and note, too, the trap and catch point arrangements in the foreground. *Ron Lumber, courtesy Dave Mitchell*

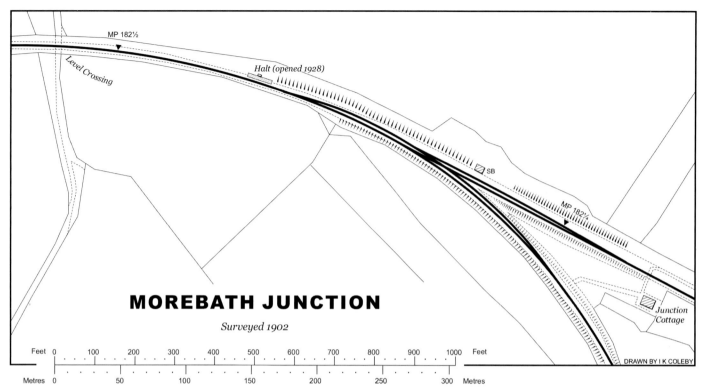

MOREBATH JUNCTION

Surveyed 1902

Morebath Junction Signal Box was situated 100 yards west of the 182¼ milepost, on the north side of the line and directly facing the junction it served. It was a GWR type 3 box, with a timber upper structure on a brick base and a slated gabled roof.

The loop at the junction was originally 600 feet in length. As was usual at such junctions, the single line Exe Valley line also split in two 225 feet from the junction, creating separate Up and Down connections for branch trains. The D&SR loop lines were extended in 1937, after which the double track section began at the Bampton to Morebath road bridge to the east of the junction and ended beyond the signal box, just before the halt.

In 1947, the loop lengths were stated in the *Appendix to the Service Time Table* as 792 feet (both Up and Down).

After the Exe Valley Branch closed on 7th October 1963, it was lifted along with the junction. Consequently, the D&SR loop here also became redundant and the Down line was taken out of use on 29th April 1964, Morebath Junction Signal Box closing on the same day.

MOREBATH JUNCTION HALT (19 MILES 17 CHAINS)

Opened to Passengers .... 1st December 1928
Closed to Passengers .... 3rd October 1966

It was now 11.01am so our train was about 4 minutes late as it arrived at this basic halt, located half a mile south of Morebath village and therefore better situated than Morebath station itself, about 2 miles to the east, which was no doubt what motivated its opening. However, the halt was sited in a field, there was no metalled road to it and no obvious footpath. Passengers had to use what, over time, became a well worn route across the fields to gain access to the platform. Given

that this unconstructed pathway was often muddy, there are stories of villagers walking to the station in their wellington boots and then changing into shoes to board the train. The 'wellies' were left in the waiting shelter until their return later in the day!

As all Exe Valley line and most weekday Taunton and Barnstaple

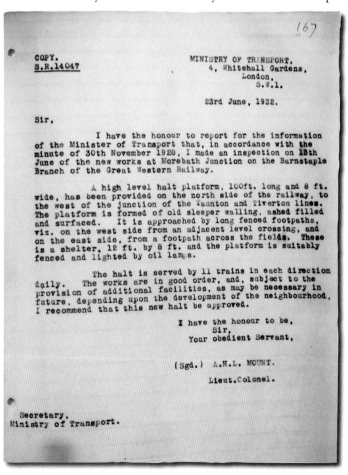

Letter confirming the MoT works inspection by Lieut. Col. A.H.L. Mount on 13th June 1932. Clearly the GWR were trusted to have carried out the work properly, as this was four years after the halt opened. *Courtesy National Archives*

No. 6327 stopped at Morebath Junction Halt with a four-coach Barnstaple Junction to Taunton train on 13th April 1964. *Peter W. Gray*

trains stopped at the halt, it and the nearby village enjoyed a good service, better than that of Morebath station itself. Unstaffed, oddly perhaps it came under the jurisdiction of the Bampton station master, on the Exe Valley line, rather than his contemporary at Dulverton, on the D&SR route. Also as a consequence of this, traffic summaries for the halt were included in the Bampton data.

The platform, 100 feet long and 8 feet wide, was positioned on the north or village side of the single line, just west of the commencement of the double track section for the junction of the Exe Valley Branch with the Taunton to Barnstaple line. The platform was originally constructed with railway sleepers as a face to the running line and in-filled. However, these sleepers were later replaced by concrete block facings. A rustic wooden-slatted and creosoted shelter with a back-sloping roof was the only cover for the travelling passenger. Originally built without any weather protection at the front, a small canopy was added later, which was supported by a slim pole at each end. The only other platform furniture were two hurricane lamps on concrete posts and the rather large station nameboard. A concrete-post and wire fence, like those along the lineside, ran along the back of the platform to prevent passengers falling off it in the dark.

A general view of Morebath Junction Halt looking in the Down direction towards Barnstaple in June 1965. A view of the halt showing it with the original sleeper-built platform facing can be found in Vol. 1, on page 146. *John Alsop*

ABOVE: A close-up of the running in board, a standard GWR design supported on concrete posts, on 4th June 1966. *Colin Caddy collection*

ABOVE: An overall view of the halt looking north-east, showing the rear of the Down 40mph speed restriction sign in the foreground and the bracket signal for Morebath Junction beyond. The arm on the right was for the Exe Valley Branch.
The Lens of Sutton Association

LEFT: No. 7337 has just left Ashtown Cutting and is now drifting down the bank towards the Exe River bridge, at the head of a three-coach westbound train on 9th September 1963,. *Derek Joanes, courtesy Roger Joanes*

BELOW: The same train in the same place on the same day! Derek's brother Roger was stood track side but just out of shot in the picture above. Ashtown Cutting is visible in the right distance. *Roger Joanes*

The train speed was restricted to 50 miles per hour between Morebath and Dulverton. On leaving the halt, the railway curved slightly to the left at 29 chains radius, gently cutting into the fields. As the line crossed a farmer's occupation crossing, it started to climb before entering the deeper, half mile-long Ashtown Cutting, which was spanned by a stone-built occupation bridge a short way along its length. The climb out of the halt was at 1 in 100 for 18 chains, rising then to 1 in 66 for 11 chains at the start of the cutting and part way through it. This was followed by a falling gradient of 30 chains at 1 in 58 and 42 chains at 1 in 68 down towards the open expanse of the Exe Valley. Coming out of Ashtown Cutting and running on to an embankment just under a mile from the halt, the hamlet of Exebridge could be seen in the open valley ahead.

Continuing out of Ashtown Cutting on the downgrade and onto an embankment, the line then passed over a stone bridge as it crossed the A396 Minehead to Exeter road. Exebridge Saw Mills were located below the embankment, to the right beyond the road bridge, as was 'Blackpool', the confluence of the River Barle with the River Exe.

At this point, on the right-hand side, was a spoil bank left behind from the construction of the line but long overgrown. The line then levelled as it passed over the single-span iron girder Exe River bridge, which was 70 yards in length. Here trains would have to cut their speed to 25 miles per hour to traverse the bridge.

A lovely panoramic view of the Exe Valley, with the 2.20pm from Barnstaple Junction to Taunton climbing towards Ashtown Cutting on 31st January 1964. The A396 Exeter to Minehead road runs on the other side of the three pairs of white painted cottages on the left and then passes under the line, through a stone arch which still survives today. Just beyond this overbridge, the railway crosses the River Exe and then curves to the right (north-west) to head towards Brushford village, in the centre distance, and Dulverton station. Just behind the train and to the right of the line, the premises of Exebridge Saw Mills are prominent; the site now houses a garden machinery centre. The train is approaching a foot crossing, marked by the white painted gates bottom right. *Peter W. Gray*

Although there were many to choose from, one of the most photogenic spots on this highly scenic route was undoubtedly alongside the bridge over the River Exe. On 30th August 1961, Class '57XX' 0-6-0PT No. 9670 was recorded rumbling across with the South Molton to Taunton pick-up goods. The photographer's viewpoint allowed a clear view of the mixed stone and brick construction of the abutments and their access arches, as well as the girder span with its walkway beneath. The 'iron mink' van third in line had been in use for cement traffic and carries an Earle's Cement label. The box van next to it has a crown motif on its side – royal warrant traffic of some description? – and that fifth in line is labelled for fruit. *Michael J. Fox, courtesy Rail Archive Stephenson*

LEFT: On the same day, an unidentified 'Mogul' was captured as it darted across the river with a westbound train.

BELOW: Class '14XX' No. 1468 propels two auto trailers over the box truss river span. Forming the 5.30pm service from Dulverton to Exeter, this selection of views provide proof that standing in the right place could deliver a certain variety in the motive power to be seen on the line.
Both Michael J. Fox, courtesy Rail Archive Stephenson

EXE RIVER BRIDGE

The River Exe was crossed at the village of Exebridge, just over half a mile to the east of Dulverton station and $183^3/4$ miles from London Paddington station. The bridge comprised stone abutments on each bank, both of which had small arches in them for foot access (a footpath ran along the east bank) but also assisted in alleviating flooding. The wrought iron, box truss girder span over the river was 70 feet in length. The design was similar to the more substantial viaducts at Waterrow and Filleigh, and also included a walkway underneath.

The numerous ponds of the Exebridge Fisheries spread out beyond the foot of the embankment on the south side of the line. The fisheries had been a feature from the early days of the railway, built during the 1800s and abandoned in the 1890s, they were re-established and expanded in the early 1900s, and still survive and thrive today. Sadly, the bridge did not survive the closure of the railway, the metal span being removed in the late 1960s but the two stone abutments still remain.

Once over the river bridge, the railway crossed the county boundary again, passing back in to Somerset for a few miles, with Hulverton Hill straight ahead. However, the line curved to the right, on a radius of 38 chains, to by-pass the hill to the north-east. On rising grades of 1 in 68 for 42 chains and then 1 in 88 for 22 chains, the railway made its way up the Barle Valley for about three quarters of a mile to reach Dulverton station, located in the village of Brushford, some 2 miles from the town itself. There was a maximum speed restriction of 40mph at the entry to the station loop but given almost all services stopped here, drivers invariably had to reduce their speed well below that. The locomotive would come to a halt at the north-west end of the station, just before the Down Starting signal and water crane, with its train alongside the waiting room and footbridge on the island platform on the Down side.

It was now 11.04am and we were scheduled to leave at 11.05am but had to cross the 10.00am Barnstaple Junction (10.11am Victoria Road) to Taunton train, which was delayed by a few minutes; it was currently on its way down the single line section from East Anstey. Simmering in the bay was the Exe Valley service, usually a Class '14XX' 0-4-2T in charge of a single auto coach, preparing to leave at 11.10am back to Exeter (due to arrive at 11.48am). This service loaded to two auto trailers on Saturdays and market days, and was occasionally worked by Class '57XX' pannier tanks or even Class '45XX' 'Prairie' tanks, neither of which were auto-fitted, so had to run round their trains at each end of the line. The goods yard was also busy, the 8.20am Taunton to Bampton goods (Mondays, Wednesdays, Fridays only), with a pannier tank in charge, was preparing to follow the Exe Valley service up the branch to Bampton at 11.16am.

Collett 0-6-0 No. 2266 leaves Dulverton for Taunton at 12.35pm on 3rd August 1953. The field to the right became the re-formed West Somerset Polo Club's ground in the 1990s. *Peter W. Gray*

Dulverton station, like Wiveliscombe, was on a left-hand curve and was the major intermediate station on the line. As noted above, the Exe Valley line trains from Exeter via Tiverton terminated here, so the station had several relatively busy periods each day, throughout most of its life. Dulverton was 19 miles from Norton Fitzwarren and just over 21 miles and 8 chains from Taunton, and therefore was just under half way along the route between there and Barnstaple. With this station stop, the driver and fireman might well obtain a

few minutes respite, as D&SR line trains often crossed here.

With the train stopped at the Down Starting signal, passengers in the front carriage would have the opportunity to glance to the right-hand side. Just outside of the station limits was the Carnarvon Arms Hotel, a popular destination at the time of the railway for those wishing to hunt, shoot and fish on Exmoor. Looking beyond the hotel, the eyes would be drawn down the narrow Barle Valley towards Dulverton itself, about 2 miles away, but little could be seen apart from the blanket of trees covering the valley sides.

Looking west towards Blights Hill, No. 6326 drifts into Dulverton with a four-coach Llanelly to Ilfracombe Saturdays only train on 27th June 1964. Note the token exchange apparatus by the second carriage. *Michael J. Fox, courtesy Rail Archive Stephenson*

DULVERTON (21 MILES 8 CHAINS)

Opened to Passengers ....1st November 1873
Opened to Goods ....11th November 1873
Closed to Goods ....6th July 1964
Closed to Passengers ....3rd October 1966

Dulverton station was actually located on the edge of the village of Brushford, about two miles south of the town from which it took its name. Unusually for the GWR in such instances, they seem to have resisted the inclination to append the word 'Road' to the name, as they did in many other places where a station was some distance from the place it was named after. The constraints of the local geography, – Dulverton is surrounded by hills – meant that the line could not be taken through the town. The station was near the mid-way point along the line and always held a prominent position on the D&SR. On the opening of the railway, it was one of the original, limited crossing places for trains. The station's prominence increased when it became the northern terminus of the Tiverton & North Devon Railway (T&NDR) when that line opened to Tiverton in 1884 (and then to Exeter, via the Exe Valley Railway, in 1885). Dulverton's population was recorded as 1,552 by the 1864 Parliamentary Select Committee. However, by 1901, this figure had decreased to around 1,300, remaining at that level up until 1961 and even today it is only a little higher at 1,408. Brushford's population would have only ever been in the low hundreds throughout the life of the line; recorded as 328 in 1864, today it stands at 535.

Dulverton's original layout was relatively simple but it expanded over the years and eventually became the most complex of the intermediate stations on the line, which was not surprising given the junction status it attained some eleven years after first opening. As originally built, Dulverton had two 300 foot stone-faced platforms serving the Up and Down lines, and there was no bay platform as the Exe Valley line did not open until 1884. Indeed, its original broad gauge layout is likely to have comprised just the two lines running through the platforms, which formed a passing loop, and the Up side goods yard but no pre-1884 plan has been found to date to confirm this.

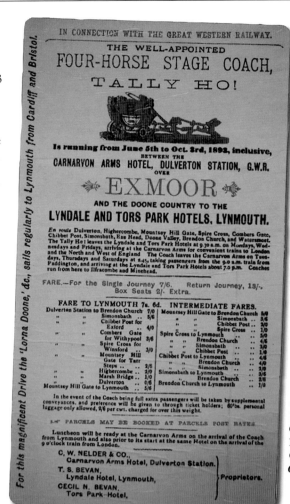

The published fares for 1893 for the Tally-Ho! stagecoach that ran between Dulverton and Lynmouth, with the proprietors' names at the bottom. The service commenced in 1890, ran until 1920 and was subsidised by the GWR to the extent of 10 shillings for each journey. It was a four-horse stage coach which traversed the wilds of Exmoor on its 26-mile run during the tourist season (broadly June to October). Departing from the Lyndale and Tors Park hotels in Lynmouth at 9.30am on Mondays, Wednesdays and Fridays, it arrived at the Carnarvon Arms Hotel around 2.00pm, connecting with afternoon trains to London. The coach returned on Tuesdays, Thursdays and Saturdays, leaving the Carnarvon at 2.45pm (to pick up passengers from the 9.00am London departure), arriving at the Lynmouth hotels at about 7.00pm. Lunch at the Carnarvon was available to travellers in either direction. The proprietors were Mr Charles Nelder (licensee of the Carnarvon Arms Hotel), Mr T.S. Bevan of the Lyndale Hotel and Mr Cecil Bevan of the Tors Park Hotel. *Courtesy Chris Nelder*

No. 7337 arriving with a Barnstaple-bound train in 1960. The noticeboard on the left advised the crews of Up goods trains to 'pick up brakes'; *i.e.* having had the wagon brakes pinned down for the journey from Barnstaple, to slacken them off for the largely up hill section to Venn Cross. Note too the Up side automatic token exchange apparatus a little further along. The signal immediately to the right of the train is unusual. The Starting signal for Exe Valley Branch trains, the arm had 'BAY' painted on it in white letters to make it clear to which line it referred. *Peter Barnfield*

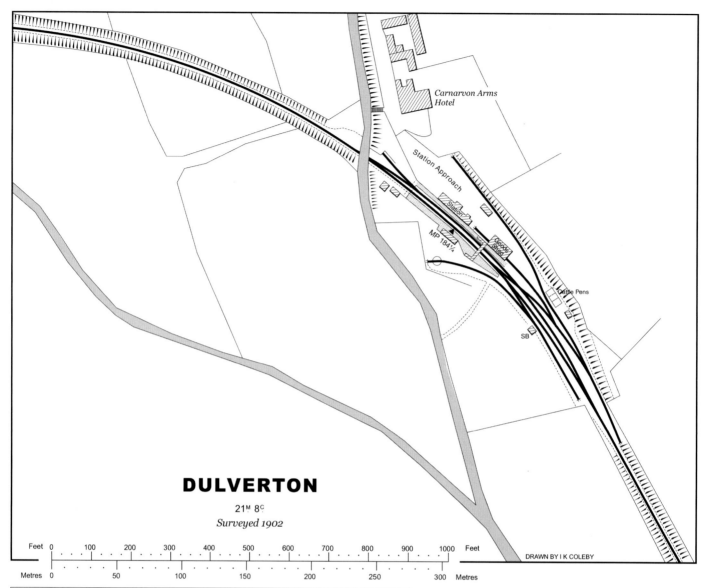

DULVERTON

21M 8C

Surveyed 1902

Feet 0   100   200   300   400   500   600   700   800   900   1000   Feet

Metres 0   50   100   150   200   250   300   Metres

DRAWN BY I K COLEBY

A close-up of the station nameboard on the Up platform and main building on 7th April 1959, with No. 6364 waiting to depart on a Down train. The exterior of the station building was slated as protection against the Exmoor weather. Changing here for Exe Valley trains would be possible only for another 4¹/₂ years. *Roger Joanes*

The main station buildings were on the Up platform and comprised the station master's house, along with the usual assortment of station offices. The house had two storeys but the ground floor of the gable ended easternmost section of it incorporated the booking office, cloak room and parcels office on the ground floor. The hipped roof portion of the house had a hallway and stairs on the ground floor behind the booking office, which led up to the bedrooms that occupied the whole of the upper storey. A sitting room completed the ground floor accommodation of the two-storey section but a scullery and kitchen were housed in a single-storey, hipped roof building adjoining at the Barnstaple end. Wooden porches guarded the doorways in to the house, one at the western end of the building and the other facing out on to the forecourt.

When first built there was an open alcove area facing on to the platform and in to the weather but this was enclosed at some stage in the 19th century. It is likely that the waiting room behind this was also added at the same time, as the stonework at the rear differs noticeably from the rest of the main building.

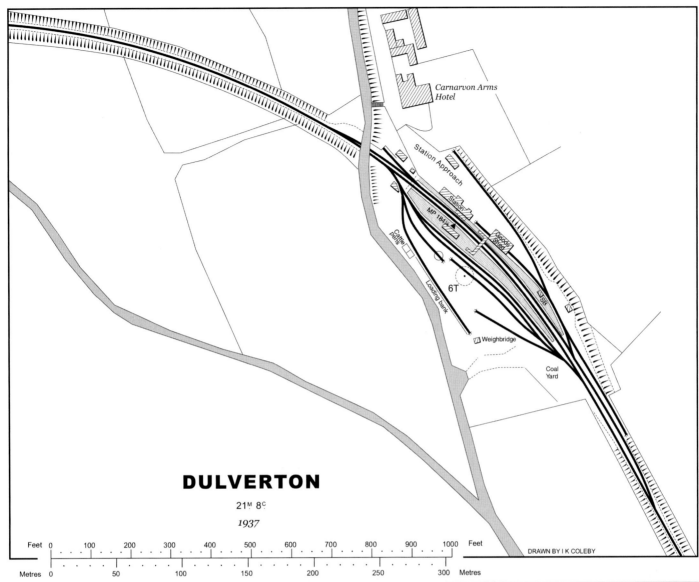

Carnarvon Arms
Hotel

Station Approach

Station

Cattle
pens

MP 184¾

Goods
Shed

USB

6T

Loading bank

Weighbridge

Coal
Yard

DULVERTON

21ᴹ 8ᶜ

1937

Feet	0	100	200	300	400	500	600	700	800	900	1000	Feet

Metres	0	50	100	150	200	250	300	Metres

DRAWN BY I K COLEBY

The platform canopy was added circa 1910. Next to the main waiting area was the ladies' toilet, whilst the gentlemen's toilets were located at the Taunton (east) end of this group buildings, in a stone-built lean-to type structure with a gently sloping flat roof, which has the appearance of being a later addition. Also at some stage in the 19th century, the platform and north-west elevations of the station master's house were clad in slates to prevent the rain and Exmoor dampness from seeping into the stonework. It is possible that many of these improvements to the station date from the opening of the Exe Valley line in 1884.

The Down platform had a substantial stone-built waiting shelter, the width of which was restricted by that of the island platform on which it stood. It had a slate roof and a small canopy on the front. The tall chimney, which was centrally located, divided the passenger area in half, the waiting room comprising one side, and the ladies' and gentlemen's toilets the other. The bay platform side of the structure had four windows, two for the waiting room and one each for the toilets.

No. 7332 reverses its train, the 10.50am Barnstaple Junction to Taunton, into the horse dock at Dulverton Station on Saturday 5th October 1963 to pick up one horse box, probably containing a racehorse. Horse boxes were normally conveyed by passenger trains but this was a rarely photographed operation. *Michael L. Roach*

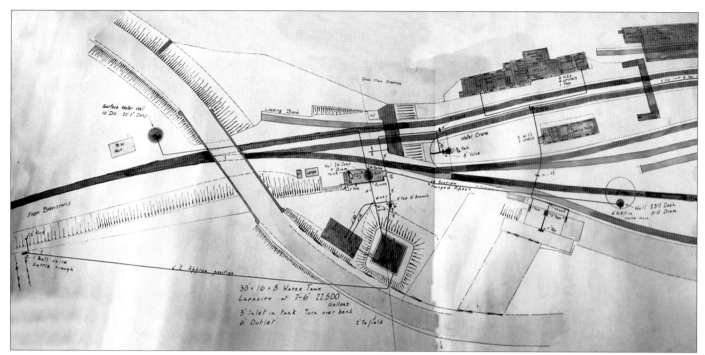

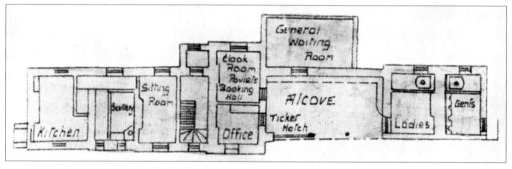

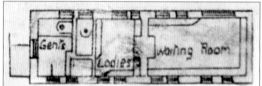

Above: A circa 1930s plan of the water supply at Dulverton station. Note the two tanks on the embankment of the road climbing up to cross over the line at the west end. Also, the pump house with its reprofiled eastern end, near the bay loop Starting signal.

Right: The plan also afforded the ground floor internal details of the main station building, above, and the Down side waiting room, below, from which these enlargements are taken. No other plans of these have been sourced to date, so this is the best that can currently be achieved for those who might require them for modelling purposes.
Courtesy Wiltshire Records Office

The station had water cranes located at the Taunton and Barnstaple ends on the Up and Down platforms respectively. The water for these cranes and for the station was provided by two reservoir tanks, located on the mound between the cattle dock and the road bridge. The largest of these tanks was surface mounted and could be seen from the road; the other was built underground. At the foot of this mound and near the Down platform ramp (at the Barnstaple end) was the pump house. This started life as a rectangular brick shed but was modified when the bay platform line was extended at the Barnstaple end in 1910; the modification consisted of part of the front wall being rebuilt at an oblique angle, effectively 'shaving' the eastern front corner off the building, which was necessary to allow for the overhang of coaches exiting the bay. The steam engine and boiler in the pumping house were replaced on 8th November 1923 by a $3^{1}/_{2}$ hp petrol engine. The budget was £330 but actual expenditure was £185 7s 3d, a saving £144 12s 9d, arising from a credit for recovered materials to reduce the cost.

The barrow crossing was also located at the west end of the platforms, whilst the short horse dock siding, of 40 feet in length and added in 1884, ran back from the Up loop line at the Barnstaple end. It had a loading bank on the road side, a carriage shoot at the end and could accommodate two vehicles.

The footbridge at Dulverton was the only one on the line and was of a similar style to others erected elsewhere on the GWR system,

Above: One of the storage tanks which fed the station and water cranes, alongside the B3222 road. There was an additional tank buried underneath it, the top of which is just visible. The pump house was behind and below the tank. *Courtesy Martin Bird*

A rare early 1920s view of the station, looking west along the Up platform from the signal box steps. The 6-wheeled stock of an Exe Valley service waits in the bay platform, with the doors open as station staff load luggage on board. The branch locomotive shunts what looks to be a horse box in the centre background. On the right, the stonework of the arched rail entrance to the goods shed had clearly fairly recently required some major repointing of the cement, if not rebuilding; further proof that there were problems with the construction of the D&SR goods sheds. The house in the left background does not feature on early 20th OS maps, so must have been fairly new at the date of this picture. *E. Wallis Collection, courtesy Kevin Robertson*

such as at Hallatrow, Wilmcote and Taplow (albeit the latter spanned four tracks). Its frame was in an ornate lattice-style, with a corrugated iron roof, and wooden treads and risers. The sides of the stairs were boxed-in with timber as far as the cast-iron support posts or 'stringers', which were used to support the half-landing of the bridge. Advertising posters were located on the sides of the wooden covers and smoke deflectors were fitted directly above the rails. The entrance to the stairs on each platform was flanked by a decorative wooden arch and the edging to the footbridge canopy was similarly decorative. Its circa 1880s design suggests that it was erected after the line opened but an exact date for its provision has so far not been ascertained. It most probably dates from the opening of the Exe Valley line, following which the need for passengers to cross the line would have been greater and more trains would have been using the station. Initially, Exe Valley trains had no separate bay.

There was a substantial single road, stone-built, 60 foot long goods shed, like those at South Molton and Wiveliscombe, which adjoined the north-east side of the Up platform. Built with a slate roof, it latterly had a corrugated asbestos sheet roof covering. A loading dock was located beyond the back of the shed and could accommodate two wagons. The shed, which could accommodate three wagons, had a 2-ton capacity crane on the internal goods platform and road access via a large door. The 1880s 2-chain survey (*see Vol. 1, page 115*) shows an additional short siding of three or four wagon capacity running parallel to the shed siding and

DULVERTON.

Station is on an Incline of 1 in 60 falling towards Morebath Junction.

No vehicle must be detached and allowed to remain on the Main Line.

Before engines of Freight trains performing work are detached from their trains, the brake of the Guard's Van must be securely applied and sufficient wagon brakes put down and sprags used, to prevent the train moving. Any wagons shunted on to the train must be immediately coupled up.

Guards of Freight trains must fully apply the hand-brake before leaving their vans.

Six sprags must be kept, 10 yards apart, between the Loop Lines.

Cattle Pens Siding.

This Siding is on a sharp curve, and when eight-wheel passenger stock is shunted over it special care must be taken to prevent the running line being fouled.

Telephones to Control Shunting Movements.

Telephones to control shunting movements in the Down Sidings are fixed in the following positions :

Up Platform.   Near Pumping House.   Signal Box.

Code

Set points for Cattle Siding	..	..	..	..	..	1–2
„ „ „ Timber Siding	..	..	..	..	..	4
„ „ „ Exe Valley Loop Line	..	..	..	..	..	1–3
„ „ „ Down Main Line	..	..	..	..	..	5

Auxiliary Electric Train Token Instrument.

An Auxiliary Electric Train Token Instrument, for the Dulverton–East Anstey Section, is fixed near the Down Platform Starting Signal.

The Instrument is provided as an additional facility for the withdrawal of a Token by the Driver of a Down train. Telephone communication exists between the Instrument and Signal Box.

When a Down train is ready to proceed to East Anstey and the Driver is not in possession of the Token for the Dulverton–East Anstey Section, he must send his Fireman to the Auxiliary Token Instrument to obtain permission by telephone to withdraw a Token.

When the Signalman at Dulverton has obtained permission from East Anstey for the train to proceed, both Signalmen must press in the plungers of their Token Instruments to permit the Fireman to withdraw a Token from the Auxiliary Instrument.

A Token can be placed in the Auxiliary Instrument at any time, but one can only be withdrawn by co-operation between the Dulverton and East Anstey Signalmen.

For instructions as to withdrawal of Token by Fireman see the General Appendix to the Rule Book.

Assisting of Freight Trains between Dulverton and East Anstey.

Freight and Ballast trains may be assisted in the rear from Dulverton to East Anstey, provided the double load does not exceed equal to 32 10-ton wagons. The assisting engine must be coupled to the brake-van.

Exe Valley Branch.

Tank engines only must be used for working the Branch Line between Stoke Canon Junction and Dulverton. A tender engine—engine leading—may, however, be worked over the branch between Stoke Canon Junction and Dulverton, on a through train.

Shunting with Auto Engines.

When it is necessary for the Exe Valley Auto Engine to be used for shunting purposes the trailers must first be detached.

Traffic Department Staff are responsible for disconnecting the coupling and vacuum pipes ; Locomotive Department Staff the regulator, gear and bell.

The Exe Valley trains were not always in the hands of Collett 0-4-2 tanks, as this 7th April 1959 view shows. Class '45XX' 2-6-2T No. 5546 waits in the bay platform for its to return run to Exeter St. Davids. Not being auto-fitted, the locomotive had run round following its arrival and will travel back bunker first. In the Down platform, a train bound for Barnstaple Victoria Road may well be exchanging one or two passengers bound to or from Bampton or Tiverton on the Exe Valley line. *Roger Joanes*

Collett 0-4-2T No 1451 propels an Exe Valley Branch service away from the bay platform on 25th July 1963. In the foreground is the 23ft turntable which was installed for turning branch engines but how much use it saw over the years is a matter of conjecture. Clearly it was useful enough to be retained when a new line was laid serving it during the 1904-1910 improvements but it was too short for the Class '45XX' 2-6-2Ts with their near 27ft wheelbase and there would have been little point in turning the auto-fitted 0-4-2 tanks. It was turned by the simple expedient of locomotive crews pushing against the white painted handles. Note the clean brickwork of the signal box base in the background. *Ron Lumber, courtesy Dave Mitchell*

terminating just in front of the eastern end of the building but this had been removed by 1902. The main goods yard or mileage siding was located to the north side of the shed. A small additional timber-sided shed stood alongside the back siding, which is shown in a photograph of circa 1907 (see *Vol. 1, page 134*).

The cattle pens were also originally located in the Up side goods yard, at the east end of the mileage siding. In its earlier incarnation, the Up yard could only be accessed via a trailing crossover point from the rear of the Down platform loop running to a headshunt from which there was a kick-back connection to the goods shed and mileage siding. The headshunt, which ran parallel to the Up loop and remained in place after the realignment described below, could accommodate three wagons. The goods shed originally had a chimney on the north-east corner, presumably for the internal goods office. The brick-built goods office at the Barnstaple end of the shed subsequently replaced this internal office and the chimney was removed.

The station went through a number of alterations over the years. In 1904, the bay platform line was added behind the Down platform to facilitate the Exe Valley service. This was

DULVERTON – PASSENGER, PARCELS & STAFF STATISTICS 1903-1958

Year	Payroll cost £ (& staff no's)	Total Receipts incl. goods £	Tickets issued (season tickets)	Passenger receipts £	Parcels etc receipts £	Total £ (incl. Parcels)
1903	455 (15)	11,625	23,330 (n/a)	2,984	2,444	5,423
1913	484 (8)	11,232	22,415 (n/a)	3,072	1,608	4,680
1923	1,510 (10)	17,985	21,920 (60)	5,027	1,698	6,725
1924	1,468 (10)	17,774	20,482 (34)	4,708	2,269	6,977
1925	1,443 (10)	19,091	20,803 (24)	4,876	2,285	7,161
1926	1,247 (10)	17,975	18,653 (26)	4,529	2,575	7,104
1927	1,300 (10)	18,044	19,658 (26)	4,651	2,487	7,188
1928	1,366 (10)	17,786	19,596 (33)	4,724	2,431	7,155
1929	1,428 (10)	19,729	19,342 (49)	4,769	2,365	7,134
1930	1,619 (12)	16,957	18,352 (56)	4,638	2,154	6,792
1931	1,806 (12)	14,767	17,285 (50)	3,999	1,848	5,847
1932	1,692 (12)	13,885	14,974 (40)	3,776	1,761	5,537
1933	1,827 (12)	12,602	13,800 (40)	3,501	1,558	5,059
1934	1,825 (12)	12,905	13,488 (54)	3,286	1,732	5,018
1935	1,827 (12)	12,130	12,421 (66)	3,289	1,197	4,486
1936	1,997 (13)	11,905	11,957 (94)	3,086	1,128	4,214
1937	2,061 (13)	11,884	12,577 (135)	3,290	1,387	4,677
1938	2,060 (13)	11,231	10,865 (117)	2,925	1,251	4,176
1939	2,109 (13)	10,620	10,754 (97)	3,101	818	3,919
1940	(13)	A	13,960 (71)	3,835	1,185	5,020
1941	2,261 (13)	A	20,747 (51)	5,942	1,389	7,330
1942	2,481 (13)	A	25,225 (60)	6,168	1,558	7,726
1943	2,806 (13)	A	27,120 (72)	7,276	1,722	8,998
1944	3,289 (13)	A	28,296 (77)	7,739	1,898	9,637
1945	3,270 (13)	A	24,049 (109)	7,560	1,949	9,509
1946	3,145 (13)	A	20,583 (102)	6,892	1,927	8,819
1947	3,252 (12+1)	A	19,769 (195)	6,497	1,902	8,399
1948	3,995 (12+1)	A	18,844 (226)	7,481	2,318	9,799
1949	4,113 (12+1)	A	16,827 (417)	6,287	2,015	8,302
1950	(11+1)	A	14,237 (410)	5,698	2,415	8,113
1951	(A)	A	15,391 (502)	5,885	2,004	7,889
1952	(12)	A	15,784 (532)	5,615	1,976	7,591
1953	(12)	A	17,389 (393)	5,471	2,161	7,632
1954	(12)	A	16,248 (475)	4,941	2,206	7,147
1955	(12)	A	15,376 (555)	4,836	1,014	5,850
1956	(12)	A	14,495 (A)	5,170	804	5,974
1957	(11)	A	15,514 (633)	5,636	745	6,381
1958	(14)	A	15,008 (608)	5,557	850	6,407
1959	(9+2+1)	A	15,314 (537)	5,806	957	6,763

A – Not recorded

LEFT: A pannier tank working the Exe Valley service replenishes its water from the crane at the Barnstaple end of the Down platform, before working back to Exeter in 1960. As the only station on the line with a footbridge, it was also the only one to have these GWR cast iron signs (there are two in view here) instructing the public to cross the line by using it. The tiny auxiliary token cabin can seen at the foot of the Down Starting signal, whilst to the right, just off the end of the Up platform is the porters' hut. Behind that is the large wooden shed used by the local Signal & Telegraph crew. The station was well kept and the flower beds were a delight. *Peter Barnfield*

OPPOSITE RIGHT: The island platform shelter in May 1965. The double doors at this end of the building gave access to the waiting room, with the ladies' toilets next door and the gents' at the far end. *Peter Barnfield*

DULVERTON – GOODS TRAFFIC 1903-1959

Year	Coal/Coke charged/ forwarded (tons)	Other minerals (tons)	General merchandise forwarded (tons)	Coal/Coke charged/ received (tons)	Other minerals received (tons)	General merchandise received (tons)	Coal/Coke not charged forwarded/ received (tons)	Total goods tonnage	Total receipts (excl. not charged) £	Livestock wagons forwarded/ received	Total carted tonnage (incl. total goods tonnage)
1903	10	0	2,116	1,100	2,511	7,107	2,167	15,011	6,197	430	1,706
1913	0	88	2,459	808	1,786	6,515	2,855	14,511	6,552	378	1,669
1923	7	42	2,071	1,247	2,404	6,451	2,167	14,389	11,260	351	1,474
1924	30	59	2,349	1,119	2,427	7,431	2,179	15,594	10,797	366	1,618
1925	34	38	2,273	1,268	3,604	7,495	2,251	16,963	11,930	431	1,756
1926	34	118	2,174	630	1,972	7,436	1,569	13,933	10,871	487	1,610
1927	9	67	2,141	800	3,241	5,811	2,942	15,011	10,906	413	1,678
1928	11	38	1,956	894	2,301	7,264	2,846	15,310	10,631	461	1,456
1929	41	112	2,849	736	2,655	9,343	3,262	18,998	12,595	400	1,528
1930	32	12	1,666	677	3,313	6,166	3,389	15,255	10,165	428	1,633
1931	8	15	1,345	780	1,992	5,433	3,223	12,796	8,920	406	1,383
1932	0	14	1,136	922	2,298	5,325	2,892	12,587	8,348	395	1,547
1933	10	68	1,349	1,098	1,786	5,106	2,304	11,721	7,543	275	3,260
1934	0	59	1,486	947	2,225	5,241	2,658	12,616	7,887	185	3,556
1935	25	61	1,474	953	1,665	4,712	2,970	11,860	7,644	156	3,599
1936	16	99	1,440	1,031	1,460	4,858	2,983	11,887	7,691	180	4,279
1937	0	111	1,327	1,049	1,277	4,471	3,263	11,498	7,207	107	4,264
1938	8	43	1,275	948	1,260	3,944	2,804	10,282	7,055	74	3,800
1939	8	119	980	956	1,112	3,502	3,598	10,275	6,701	119	Not recorded
1940	35	77	4,730	1,940	1,099	3,048	2,953	13,882	Not recorded	165	Not recorded
1941	86	36	5,468	2,223	681	2,030	3,724	14,248	Not recorded	146	Not recorded
1942	17	30	6,397	1,469	704	2,189	3,054	13,860	Not recorded	174	Not recorded
1943	11	4	7,887	995	745	2,441	3,755	15,838	Not recorded	216	Not recorded
1944	0	0	9,673	63	413	2,137	4,053	16,339	Not recorded	208	Not recorded
1945	0	0	4,094	63	171	2,863	3,999	11,190	Not recorded	177	Not recorded
1946	68	0	5,104	37	271	3,596	3,935	13,011	Not recorded	155	Not recorded
1947	0	37	3,088	0	341	2,595	3,003	9,064	Not recorded	18	Not recorded
1950	Goods zoned at Tiverton from 1st August 1947										
1959	20	16	220	0	2,157	1,104	4,178	7,695	Not recorded	78	Not recorded

ABOVE: A view from the B3222 road bridge at the west end, with a Down train departing behind No. 7333 sometime in the summer of 1963. Note the ventilated vans in the mileage siding, which will have brought in supplies for the provender store at the end of the siding.
E.T. Gill, courtesy Rob Blencowe

LEFT: No. 7337 arrives with the four coaches of the summer Saturdays only 11.05am train from Ilfracombe to Wolverhampton on 27th July 1963. This view from the footbridge shows good detail of the waiting area beneath the Up platform canopy, with posters visible for York and the Channel Islands amongst other places. Note too the position of the 184 milepost, next to the platform bench.
Ron Lumber, courtesy Dave Mitchell

initially a dead-end bay and was provided to reduce the shunting of Exe Valley services and keep the main platform lines clear for Taunton to Barnstaple trains; a set-back siding had originally been provided at the Taunton end to hold the Exe Valley trains. Also at this time the cattle pens were moved from the Up yard to the loading dock siding at the Barnstaple end on the Down side, this siding running back to the south west of the existing station layout. Additionally, a

run round loop was provided on the outside of the bay platform line.

Further developments led to the Down platform becoming an island in 1910, as the bay platform line was extended towards the cattle dock siding also to form a second loop. There were further improvements on the Down side too. The platform was widened and extended in length to 435 feet, with the Up platform extended to 445 feet at the same time; the faces of both of these extensions were

A fine overall view of Dulverton station from the road bridge during one of its busy periods, at around 5 o'clock on Saturday 15th June 1963. In the right background, the 4.10pm from Barnstaple heads away east to Taunton, having waited for the arrival of classmate No. 7304 with the 4.20pm Taunton to Barnstaple Junction service. Meanwhile, Class '14XX No. 1421 will wait in the bay until No. 6372 has cleared the section to Morebath Junction, before departing with the 5.15pm auto-train to Exeter via Tiverton, after which peace and quiet will descend on the station for an hour or so. In the right foreground, the 'shaved' corner of the pump house is clearly shown and note too the trolley on the Up platform with a tented canvas cover. For the modeller, there is much other detail in the picture, which therefore merits careful study. *Peter W. Gray*

ABOVE: Looking northwards across the Down side goods yard from above the cattle dock and loading bank, with No. 1471, in BR lined green passenger livery, alongside the Exe Valley bay awaiting departure with the 1.35pm to Exeter on 14th July 1962. The flat roofed extension to the Up side building housed the gentlemen's toilets. *John Spencer Gilks*

LEFT: Taken from the half landing of the footbridge, the Exe Valley service on 10th October 1959 was again in the hands of a Class '45XX' tank, No. 5524 of Exeter shed. Also featured on the right is the 6-ton yard crane installed circa 1928, with the coal yard beyond. *Peter W. Gray*

constructed of brick. Meanwhile, extra sidings were also added. In the first instance, a storage/ Exe Valley exchange siding that could hold fourteen wagons was built between the run round loop (which had a capacity for eighteen wagons) and the bay platform loop. However, this was later switched around, with the exchange siding becoming the run round loop, whilst the existing goods loop was truncated to make a new storage/exchange siding; the 1937 track plan should make all this clear. The coal yard siding, accommodating nine wagons, was located at the Taunton end, to the south of the station area and was again added at the time of these improvements.

A small turntable was installed by the GWR following a request by Colonel Yolland of the Board of Trade (BoT), when reporting on the arrangements of the Tiverton & North Devon Railway (T&NDR) in 1884. Having just one turntable at Dulverton to serve the T&NDR was apparently a compromise solution, as the BoT had wanted one at Tiverton as well. The turntable was small, with a diameter of just 23ft 7 inches and was therefore only suitable for tank engines. It was little used after 1923, when auto trains commenced working on the Exe Valley Branch. When it was first installed, locomotive access was from the Taunton end of the station, via the set-back siding. When the layout was restructured in 1910, the turntable was retained but a new approach to it was laid in from the Barnstaple end of the station. However, this left the engine inspection pit on the original approach line to the turntable located on the wrong side, so it was made redundant and filled in. Following the restructuring, the turntable access line now branched off from a siding leading to an extensive new platform on the south west side of the yard, holding the repositioned cattle pens and a general loading dock of 225 feet in length. There was an additional carriage shoot at the end of the new dock platform and the siding could accommodate twelve wagons. A weighbridge and weighhouse were installed at the entrance to the new goods yard, at the south end of the site.

Work carried out in 1937 further extended both platforms to a length of 500 feet and the running loop was also extended. There were a number of consequential changes to facing point work at each end to enable running in at 40mph and also to signalling, with both Home signals being renewed. In 1947, the loop lengths were stated in the *Appendix to the Service Time Table* as 972 feet (Up) and 735 (Down), with the bay measured at 693 feet. A 6-ton capacity crane was erected in the new yard alongside the outer siding, to replace the existing 5-ton capacity crane, although for a period of time the two were *in situ* together (*see Vol. 1, page 145*).

The first recorded signal box here (there was probably an earlier one – *see page 422*) was located on the Down side at the Taunton end, facing the Exe Valley lay-over siding and some distance from the end of the platform (*see Vol. 1, page 18*); this picture appears to show it had a brick base and chimney, with a timber upper storey. It was

ABOVE: Another busy scene at Dulverton, on 10th October 1959, with contrasting ex-GWR and SR 'Moguls'. No. 6398 arrives with an Up goods, whilst 'N' Class No. 31846 waits with the 3.35pm departure to Barnstaple. On the right, 'Prairie' tank No. 5524 will be leaving at 3.42pm to trundle down the Exe Valley to Exeter. *Peter W. Gray*

BELOW: Viewed from the first coach of the 3.50pm Barnstaple Junction to Taunton train behind No. 7307, classmate No. 6345 waits to cross with it in the Down platform loop on 15th August 1964. *Tim Stephens*

replaced circa 1904 by a new box mounted on the Up platform near the goods shed. A glimpse of it appears in a circa 1907 photograph (*Vol. 1, page 134*) which shows a timber structure with a hipped slated roof. The lower half of the box was painted a much darker shade at this time. It was to be a short lived installation, however, being replaced in January 1910 by another box of all wooden construction (GWR type 27C), which was located further east along the Up platform, almost opposite the site of the first signal box. The still relatively new second box was not wasted, though, being dismantled and re-used at Bilston in Staffordshire (where it survived until circa 1970), at a cost of £232 15s. In BR days, the wooden base of Dulverton's third signal box was rebuilt in brick; an exact date for this has not been ascertained but it

No. 5326 at Dulverton on 27th June 1964 with a four-coach train from Ilfracombe to Taunton. Nicely framing the train is Dulverton's fine ornate lattice style footbridge. Of a type erected elsewhere by the GWR in the 1880s, its provision here is thought most likely to date from the opening of the Exe Valley line. Note the bay platform Starting signal on the left, behind which can be seen the Down side cast-iron footbridge support columns. The concrete lampposts dated from 1950, when electric lighting replaced the Tilley oil lamps. *Michael J. Fox, courtesy Rail Archive Stephenson*

RIGHT: A general view through the station from the end of the Down platform in May 1965. On the left, the slate-clad station master's house also included the booking office on the ground floor of the gable ended section, with the booking hall and waiting room adjacent beneath the canopy and the ladies' and gents' toilets beyond. Note the typical B&ER ventilation pipe at the top of the nearest drainpipe. *Peter Barnfield*

BOTTOM: The original 'half-shed' provender store at Dulverton, with Silcock's branding, as featured in the *Great Western Railway Magazine.*

BOTTOM RIGHT: The extended shed in a sorry state a few years after closure. It survived for many years but has now been demolished. *Author*

BELOW: Moody skies above Dulverton in 1960, looking towards Barnstaple and illustrating the steps end of the signal box and also showing how narrow the island platform was at this end. The van was attached to the rear of an Exe Valley service. *Peter Barnfield*

still had its wooden base in the early 1950s. The box had a 54-lever frame, with 48 in use and 6 spare in case of future changes.

After the layout of the goods sidings was changed, the Up yard mileage road, leading towards the station entrance, lost the timber-sided shed mentioned earlier but a new shed was erected (circa 1930) at the end of the siding. Built of corrugated iron sheet and raised on wooden stilts, it was used for the storage of animal feed stuffs and carried branding for Silcocks, Fulford & Philips and Bibby's. Typical of such sheds appearing in goods yards throughout the GWR in the 1930s, it was later more than doubled in size, with other such provender stores on the line being erected at Wiveliscombe, Morebath and South Molton. Also provided, near this shed, just inside the station entrance, was a petrol pump. For station use only, it was operated by a brass handle which was kept in the office until needed. In 1950, the Tilley oil lighting was replaced by electricity on the platforms and in the station.

Dulverton was usually the busiest station on the line. In 1903, 23,330 passenger tickets were issued and this remained relatively stable for the next twenty years, with a small drop to 21,920 in 1923. Thereafter, however, a steady decline set in and the figure had halved by the onset of war in 1939, to 10,754. However, the war was then to see a dramatic increase

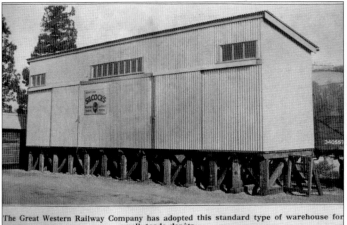

The Great Western Railway Company has adopted this standard type of warehouse for small goods depôts.

RIGHT: A close-up of the water crane and its attendant brazier at the east end of the Up platform, with a backdrop of some more fine Somerset countryside and Perry Farm in the distance framed by the water crane.
Hugh Davies collection

BELOW: A closer view of the somewhat untidy area around the horse dock. The porters' hut is nearest, with the larger S&T shed behind and the station coal bunker in between. Note too the drums for signal lamp oil and the station wheelbarrow. The wagon alongside the dock looks to be a van rather than a horse box, which was probably left here for convenient collection by an Up train.
Author's collection

which produced the station's peak of 28,296 passenger tickets sold (plus 77 seasons) in 1944. The usual post-war decline saw this drop to around 15,000-16,000 during the 1950s but this was still higher than in the 1930s. Season tickets, however, grew though the 1950s, peaking at 633 in 1957, presumably reflecting the growth in commuter traffic to Taunton and perhaps Tiverton and Exeter as well.

SAMPLE FARES DULVERTON TO PADDINGTON				
YEAR	ORDINARY SINGLE (1ST)	ORDINARY SINGLE (3RD)	MONTHLY RETURN (1ST)	MONTHLY RETURN (3RD)
1901	30s 9d	15s 4½d †	53s 10d	33s 9d *
1947	47s 11d	28s 8d	57s 11d	38s 7d
1955	35s 11d	23s 11d		
1958	41s 0d	27s 4d		
* Second Class † A Second Class fare at this time was 19s 3d				

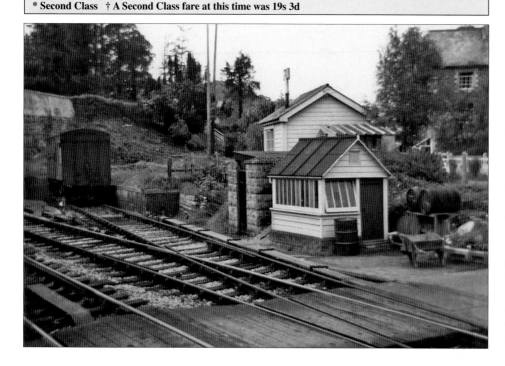

In 1903, there were fifteen staff, on salaries totalling £455 for the year. In later (BR) years, the station master was supported by a chief goods clerk, a booking clerk, two signalmen (on shift), six porters and three Signal & Telegraph (S&T) staff, who were responsible for the whole branch. In 1963, there were ten staff at the station. Some of the work at Dulverton will be detailed in Dennis Bending and John Howard's recollections in the next volume.

Goods traffic was substantial, with outwards consignments including timber from the nearby Exebridge saw mills, pit props for Welsh coal mines from the Pixton Estate and agricultural produce. Goods inwards included coal, fertiliser, cattle feed and agricultural equipment. Fulford Phillips, millers and suppliers of animal feedstuffs, had their head office near the station, their mill being located in Minehead. Messrs Goodlands were the local coal merchants, their offices being located across the road from the goods yard entrance gate, south-west of the station. Cattle trains were assembled on market days and horse box traffic (including horses for hunting) would be received and dispatched here. Such traffic often peaked with the annual Horse Fair at Bampton in late October. Cattle from Brushford market (next door to the Carnarvon Arms Hotel) and Cutcombe market, 10 miles up on the hill at Wheddon Cross, were also despatched by train.

A set of white painted double gates at the main entrance to the Up platform were shut every night following the departure of the last train of the day.

The roadside elevation of the main station buildings in June 1965. Being sheltered from the direction of the prevailing winds and rains, this side was never clad in slate. Note the stonework of the waiting room, on the left, differs markedly from the rest of the building, strongly suggesting that it was a later addition. The drainpipe on the gable ended section runs through the roof slates to another B&ER ventilation pipe. *John Alsop*

Between the gates and the horse dock was a small porters hut (it resembled a modest green house), which may have previously existed as a ground frame hut somewhere. Adjacent to this was a stone-built coal bunker, which served the station buildings in winter, and at the rear of the horse dock was a white painted wooden shed, which housed the local S&T office.

Exe Valley services ceased on 7th October 1963 and goods services on the D&SR were withdrawn from 6th July 1964. By April of that year, the headshunt, horse dock siding and turntable road had been lifted. On 5th August 1964, the dismantlers moved in again and all other sidings, except that serving the long loading dock, were lifted.

The dock siding was later used by those dismantling the line after closure, for storing bogie wagons holding the lifted rails.

The *February 1947 Service Time Table* notes that a steam lance was stored at Dulverton signal box, to facilitate the clearance of snow from points. This would have been particularly useful given the heavy snowfalls in the period January to March of that year. Dulverton also retained a re-railing ramp and this was stored in the goods yard.

Prior to 1939 Dulverton had three GWR Thorneycroft motor lorries, collecting and delivering goods locally on the Country Lorry Service, around Exford, Winsford, Withypool, Simonsbath and Exmoor generally. One lorry would deliver to and from East Anstey

Two modern views of the weighbridge hut, from the road side, left, and from the station yard side, right. The stonework, which looks modern but is in fact original, matched that used for the waiting room (above). *Both author*

and Morebath stations. After the war, two lorries did the job but they were stretched when large amounts of fertiliser and slag were awaiting delivery to outlying farms.

The *1901 Passenger Time Table* published coach times from Dulverton station to the town on weekdays. The price of the horse-bus was 9d.

STATION TO TOWN	TOWN TO STATION	ARRIVAL TIME
	11.30am..	11.50am
12.45pm..	1.40pm..	.1.55pm
2.35pm..	4.05pm..	.4.30pm
4.45pm..	7.25pm..	.7.45pm
8.30pm		

In the late 1950s the town to station bus was run by Greenslades and the bus was driven by a Mr Danny Roberts.

Having rested for a couple of minutes at the station and waited for a late running Up train to cross, during which we would perhaps have taken on water from the platform-mounted water crane, the Barnstaple-bound train crew would be ready for the road 'up the cutting', as it was colloquially known by the Dulverton staff. With a steady 4-mile climb ahead, at largely 1 in 58, the fireman would need to stoke the locomotive's firebox and be prepared to work hard again.

The delayed Up train from Barnstaple having arrived, we got the right of way at 11.10am, five minutes late. With the Starting signal 'off' and a blast on the whistle, the train would pull away, first negotiating the points at the west end of the station throat as it passed under the stone-built arch of the B3222 road bridge. The line

continued on a left-hand curve of 12 and 24 chains radius as it passed into a shallow cutting behind Brushford village. Here, a 50mph speed restriction began, which lasted for just half a mile.

About a quarter of a mile out of the station, the line went under a second stone-built road bridge and emerged onto an embankment. To the right, St. Nicholas church could be seen, parts of which are believed to have been built in the 13th century, along with the village primary school and some stone-built cottages which comprised 'Old Brushford'.

The embankment grew in height as the line started to curve back to the right at 27 chains radius, passing over the narrow and winding Brockey stream and then over a stone bridge taking a narrow road up Langaller Hill and leading to a number of farms. Looking on the left-hand side down the Brockey Valley, in the distance was Kentshill

Looking north-west from the B3222 road bridge, as No. 6326 heads away with the 4.20pm Taunton to Barnstaple service on 3rd September 1964. Brushford village is in the background. By this date, the Home signal was no longer a bracket. *Steve Linney, courtesy Richard Derry*

Above: No. 6363 heads beneath the road overbridge with the Saturday's only Wolverhampton to Ilfracombe train on 22nd August 1964. *Tim Stephens*

Right: Viewed from the train, No. 7307 approaches Dulverton with the 3.50pm from Barnstaple Junction to Taunton on Saturday 15th August 1964. *Tim Stephens*

Quarry, stone from which was used to build some of the early village properties and, most likely, the station buildings themselves. On the right, the railway skirted the edge of a small copse named Beer Wood.

The line then ran straight for about half a mile, at the end of which section a glimpse along Combe Farm drive was possible, before the line curved back to the left on a 30 chains radius and then back gently to the right. The line was now 1¹/₄ miles out of Dulverton (milepost 185¹/₂) and the 1 in 58 climb was apparent. Despite the gradient, the speed restriction had by this point eased to 55mph, which now applied all the way to East Anstey.

The sides of the Brockey Valley to the right were largely steep farmland, used for grazing and belonging to Ashill Farm. Further on and just visible on the right was Nutsford House, then Gilmore Farm. The line hugged the left-hand or southern side of the valley, which was more tree covered with the occasional coppice, then straightened for the next half mile as it cut through fields, before passing over a stone-built road bridge near Nightcott Farm.

It then entered a deep wooded cutting and the short Knackershole or Nightcott Tunnel was a quarter of a mile away. The tunnel was only 44 yards long and in reality was a substantial road bridge for the single track road running between Oldways End and Dulverton but as the cutting at this point was very deep, the short tunnel was therefore a suitable civil engineering compromise.

The 4.10pm from Barnstaple to Taunton train arrives at Dulverton on 26th March 1963, with ex-GWR power in charge on this occasion. No. 6327's train consists of two loaded 6-wheeled milk tank wagons and four coaches. The tanks would have originated from the Cow & Gate milk depot and creamery at Torrington, from where they were tripped to Barnstaple Junction for onward transfer by this train. Most of Torrington's output went via the ex-SR route to Exeter and then on to London via Salisbury, as they were destined for the United Dairies plant at Vauxhall or the Express Dairies creamery at Morden. However, some tanks also came this way, transferring to the Cornwall to London milk train at Taunton, from where they travelled via the WR route to the Express Dairies depot at Kensington. Milk traffic by rail from Torrington ceased in 1978, by which date the depot had been taken over by Dairy Crest. It closed completely in 1993. *Michael L. Roach*

No. 6375 passes the Advanced Starting signal in the cutting behind Brushford, as it heads away from the station with the 12.15pm Taunton to Barnstaple train on 28th August 1961. This signal was positioned to allow shunting in to the Down sidings without leaving the control of Dulverton signal box. The leading coach with its distinctive domed roof ends is a Hawksworth design, Diagram D133, gangwayed Brake or Van Third, with four passenger compartments, one of 125 examples built. The end of the coach nearer the camera has no end steps or handrail and appears to have been built like that. Next to it is what looks to be a Collett Composite with seven compartments. *Michael J. Fox, courtesy Rail Archive Stephenson*

No. 7304 heads past Brushford's St. Nicholas church and part of the old village, as it starts to slow for the station stop with the 10.20am Barnstaple Junction to Taunton service on 30th August 1961. The train, which is formed of a set of three green-liveried Bullied coaches, is about to pass beneath the first stone bridge on the approach to the station, a stone arch carrying a minor lane between the B3222 and Brushford New Road. It still remains today, although the trackbed on either side is now covered by the gardens of new properties built along Brushford New Road since the railway closed. *Michael J. Fox, courtesy Rail Archive Stephenson*

A circa 1965 view of the line running down the Brockey Valley, looking east towards Dulverton station and the Carnarvon Arms Hotel in the centre distance. The Exe River Bridge and Ashtown Cutting can be made out upper right and in the very top corner, Morebath Junction, with the line to Taunton heading straight off the top of the picture and the course of the Exe Valley Branch curving to the right. Combe Drive can be seen bottom left running through the copse named Beer Wood. On the right is Langaller Farm and the dwelling about a quarter of a mile to the north of it is Rocks Cottages; the trackway heading south from here led to Kentshill Quarry, just off the right-hand edge of the picture. Centre left, on the northern edge of Brushford village, a distinctive tree-lined driveway leads up to a 1930s-built property, which is now the Three Acres Country House B&B. *Aerofilms/Historic England*

After the bird's eye view, a sheep's eye view of the same stretch of the line! Seen from the fields to the side of Langaller Hill, an unidentified 'Mogul' heads west towards East Anstey on 14th July 1962. The six coach train is thought to be the 10.55am Wolverhampton Low Level to Ilfracombe Saturday's only service. The difference in architectural styles between the old and new parts of Brushford village is clear and there is also a ground level view of the evergreens leading up to Three Acres House. *John Spencer Gilks*

LEFT: A driver's eye view of Knackershole or Nightcott Tunnel, looking east towards Taunton circa 1950. The hedge running diagonally over the top of the tunnel borders the road, giving an indication of how high an overbridge would have been if one had been built instead and the cutting opened right out. It would also have required three arches to span the cutting. It can be seen that the line was level through the tunnel, dropping away to Dulverton on the far side and climbing again towards East Anstey behind the photographer.
Roger J. Sellick,
courtesy National Railway Museum

BELOW: No. 7333 exits the eastern portal of the tunnel with the 2.24pm Barnstaple to Taunton train on 26th March 1963. Note the female figure sat high up the bank above the tunnel mouth. With the driver having shut off steam as his train breasted the summit to begin the mile long descent to Dulverton station, she has not been engulfed in smoke. *Michael L. Roach*

KNACKERSHOLE OR NIGHTCOTT TUNNEL

Nightcott Tunnel, which was also known as Nightcote, West Knowle and, most commonly, Knackershole Tunnel, was the shortest tunnel on the line at 44 yards. Located between Dulverton and East Anstey stations, it tunnelled beneath a country lane that led from the town of Dulverton to Oldways End, a hamlet near to East Anstey. The short tunnel was in a deep cutting but it avoided the excavation of the deepest part and the consequent requirement for a high overbridge. Its eastern portal was 186 miles and 38 chains from London and although it was the shortest tunnel on the line, it had the most alternative names. Situated to the west of the hamlets of East and West Nightcott, on the north side of the railway, Nightcote may simply have been a miss-spelling of Nightcott, whilst West Knowle came from another hamlet, of the same name, just to the west of the tunnel, on the south side of the line. However, the 1890 Ordnance Survey indicates that this hamlet was previously named Knacker's Hole and shows the

tunnel as Knackershole; the OS continued with this name for it right up to its 1970 map, after the railway had been dismantled. The hamlet was renamed West Knowle circa 1900, this presumably being deemed more acceptable than its rather crude predecessor, although the Knackershole name survives with a nearby barn that has been converted for use as a local theatre venue.

In the blink of an eye, the train was through the tunnel and back into the cutting, which soon opened up on to an embankment on a left-hand bend. As the line headed towards East Anstey, it passed close to several farms, in particular Venn Farm and Anstey Farm, as its 1 in 58 climb continued. The railway was now one mile from East Anstey and the steep gradient was maintained all the way. Sweeping first to the right and then back to the left on a 36 radius curve, the line went back into a cutting and passed under a narrow farm occupation bridge, built with straight stone pillars but with a wood boarded span providing access across the top. Emerging out of the cutting and passing briefly into open fields by another farm, the line then ran

into another cutting on a left-hand bend which, after a quarter of a mile, led to another deep-sited road bridge, masquerading as a tunnel but of only 22 yards in length. Here, as the line made its way out of Somerset again for the final time, it stayed in the deep cutting for a further short distance until passing under the Oldways End to East Anstey road bridge and into East Anstey station, 188 miles from Paddington and 22^3/$_4$ miles from Norton Fitzwarren. This was the summit of the line at 699 feet above sea level and a short stop here for any train crew was a welcome breather.

Our arrival was at 11.18am, still carrying the five minutes lost at Morebath and Dulverton. East Anstey station was partly situated in the cutting at the east end but opened out at the west end. The Froude Arms public house was situated right next to the station, whilst the village spread over the years to both sides of the railway, although its centre was to the north of the line and comprised a primary school (still open), St. Michael's church and rectory, Parsonage Farm (now a private house), and a small cattle market and sheep pens.

East Anstey (24 miles 67 chains)

Opened to Passengers ....1st November 1873
Opened to Goods ....11th November 1873
Closed to Goods ....30th September 1963
Closed to Passengers ....3rd October 1966

East Anstey station was one of those on the line that was actually located close to the community it was named after; the village was just half a mile to the north of the line when it first opened. The population was only ever at the 200 level during the life of the railway (recorded as 227 in 1864) and the station was the highest point on the line, at 699 feet above sea level. The eastern end by the bridge was in Somerset, with the station located in Devon.

The line through the station was single track when first opened, with the platform and associated buildings located on the south (later Down) side. Improvements followed soon after opening, with the building of a passing loop in 1876 and the provision of an Up platform with waiting shelter. The loop was lengthened twice (in 1910 and 1937) at both the east and west ends. The Up and Down platforms each measured 245 feet in the 1920s. In the 1937 improvements, the Up refuge siding was added at the Barnstaple end, which could hold twenty-eight 10-ton wagons plus an engine

RIGHT: No. 7333 waits with an Up train at East Anstey station to cross with the arriving Down train from which this photograph was taken on 22nd July 1963. Note the brick facing of the bridge, dating from when it was widened when the passing loop was lengthened. *The late Owen Mogg, courtesy Peter Triggs*

BELOW: A general view through the station, looking in the Down direction on 9th July 1962. Note the start of another downgrade beyond the end of the platforms. *C.J. Gammell, courtesy Roger Joanes*

Another view on 9th July 1962, looking back towards Taunton with No. 6340 calling on a Barnstaple-bound service. The Down Starting signal is off and the signalman is exchanging the single line token and no doubt a word or two as well with the footplate crew. *C.J. Gammell, courtesy Roger Joanes*

and brake van. In 1947, the loop lengths were stated in the *Appendix to the Service Time Table* as 810 feet (both Up and Down), being an increase on the 650 feet lengths *in situ* prior to this.

The station building was constructed of stone and was single storey, similar to the one at Morebath. There was a central section which projected beyond the main buildings towards the edge of the platform, which had an apex roof at right angles to the line. There were two wings either side which were set back slightly from the central portion, with their roofs running parallel to the line. This building contained the waiting room, booking office, and ladies' and gentlemen's toilet facilities.

The Up platform had a small wooden shelter positioned centrally.

It was set back into the bank behind the platform and had a simple opening at the front. There was no footbridge, so passengers had to cross the line by means of the barrow crossing at the west end of the station.

The stone-built goods shed was situated at the west end, on the Down side behind the platform. It was 40 feet in length, could accommodate two wagons and had a 2-ton crane located on the loading platform inside. There was a loading dock area at the back of the shed (behind the signal box), which could accommodate a single wagon. A cattle dock was situated adjacent to the shed but on its west side, with a loading bank of 35 feet in length. The loading bank siding in front of the shed had a capacity for eight wagons. The rest of the

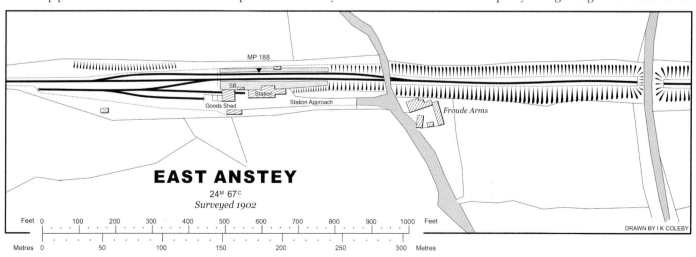

EAST ANSTEY

24^M 67^C

Surveyed 1902

DRAWN BY I K COLEBY

No. 7333 starts away from East Anstey on 2nd October 1962, with the 1.15pm service from Taunton to Barnstaple Junction. The short 22-yard tunnel can be seen in the far distance, through the arch of the road bridge at the end of the platforms. Having already seen how the line drops away to the west, towards Barnstaple, the station's position as the summit of the route is confirmed by the rails also descending just beyond the east end of the platforms and through the tunnel. Note, too, that the Down Home signal is still showing 'off'. On the right, the rail entrance to the goods shed retained its arch but the ends of wall ties show the usual structural problems we have come to expect from the other stations we have already visited. *R.A. Lumber, courtesy Dave Mitchell*

modest goods yard was on the west side, behind the Down platform and was reached by a headshunt branching off the Down loop. The headshunt could accommodate six wagons and the siding running parallel to the goods shed line and back to the loading dock could hold eleven wagons. Goods in comprised mainly slag, fertiliser and cattle food but coal traffic was light. There was a monthly market situated next to the station and this provided a reasonable amount of livestock traffic, with the despatch of loaded cattle wagons and also sheep, along with regular consignments of rabbits and poultry. Through the 1920s and up to 1931, around 300 livestock wagons a year were forwarded, an average of about twenty as a result of each market day. However, this dropped to a third of that figure by 1938, when just ninety-one wagons were despatched, but then climbed back to 1920s levels during the war years.

The signal box opened in 1876 when the loop was built and was located at the east end of Down platform. It was replaced circa 1901 (see Chapter 9) by a new box located at the west end of the Down platform, between the station buildings and the goods shed. It was a brick-built GWR type 5 box.

No. 7337 trundles into the Up platform at East Anstey with a substantial summer Saturday train, the 8.35am from Ilfracombe to Manchester on 7th July 1962. Note the fairly rudimentary timber-built shelter that provided the accommodation on the Up platform. The steps on to the Up platform, just glimpsed in the right foreground, led to the livestock market, which seems to have been established circa the 1920s. *Peter W. Gray*

EAST ANSTEY – PASSENGER, PARCELS & STAFF STATISTICS 1903-1958						
Year	Payroll cost £ (& staff no's)	Total Receipts incl. goods £	Tickets issued (season tickets)	Passenger receipts £	Parcels etc receipts £	Total £ (incl. Parcels)
1903	173 (7)	2,936	6,807 (B)	728	836	1,564
1913	198 (3)	2,754	7,117 (B)	694	440	1,134
1923	492 (4)	4,057	6,740 (7)	833	331	1,164
1924	568 (4)	3,502	6,297 (4)	752	273	1,025
1925	509 (4)	3,667	6,098 (2)	771	296	1,067
1926	519 (4)	3,507	5,095 (3)	680	342	1,022
1927	538 (4)	3,163	4,576 (8)	635	283	918
1928	592 (4)	2,914	4,766 (0)	578	222	800
1929	584 (4)	2,782	4,269 (2)	501	272	773
1930	589 (4)	2,948	4,296 (1)	501	248	749
1931	595 (4)	3,105	4,028 (3)	505	283	788
1932	604 (4)	2,214	4,046 (10)	439	170	609
1933	581 (4)	2,214	4,949 (16)	453	184	637
1934	566 (4)	2,324	4,635 (16)	500	165	665
1935	581 (4)	2,586	3,918 (12)	441	170	611
1936	615 (4)	3,251	4,315 (15)	434	118	552
1937	674 (4)	2,540	3,749 (17)	441	118	559
1938	631 (4)	2,322	3,608 (10)	409	85	494
1940	685 (4)	A	3,204 (B)	456	405	861
1945	998 (3)	A	5,759 (B)	1,073	381	1,454
1950	B (4)	A	4,728 (7)	1,170	571	1,741
1955	B (4)	A	3,141 (40)	718	134	852
1958	B (4)	A	3,392 (46)	918	116	1,034
A – Goods receipts not recorded; B – Not recorded						

LEFT: Looking westwards from the road bridge at the east end of the station, across the county boundary in to Devon, in October 1952. The bridge, which still remains, carries a lane from Hawkwell Cross to East Anstey. The station master's house sat above the platforms, up on the bank on the left. The noticeboard on the platform advised train crews that they were approaching a set of catch points.
P.J. Garland, courtesy Roger Carpenter

BELOW: The signal box and Down side station buildings in September 1966, looking eastwards towards the road bridge and tunnel. The line falling away beyond the bridge was on a gradient of 1 in 60. Notice how the station master's house rather dominated the scene. Apart from the signal box, all of the buildings at East Anstey survive today, converted for use as dwellings, and the platforms also remain. *Colin Caddy collection*

The bridge at the east end of the station was originally constructed of stone but was later widened, when the loop line was extended through it in 1937. The rebuilding work included a reprofiled arch and a new brick abutment on the north or Up side, the other abutment apparently being left as built.

In terms of passenger numbers, the station was busier than many of the other small intermediate stations on the line, with a peak of 7,117 in 1913. The usual gradual decline then through the 1920s and 1930s followed, down to 3,204 in 1940. This decline is further emphasised by the fact that the figures included tickets issued for passengers using Yeo Mill Halt from its opening in the summer of 1932. The Second World War spike saw a climb back up to 5,759 in 1945, dropping again

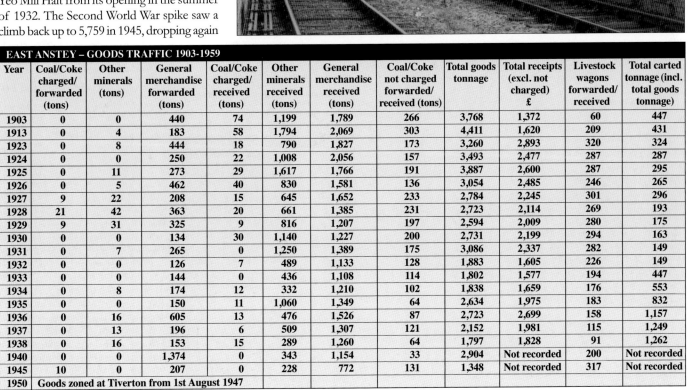

EAST ANSTEY – GOODS TRAFFIC 1903-1959											
Year	Coal/Coke charged/ forwarded (tons)	Other minerals (tons)	General merchandise forwarded (tons)	Coal/Coke charged/ received (tons)	Other minerals received (tons)	General merchandise received (tons)	Coal/Coke not charged forwarded/ received (tons)	Total goods tonnage	Total receipts (excl. not charged) £	Livestock wagons forwarded/ received	Total carted tonnage (incl. total goods tonnage)
1903	0	0	440	74	1,199	1,789	266	3,768	1,372	60	447
1913	0	4	183	58	1,794	2,069	303	4,411	1,620	209	431
1923	0	8	444	18	790	1,827	173	3,260	2,893	320	324
1924	0	0	250	22	1,008	2,056	157	3,493	2,477	287	287
1925	0	11	273	29	1,617	1,766	191	3,887	2,600	287	295
1926	0	5	462	40	830	1,581	136	3,054	2,485	246	265
1927	9	22	208	15	645	1,652	233	2,784	2,245	301	296
1928	21	42	363	20	661	1,385	231	2,723	2,114	269	193
1929	9	31	325	9	816	1,207	197	2,594	2,009	280	175
1930	0	0	134	30	1,140	1,227	200	2,731	2,199	294	163
1931	0	7	265	0	1,250	1,389	175	3,086	2,337	282	149
1932	0	0	126	7	489	1,133	128	1,883	1,605	226	149
1933	0	0	144	0	436	1,108	114	1,802	1,577	194	447
1934	0	8	174	12	332	1,210	102	1,838	1,659	176	553
1935	0	0	150	11	1,060	1,349	64	2,634	1,975	183	832
1936	0	16	605	13	476	1,526	87	2,723	2,699	158	1,157
1937	0	13	196	6	509	1,307	121	2,152	1,981	115	1,249
1938	0	16	153	15	289	1,260	64	1,797	1,828	91	1,262
1940	0	0	1,374	0	343	1,154	33	2,904	Not recorded	200	Not recorded
1945	10	0	207	0	228	772	131	1,348	Not recorded	317	Not recorded
1950	Goods zoned at Tiverton from 1st August 1947										

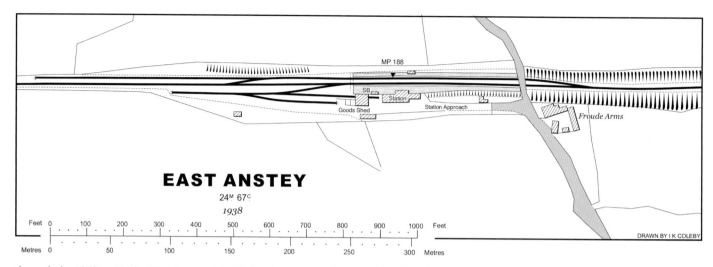

EAST ANSTEY

24ᴹ 67ᶜ

1938

Feet 0 100 200 300 400 500 600 700 800 900 1000 Feet

Metres 0 50 100 150 200 250 300 Metres

DRAWN BY I K COLEBY

through the 1950s, with the 1958 figure of 3,392 closely matching that of 1940. Season tickets were generally low, in single figures up until the 1930s and then in the teens throughout that decade. The peaks occurred latterly, with totals in the forties during the 1950s.

Staff at East Anstey included a station master until the 1950s but in its final years, like Morebath, it became the responsibility of the Dulverton station master. He was supported by two signalmen on shift and a lad porter. The station had a brief moment of fame when it appeared in the film *Halfway House*, staring Mervyn Johns and his daughter Glynis, and produced by Ealing Studios in 1944. Oddly, although it is actually set in South Wales and the station was renamed Ynysgwyn for the purposes of the film, it was actually shot on location at Barlynch Abbey, on the boundary between Devon and Somerset. The film can be viewed on YouTube, with the station appearing about 19¹/₂ minutes in and featuring for just under two minutes; the train seen arriving is hauled by GWR 'Mogul' No. 6364.

The stations between Dulverton and Swimbridge (inclusive) had their woodwork and possibly other fittings painted in green by the GWR in the mid-

1940s, East Anstey being so treated on 16th November 1946. Little is known about this, whether it was done as an experiment or whether the GWR were simply using up available paint stocks at a time of national shortages at the end of the war. Around the same time, some stations in former Cambrian Railways territory, along with Yarnton, Eynsham and South Leigh on the Fairford Branch in Oxfordshire, were painted in a two-tone livery using cream and a shade of blue-green, again for reasons which are not clear.

EAST ANSTEY.

Station is on the Summit of Inclines of 1 in 60 in both directions, and in the Station the line falls slightly towards Bishop's Nympton & Molland.

No vehicle must be detached and allowed to remain on the Main Line.

Vehicles attached to Down Passenger Trains must be formed next to the engine, except as shewn on page 102, and placed in the Siding by the engine.

Unless absolutely necessary, non-vacuum vehicles must not be used for Passenger Train Traffic.

In the event of non-vacuum stock being loaded the traffic must be unloaded on the platform, the vehicle remaining on the train.

Unless horses for Up trains can be loaded or unloaded at the Loading Bank, the vehicle must be formed in the Up train at the rear. and the horses dealt with at the Down platform.

When a Freight train has come to a stand on the Down Loop, the brake of the Guard's Van must be fully applied, and sufficient wagon brakes put down and sprags used to prevent the train moving. The two leading wagons next to those detached must be securely braked and sprags used. Any wagons shunted on to the train must be immediately coupled up.

An Up Freight Train having to perform shunting must be drawn into the Up Loop or shunted into the Up Refuge Siding and secured in accordance with the instructions for Down Trains.

Guards of trains must fully apply the hand-brake before leaving their vans.

Whenever possible, a brake-van, with a man riding in it, must be at the Taunton end of wagons which have to be propelled from the Yard to the Down Loop. When a brake-van is not available, brakes must be securely applied on the leading wagons and a competent man walk alongside. The wagons must remain attached to the engine until they are brought to a stand on the Down Loop, where they must be secured by a sufficient number of brakes and sprags. When wagons so propelled have to be taken away by an Up Freight Train the engine must run round them via the Up Loop or the engine must stand towards the Down Advanced Starting Signal and the wagons be pushed into the Yard and picked up by the engine.

A sufficient number of sprags must be kept, 10 yards apart, between the Loop Lines.

The west end of the station in the early 1950s, showing the headshunt for the goods yard on the left and the refuge siding beyond the Up loop on the right. The headshunt and goods yard was on the level and the line once again drops away from the station, on a gradient of 1 in 58 towards Yeo Mill Halt and Bishop's Nympton & Molland. In the centre, the nearer post holds the Advanced Starting signal and in the right distance the Up Home can also be seen. Note, too, the token apparatus on both sides of the line. *Joe Moss, courtesy Roger Carpenter*

Heading away again at 11.19am, westwards from East Anstey there was an initial falling gradient of 1 in 58 for just over one mile towards Yeo Mill Halt, so the fireman had some further respite. The line was almost straight, passing by some woods on the right, then through fields on the level before going onto a low embankment, which increased in height as the fields dropped away below. The line was now in the Yeo River Valley and one of the tributaries passed under it at this point, about a mile out of East Anstey. The view to the right gave passengers their first glimpse of the lower reaches of Exmoor. The moor proper was still about two miles away to the north but the change in scenery, from cultivated farmland to more rugged moorland in the distance, was noticeable, as would have been the purple heather for travellers in late August and September. The line now felt isolated and, indeed, this probably was the most remote section of the forty-five miles of its route. Farmland remained in the near foreground on both sides. For about another half mile, the line curved gently to the right at 36 chains radius and then straightened, cutting though fields until reaching the isolated halt of Yeo Mill. The single platform stood on the north side of the line and to the east of the bridge which carried the railway over the narrow country road to West Anstey. There were few dwellings nearby. Yeo Mill village was a short walk away but West Anstey village was just over a mile to the north.

YEO MILL

Surveyed 1903

Yeo Mill Bridge

Halt (opened 1932)

Feet 0   100   200   300   400   500   600   700   800   900   1000 Feet

Metres 0   50   100   150   200   250   300   Metres

DRAWN BY I K COLEBY

No. 6372 approaches Yeo Mill Halt with the 9.20am Ilfracombe to Taunton train on 7th July 1962. The iron parapet railings of the bridge over the lane at the west end can just be made out behind the platelayers' hut and the roofs of some of the houses of Yeo Mill village can be seen on the right. *Peter W. Gray*

YEO MILL HALT

Opened to Passengers ....27th June 1932
Closed to Passengers ....3rd October 1966

Yeo Mill Halt comprised a single platform and was provided by popular local request, at a time when the GWR were opening a number of small halts to counter the growing impact of road transport. It was located close to the hamlet of Yeo Mill but was also relatively convenient for those living at West Anstey, just over one mile away, and neighbouring farms in this isolated area. West Anstey was recorded as having a population of 299 in 1864 (Parliamentary Select Committee).

The station platform and shelter were located on the north side of the single line. The platform, of one coach length, was built of timber, as was the small passenger shelter, which also had a tiny canopy over the entrance. A wooden fence ran along the back of the platform and the halt's nameboard was to the west of the shelter.

Lieut Col A.H.L. Mount's inspection report for the halt, carried out on 17th June 1938, although it had in fact opened in 1932. *Courtesy National Archives*

There was a lamp adorning the platform at either end and a third at ground level at the west end at the top of the steps up from the lane. It was indeed basic.

As with all such facilities, the halt was never staffed, coming under the jurisdiction of the East Anstey station master. Passenger tickets could be issued by the guard or at East Anstey. The last train of the day stopped here in order for the guard to put out the oil lamps, a common practice for unstaffed halts, and there were never any goods or parcels facilities here. However, as the photographs show, it faced on to a platelayers' hut which pre-dated the halt.

Lieut Col Mount's letter to the Ministry of Transport recording the outcome of his inspection of the halt, carried out in 1938 six years after it opened, did suggest that it could be improved if future traffic demands merited it but this clearly never happened. Also, his

COPY.

MINISTRY OF TRANSPORT,
Metropole Buildings,
Northumberland Avenue,
London, W.C.2.

S.R.19421.

28th June, 1938.

Sir,

I have the honour to report for the information of the Minister of Transport that in accordance with the appointment of 29th June, 1932, I made an inspection on the 17th June, 1938 of the new works at Yeo Mill Halt between East Anstey and Bishop's Nympton and Molland on the Barnstaple branch of the Great Western Railway.

A high level halt platform 60 ft. long and 8 ft. wide with ramps 24 ft. and 14 ft. long has been provided at 189 m. 50 chs., on the east side of the bridge over the road leading to West Anstey. The platform is built with timber trestles and surfaced with 9 ins. x 3 ins. timber decking. It is lighted by 3 oil lamps and is adequately fenced with timber posts and timber rails. There is a shelter 8 ft. 6 ins. by 6 ft. 6 ins. and the halt is approached by timber steps with a wicket gate at road level. The gradient of the line is 1 in 60 falling towards Bishop's Nympton and Molland.

The Halt is served by 6 trains (rail motors) in each direction daily, and is used by some 120 to 150 passengers per week. The works are of adequate construction, and I recommend that they be approved, subject to the provision of any additional facilities in future depending upon the development of traffic.

I have the honour to be
Sir,
Your obedient Servant,

(SGD) A.H.L. MOUNT.

Lieut. Colonel.

The Secretary,
Ministry of Transport.

ABOVE: Yeo Mill Halt in its idyllic setting on the edge of Exmoor. *Peter W. Gray*

RIGHT: A close-up study of the simple wooden platform and shelter in later years, after one of the lamps had been removed. Note the slatted ramp to facilitate access in wet weather. The purpose of the square board with a circle on it (red outer/white inner?) is not clear. There was a similar one at the west end too. Were they indicator boards to show drivers exactly where to halt, so that when aligned next to the footplate, the first carriage was lined up with the platform? *Courtesy The Lens of Sutton Association*

note that the halt was served by six rail motors a day was incorrect, as such trains did not run on the D&SR line. The service was provided by the ordinary Taunton to Barnstaple line stopping trains.

After a brief stop, we leave Yeo Mill at 11.23am. The line cut gently though fields and was initially straight for about half a mile, beyond which it gently snaked its way down the Yeo Valley, with first a left and then a right-hand shallow curve. As it curved to the right it ran behind West Barton Farm, on the south side of the line, and then over a stone road underbridge, which was rebuilt with a pre-cast concrete span and parapets in its later years, and which still survives. The lane beneath it went to the hamlet of Bottreaux Mill, a couple of hundred yards north of the line, where there was a corn mill, a methodist chapel and a handful of houses. The mill no longer exists but West Barton Farm has been renamed Bottreaux Mill Farm.

The general direction of the gradient in this section was down hill, the steepest being at 1 in 70 for 62 chains but a range otherwise of broadly 1 in 90 to 1 in 192. The line ran almost straight for two miles, passing though fields and the occasional coppice, but near Kipscott Barton it became surrounded by trees again. About a quarter of a mile from Bishop's Nympton & Molland, the railway curved to the right at 30 chains radius and then, just before entering the station, passed over the stone bridge spanning the road leading to Molland village. Trains were restricted to 40mph entering and leaving the station loop.

Bishop's Nympton & Molland station was 193 miles from London and 27³/₄ miles from Norton Fitzwarren. The Black Cock Inn was immediately adjacent but the two villages that it purported to serve were three and two miles away respectively. Arriving here at 11.20am, a minute had been saved on the downgrade and on departure at 11.29, we were only four minutes down on the booked time. The working time table showed the 9.55am Up goods from Barnstaple to Taunton crossing our train here around 11.25am but it had been temporarily suspended at this date.

BISHOPS NYMPTON & MOLLAND (29 MILES 70 CHAINS)

Opened to Passengers ....1st November 1873
Opened to Goods ....11th November 1873
Closed to Goods ....3rd August 1964
Closed to Passengers ....3rd October 1966

The station was one of the most isolated on the line. Molland village (population recorded as 598 in 1864) was nearly two miles away to the north-east and Bishop's Nympton village (population 1,198 in 1864) was three miles to the south, on the far side of the A361 Taunton to Barnstaple road from the railway. It was initially called just Molland but its name was changed to Bishops Nympton & Molland from 1st March 1876. It is occasionally referred to as Molland & Bishops Nympton (for example in the accident report that will feature in Volume 3). It should be noted that the railway never used the apostrophe that the Ordnance Survey does in Bishop's Nympton.

No. 6340 arrives at Bishop's Nympton & Molland over Hilltown Hill road bridge, with the 12.44pm Taunton to Barnstaple train on 6th May 1961. *Edwin Wilmshurst*

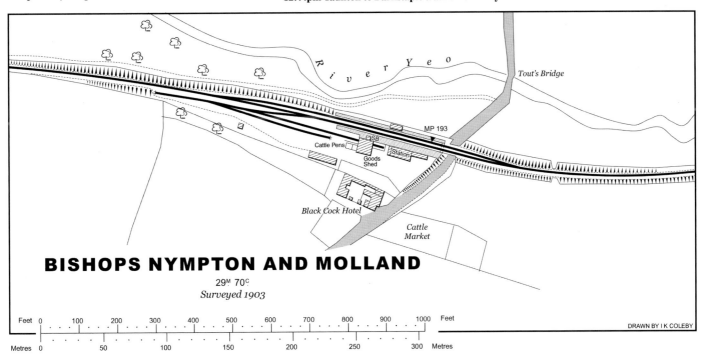

BISHOPS NYMPTON AND MOLLAND

29ᴹ 70ᶜ
Surveyed 1903

Feet 0   100   200   300   400   500   600   700   800   900   1000 Feet

Metres 0   50   100   150   200   250   300 Metres

DRAWN BY I K COLEBY

On 31st August 1963, a wet Exmoor day with the rain teeming down at Bishops Nympton & Molland, No. 7326 arrives with the six-coach 8.00am Saturday's only Wolverhampton Low Level to Ilfracombe train. Note the nameboard gave Molland second billing in letter size as well. *Stephen P. Derek*

The station buildings and platform were built on the south (Down) side of what was originally a single line though here. The crossing loop and Up platform were constructed in 1876. However, the land behind the Up loop was dropping away from the railway, so a series of brick arch supports were built buttressing the Up platform.

The main station building was a single-storey stone structure, along a similar design to the buildings at Morebath and East Anstey, the central part being flanked by two wings set back from the middle section. The roof apex of the central portion was again perpendicular to the line, with those of the wings parallel to it. The booking office, waiting room

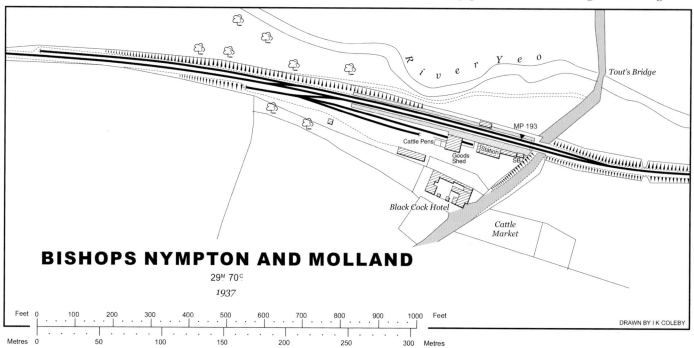

BISHOPS NYMPTON AND MOLLAND

29ᴹ 70ᶜ

1937

Feet   0   100   200   300   400   500   600   700   800   900   1000   Feet

Metres   0   50   100   150   200   250   300   Metres

DRAWN BY I K COLEBY

BELOW: **In its final year, the station did not appear quite as run down as others on the line, as shown by this view of the signal box and main buildings taken on 1st October 1966, the final day of services. Note the brick-built wall behind the man on the platform, suggesting that this part of the building may originally have been open to the platform. The signal box door was in the end wall just to his right, with an internal staircase.** *Michael L. Roach*

BISHOP'S NYMPTON & MOLLAND.

Station is on an Incline of 1 in 155 falling towards South Molton.

No vehicle must be detached and allowed to remain on the Main Line.

Vehicles attached to Down Passenger trains must be formed next the engine, except as shewn in the next paragraph, and placed in the Siding by the engine.

Unless absolutely necessary, non-vacuum vehicles must not be used for Passenger train traffic. In the event of non-vacuum stock being loaded, the traffic must be unloaded on the platform, the vehicles remaining on the train.

When horses are loaded for Bishop's Nympton & Molland, an advice must be sent that Station.

Before an engine of a Down Freight train performing work is detached from the train, the brake of the Guard's Van must be fully applied, and sufficient wagon brakes put down and sprags used to prevent the train moving. Any wagons shunted on to the train must be immediately coupled up.

An Up Freight Train having to perform shunting must be drawn into the Up Loop or Shunted into the Up Refuge Siding and secured in accordance with the instructions for Down Trains.

Guards of trains must fully apply the hand-brake before leaving their vans.

A sufficient number of sprags must be kept, 10 yards apart, between the Loop Lines.

and ladies' toilets were housed in the building, with the gentlemen's toilet facilities in a flat-roofed extension at the west end. There is the likelihood here, too, that there was originally an open-fronted alcove to the eastern wing, which had a brick frontage that did not otherwise

The stone arches supporting the Up platform, built in 1876 and photographed in 2014. The station buildings, to the left, and the goods shed, to the right, are both now residential properties. *Author*

match the stonework of the rest of the station building. The Black Cock Inn stood at the entrance to the station forecourt area, along with the station master's house. The Up platform was provided with an open-fronted, wooden waiting shelter, the roof of which sloped down towards the line. The platforms sported GWR blue and white station nameboards and there was no footbridge, so passengers had to cross the line by the barrow crossing at the east end of the station.

The station layout was built on a falling gradient of 1 in 77 towards South Molton. The platforms were originally some 245 feet in length and the loops were 650 feet long but these were all subsequently extended (see below). The station staff comprised a station master, two signalmen (on shift) and a lad porter.

The goods shed was on the south side of the Down platform at the Barnstaple end and behind that was the modest goods yard, which was of a similar layout to many of the other intermediate stations. The shed was stone-built, 40 feet in length (holding two wagons) and again of a design that matched the others on the D&SR; it housed a 2-ton crane on the loading platform. A loading bank of 35 feet to accommodate one wagon was behind the goods shed, whilst at the west end of it were the cattle pens and another loading bank, which was 40 feet in length; the siding accommodation outside the shed was ten wagons. Parallel to this was a siding with a capacity for eleven wagons, running back from the headshunt to the end of the loading bank. Coal traffic was minimal but there was a reasonable trade in other minerals, probably building and roadstone, handled through the local coal and builders' merchants, Henry Shapcott & Co., who also had offices in South Molton. A cattle market was established adjacent to the station when the line opened, situated just across the road from the Black Cock Hotel, which ensured a certain amount of livestock traffic from the monthly markets, the number of wagons sent out being slightly less than at East Anstey. As at the latter place, agricultural supplies inwards, and chickens and rabbits outwards were amongst other regular loads.

The original signal box stood at the east end of the Down platform, next to the main station buildings.

BISHOPS NYMPTON & MOLLAND – PASSENGER, PARCELS & STAFF STATISTICS 1903-1958						
Year	Payroll cost £ (& staff no's)	Total Receipts incl. goods £	Tickets issued (season tickets)	Passenger receipts £	Parcels etc receipts £	Total £ (incl. Parcels)
1903	163 (3)	2,402	7,790 (B)	597	427	1,024
1913	200 (3)	2,462	7,149 (B)	587	407	994
1923	445 (3)	4,011	7,274 (0)	791	585	1,376
1924	481 (3)	4,393	6,769 (2)	806	484	1,290
1925	498 (3)	4,121	6,854 (1)	816	348	1,164
1926	593 (3)	3,777	6,313 (2)	729	392	1,121
1927	479 (3)	3,954	6,559 (1)	765	361	1,126
1928	475 (3)	3,966	6,108 (0)	699	296	995
1929	465 (3)	3,840	5,756 (0)	657	315	972
1930	481 (3)	3,637	5,084 (0)	552	304	856
1931	459 (3)	3,546	4,479 (0)	509	264	773
1932	442 (3)	3,040	4,648 (0)	534	242	776
1933	444 (3)	2,621	4,875 (0)	530	189	719
1934	449 (3)	2,693	4,733 (0)	508	214	722
1935	442 (3)	2,707	4,680 (0)	497	173	670
1936	468 (3)	3,116	4,800 (0)	514	180	694
1937	538 (3)	2,577	4,142 (2)	492	106	598
1938	526 (3)	2,397	3,847 (4)	438	122	560
1940	598 (3)	A	4,496 (2)	568	134	702
1945	898 (3)	A	7,298 (B)	1,229	230	1,459
1950	B (3)	A	4,567 (7)	892	266	1,158
1955	B (3)	A	3,976 (4)	689	216	905
1958	B (2)	A	1,681 (2)	563	89	652
A – Goods receipts not recorded; B – Not recorded						

However, the track alterations to the Down side carried out in 1902, which saw the restructuring of the goods yard and its entrance, along with the extension of the platforms and loop line, brought the need for a new box, which was built at the west end, just off the end of the Down platform. Further improvements occurred in 1937, namely the lengthening of the crossing loop, the extension of both platforms to 500 feet and the laying of a new refuge siding on the Up side, which could hold twenty-eight 10-ton wagons, and an engine and brake van. In conjunction with these works, another new signal box was built, back at the east end of the station near the site of the original box. This final box was of brick construction and a GWR type 12B. In 1947, the loop lengths were stated in the *Appendix to the Service Time Table* as 742 feet (both Up and Down).

Passenger numbers at the station closely matched those at East Anstey, although the number of season tickets sold over the years was almost non-existent, with none at all between 1928 and 1936, and a peak of just 7 in 1950. The 1945 tickets issued total rose to the levels of the first two decades of the 20th century but after that, the drop was sharp, with the 1958 figure of 1,681 clearly not a viable number and one of the lowest on the line for that year.

On leaving Bishop's Nympton & Molland, the line ran almost dead straight for about 2¹/₂ miles. The first mile was on a series of slight downgrades (1 in 72 to 1 in 155) and then short grades up of 1 in 60 (21 chains) to 1 in 180 (a brief stretch of just 11 chains). Near Veraby Farm, the line crossed the River Yeo, on its winding way south to join the Mole River below South Molton, by way of a double span stone-built bridge. Running over the farm access road to Veraby and, shortly after, the lane to Mornacott, the line then started to climb at 1 in 66

The view west from the Down platform at Bishops Nympton & Molland in the early 1950s, with the entrance to the goods yard just beyond the end of the ramp. In the right middle distance, the refuge siding can be seen running back from the Up loop line. Note that, in similar fashion to East Anstey, the running line drops away towards Barnstaple, from the goods yard which was on the level. However, the downgrade was slight and west-bound goods trains were required to stop here and pick up their brakes. Notices at the end of each platform advised passengers to cross the line at the other end of the station, under the watchful eye of the signalman.
P.J. Garland, courtesy Roger Carpenter

BISHOPS NYMPTON & MOLLAND – GOODS TRAFFIC 1903-1959

Year	Coal/Coke charged/ forwarded (tons)	Other minerals (tons)	General merchandise forwarded (tons)	Coal/Coke charged/ received (tons)	Other minerals received (tons)	General merchandise received (tons)	Coal/Coke not charged forwarded/ received (tons)	Total goods tonnage	Total receipts (excl. not charged) £	Livestock wagons forwarded/ received	Total carted tonnage (incl. total goods tonnage)
1903	0	0	477	76	390	1,687	254	2,884	1,378	260	338
1913	0	8	353	65	883	1,855	242	3,406	1,468	202	340
1923	0	12	338	30	1,719	1,845	267	4,211	2,635	195	231
1924	0	0	701	37	1,432	2,244	328	4,742	3,103	268	261
1925	0	0	926	16	1,152	2,169	295	4,558	2,957	260	317
1926	3	0	620	16	1,081	1,976	215	3,911	2,656	239	246
1927	10	4	341	39	847	2,119	406	3,766	2,828	268	269
1928	0	3	1,517	15	1,224	1,711	291	4,761	2,971	283	209
1929	0	24	2,085	34	986	1,481	277	4,887	2,868	266	182
1930	0	0	493	20	1,546	1,596	317	3,972	2,781	286	165
1931	0	0	155	21	1,175	1,958	332	3,641	2,773	289	191
1932	0	0	148	5	716	1,946	323	3,138	2,264	217	307
1933	0	0	156	9	675	1,531	334	2,705	1,902	160	1,255
1934	0	9	134	13	735	1,504	265	2,660	1,971	157	1,223
1935	0	17	162	46	568	1,600	307	2,700	2,037	171	1,076
1936	0	0	173	44	729	2,200	350	3,496	2,422	167	1,688
1937	0	0	126	56	350	1,730	299	2,561	1,979	115	1,701
1938	0	0	152	66	539	1,377	365	2,499	1,837	78	1,420
1940	0	16	153	0	292	865	398	1,724	Not recorded	180	Not recorded
1945	65	0	441	0	429	307	646	1,888	Not recorded	170	Not recorded
1950	Zoned at Barnstaple from 1st August 1947, then zoned at South Molton from 1st June 1948										
1959	0	0	1	0	702	552	517	1,772	Not recorded	1	Not recorded

as it passed through Whitechapel Moors, a substantial wooded area, before entering open pasture land for about half a mile. The line passed under the stone-built Bicknor Bridge, carrying the South Molton to Twitchen road, three miles out of Bishop's Nympton & Molland station and then, in turn, gently curved to the right, back round to the left and crossed over the River Mole about half a mile further on.

Just beyond this point was the site of the loading bank and transshipment siding with the old mineral tramway up to Florence Mine. On close inspection, some remains could be seen amongst the trees on the right of the line, despite the fact it ceased to be used in 1894 when the last of the mines it served were abandoned.

After passing through more farmland more or less on the level, the line then began to climb again at 1 in 60 on the final approaches to

South Molton. As it passed alongside the Mole River and just before the station, the line bent round to the right on a 25 chains radius curve and passed over a substantial stone bridge, which carried it over the South Molton to North Molton road; the station was $197^1/_2$ miles from London and $32^1/_4$ miles from Norton Fitzwarren. There was a 40mph speed restriction into and out of the station loop but stopping trains had to slow more abruptly as they entered. We had made up more time on the downgrade from Bishops Nympton & Molland and were now only two minutes down on the time table, arriving at 11.34am, our scheduled departure time.

South Molton station was built on a slight right-hand curve. Water cranes were located here if needed but the stop was normally limited to two minutes.

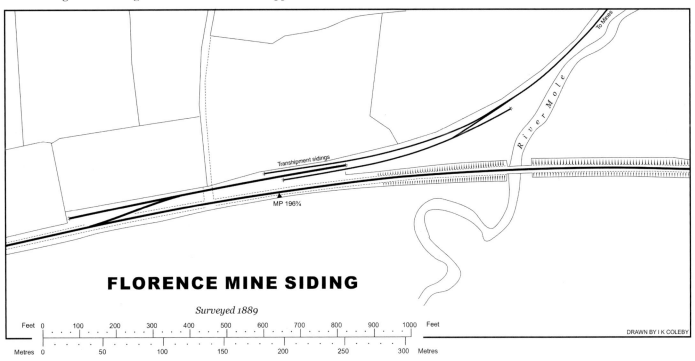

FLORENCE MINE SIDING

Surveyed 1889

DRAWN BY I K COLEBY

An overall view of the Down side platform and buildings at South Molton station, taken from the west end of the Up platform circa 1905. Note the open fronted waiting area next to the station master's house. Wooden paling fencing runs along the rear of the platform, there is a sprinkling of enamelled advertising signs and a rake of cattle wagons, with their lime-washed lower panels, can be seen in the goods yard in the right background. At this date, the Down Starting signal was on a bracket and whilst the modified stonework to the end of the goods shed stands out, it is also apparent that the work to rebuild the rail arch had not been carried out recently, so was probably done in the late 1890s. *Courtesy Rob Blencowe*

SOUTH MOLTON (34 MILES 18 CHAINS)

Opened to Passengers ....1st November 1873
Opened to Goods ....11 November 1873
Closed to Goods ....3rd August 1964
Closed to Passengers ....3rd October 1966

The station was located about one mile north of the town of South Molton, just off the road linking it with North Molton, around two miles to the north-east. In the early days of the railway, a horse-bus met the trains and charged 6d for taking passengers to and from the town. Later, this was replaced by a combined motor bus/van that ferried passengers and parcels between the station and town, which was run by the George Hotel. Subsequently, in the 1930s, a bus service was run by Terraneaus Tours of South Molton. The Tinto Hotel was located near the entrance to the station, being the only habitation in the vicinity; it is likely to have been opened at around the same time as the railway but closed in the 1930s and no longer exists. The Parliamentary select committee referred to a population of 3,830 for South Molton in 1864, whilst the figure for North Molton was 1,842. There was then a decline with South Molton's inhabitants numbering between 2,500-3,000 in the early 20th century but this has since grown again, the current figure being just over 5,000.

South Molton suffered from the delay in opening of the D&SR, as the L&SWR was already established about seven miles to the south

of the town, at Kings Nympton (or South Molton Road as it was referred to at the time) on the Exeter to Barnstaple Junction line. It was the subject of a projected branch from there to the town but powers lapsed. This isolation from the railway had, in turn, aided the success of the Eggesford cattle market, which had pulled business away from South Molton. The establishment of Molland cattle market, which opened on the coming of the D&SR, did not help the community either. South Molton was also the focus of a further battle between the L&SWR and the D&SR in 1864, as the former company looked to build a connection from Umberleigh, again on their Barnstaple line, to South and North Molton. The aim was to protect what they saw as their territory and to prevent the D&SR opening to Barnstaple.

When the D&SR first opened to Barnstaple, South Molton was one of only three passing places, along with Wiveliscombe and Dulverton. The passing loop was originally 660 feet in length but was extended at the east end in 1907 and at both ends in 1937. The platforms were recorded as 464 feet in length in the 1920s and these were also extended in 1937. In 1947, the loop lengths were stated in the *Appendix to the Service Time Table* as 873 feet (both Up and Down).

The buildings were on the Down side and comprised a substantial stone-built, two-storey house for the station master, similar to the one at Dulverton. On either side of the house were single-storey wings, the east wing housing an open fronted waiting area. The main building accommodated the booking office, waiting room, a

Although at first glance this view of the station looks very similar to the picture opposite, it dates from circa 1960 and shows a number of detail differences. The open fronted waiting area had been enclosed in 1907, whilst a very non-railway style concrete post and railing fence now ran along the rear of the Down platform at its eastern end. The Down Starting signal was also now on a single tubular post (the bracket was replaced in 1958) and the photographer had managed to include the timber-built Up side waiting shelter as well. Note the BR(WR) totems on the lamp posts. *E.T. Gill, courtesy Rob Blencowe*

small ladies' room, parcels office (with a large sliding door onto the platform) and the station master's office. The gentlemen's toilet was in the west end annex. When improvements were carried out in 1907, a new waiting room and screen were provided.

Both platforms were stone faced but when the Up side extension was built it ran onto an embankment, so had to be lighter and was therefore constructed of timber (similar to that at Morebath); the cheapness of the materials used no doubt played a part too. On the Up platform was a small wooden waiting shelter, the roof of which sloped towards the line and extended beyond the supporting

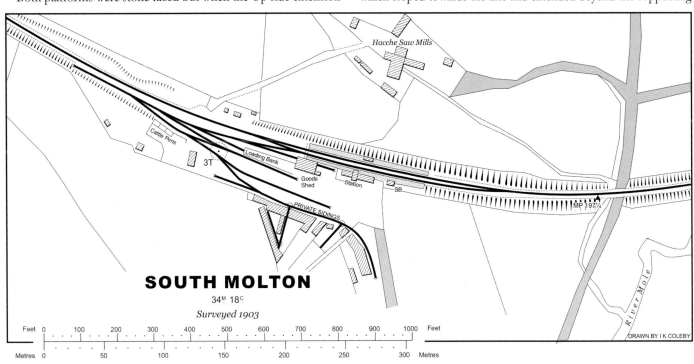

SOUTH MOLTON

34ᴹ 18ᶜ

Surveyed 1903

DRAWN BY I K COLEBY

The main station buildings, looking east towards Taunton from the Up platform on 12th August 1953. Unlike at some of the other intermediate D&SR stations where the waiting area was rebuilt with a brick frontage, here at South Molton it was enclosed behind a wood and glass screen. This view also reveals that the exposed upper section of the east end of the main building was clad in slate as a protection against the weather, with only one other wall of the structure being so treated. The concrete post fencing bordering the rear of the platform in the background dated from the construction of the extensions to both platforms at the Taunton end in 1937. Note the slight downgrade at that end too. Unlike at Bishops Nympton & Molland, there was enough space for the steps up to the signal box here to be fitted externally. *Locomotive & General Railway Photographs, John Alsop collection*

As mentioned in the text, the GWR signalled the Down platform line for bi-directional working in 1928, with Up workings being permitted to use it when trains were not time tabled to cross here. It made the loading of parcels much easier, without the need to barrow them over the crossing at the east end of the station, and was obviously more convenient for passengers too, with more straightforward access to the booking hall. Here illustrating the practice, No. 7326 arrives at the Down platform from Barnstaple with an Up train bound for Taunton in the early 1960s, as one of the station staff gets ready to load a package on board and a passenger makes the short stroll from booking office to carriage door. Pictures taken from the Up platform show the telegraph pole near the goods shed with an apparent lean, which is graphically confirmed by this view. *Gordon Bray*

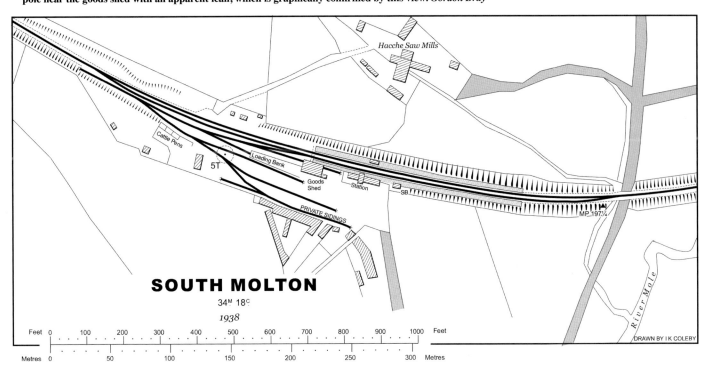

SOUTH MOLTON

34ᴹ 18ᶜ

1938

DRAWN BY I K COLEBY

The west end of the goods shed and a glimpse of the goods yard, access to which was via the point under the first coach. Note the grounded 'Iron Mink' van body on the loading dock on the right, whilst beyond it part of the provender store, built of concrete sections, can just be seen. Given the road by the Down Starting and Down Advanced Starting signals, No. 6398 heads off to Barnstaple on 3rd September 1960. *E.T. Gill, courtesy Rob Blencowe*

sides, forming a small canopy at the front. The Down platform was also extended at the east end in 1937, utilising the same wooden construction. There was no footbridge, despite a request from the local council in 1911, so the barrow crossing at the west end of the platforms had to suffice. The station was situated on an incline of 1 in 60 falling towards Bishops Nympton & Molland.

The station lamps were paraffin vapour lit until 1936, when they were converted to gas at a cost of £222. There were two water cranes, one each at the end of each platform. These were supplied by a large 9,375 gallon capacity water tank sat on tall metal supports, which was located on the north side of the line at the west end. In

1928, the Down loop was signalled to take Up trains after which, provided there was no Down train timetabled, Up services could run into the Down platform. This provided easier access for passengers and staff alike, and obviated the need to cross the line with luggage and parcels. In 1947, £920 was provided to extend the parcels office and construct a veranda.

The wooden extensions to the Up and Down platforms had been barricaded off by 1963 for safety reasons. Also, it is understood that South Molton was the only station on the line to be given BR(WR) style totem signs.

The goods shed was a 60-foot long, stone-built structure on the south side of the line which, along with the extensive goods yard, was located at the west end of the station. The shed had a through road and a 2-ton crane. This siding had a capacity for up to ten wagons – five in front of the shed, alongside a 140 foot loading bank, three in the shed and two beyond it. As elsewhere on the line, the shed's rail entrances were arched when first constructed but these were later rebuilt with straight, steel girder lintels over the doorway entrances. The goods clerk and his assistant had a separate office next to the goods shed. The 125 foot long loading bank outside also had the facility for both end-loading from a short siding (capacity four wagons) abutting it and side-loading, where a separate adjacent siding with a capacity for fifteen wagons ran alongside the bank on the south side.

SOUTH MOLTON.

Station is on an Incline of 1 in 60, falling towards Bishop's Nympton & Molland.

No vehicle must be detached and allowed to remain on the Main Line.

Before engines of Freight trains performing work are detached from their trains, the brake of the Guard's Van must be fully applied, and sufficient wagon brakes put down and sprags used, to prevent the train moving. Any wagons shunted on to the train must be immediately coupled up.

Guards of trains must effectively apply the hand-brake before leaving their vans.

Whenever possible, a brake-van, with a man riding in it, must be at the Taunton end of the wagons which have to be propelled from the Yard to the Down Loop. When a brake-van is not available, brakes must be securely applied on the leading wagons, and a competent man walk alongside. The wagons must remain attached to the engine until they are brought to a stand on the Down Loop, where they must be secured by a sufficient number of brakes and sprags. Should the destination of a train so propelled be for Taunton or any Up Line station, the engine must, when the brake-van is at the Taunton end, run round the train through the Up Loop and propel the wagons into the Siding, placing the van on the Down Loop, the Barnstaple side of the Siding points, and after the brake has been fully applied, the engine must pick up the train from the Siding and couple to the van.

Six sprags must be kept, 10 yards apart, between the Loop Lines.

Vehicles attached to Down Passenger Trains must be formed next the engine, except as shewn below, and placed in the Siding by the engine.

Unless absolutely necessary non-vacuum vehicles must not be used for Passenger Train traffic. In the event of non-vacuum stock being loaded the traffic must be unloaded on the platform, the vehicle remaining on the train.

The hand-points leading to the Spur from the Back Road Siding must be kept padlocked for the Back Road Siding, except when vehicles have to be placed in or taken from the Spur.

The view eastwards from the Down platform, taken on Saturday 1st October 1966 and showing the well kept state of the track, even at this late date. Also illustrated are the timber platform extensions, the 40mph speed restriction sign, the trap points, the two Starting signals – that on the right being for Up trains using the Down platform – the Home signal beyond the underbridge, the GWR board on the left with the 'G' painted out, the headless concrete lamp column which was representative of the lighting provided with the platform extensions and the Up side water crane. *Michael L. Roach*

South Molton station forecourt on 12th August 1953, showing the only other part of the building to be clad in slate, the east facing wall of the gable ended section. This view also shows the waiting room extension added in 1907 and built of red brick, with a blue brick base. *Locomotive & General Railway Photographs, John Alsop collection*

There were cattle pens located at the west end of the yard on a siding with a capacity for eight wagons that led back to the crane and the middle and warehouse sidings. The yard crane, situated by the point where the back siding split and by the end of the private Shell-Mex/Anglo-American Oil Co. siding spur, was initially a 3-ton version but it been replaced by 1938 with one of 5-ton capacity. This section of the siding could accommodate three wagons, whilst the middle siding in the yard was capable of holding thirteen wagons. There were entrances to serve the warehouses and the back (private) siding did, at one point, have two wagon turntables along it, to enable direct access to the warehouse and stores. The private siding was initially for Messrs Saunders, Mountjoy & Cock but a Mr T.H. Vicary was using them from around 1927. The GWR purchased these facilities circa 1945 for £177. Finally, the petroleum siding ran back from the warehouse siding on a short spur; it closed in 1959 in advance of the rest of the goods yard. *BR(WR) Supplementary Operating Instructions* in that year stated that the instruction for berthing vehicles of the Anglo-American Oil Co. (who had become Esso in 1951) be deleted. The yard was reached by a headshunt with a sixteen wagon capacity, which ran off the Down loop. There was also a weighbridge located in the yard.

SOUTH MOLTON – PASSENGER, PARCELS & STAFF STATISTICS 1903-1959						
Year	Payroll cost £ (& staff no's)	Total Receipts incl. goods £	Tickets issued (season tickets)	Passenger receipts £	Parcels etc receipts £	Total £ (incl. Parcels)
1903	492 (12)	11,895	24,099 (A)	2,655	1,828	4,483
1913	545 (8)	14,280	25,932 (A)	3,064	1,885	4,949
1923	1,229 (9)	22,177	23,490 (37)	4,392	2,475	6,867
1924	1,234 (9)	21,012	21,005 (16)	4,321	2,338	6,659
1925	1,362 (9)	21,872	19,570 (17)	4,051	2,319	6,370
1926	1,320 (9)	20,406	15,187 (14)	3,411	2,966	6,377
1927	1,379 (9)	21,262	14,824 (25)	3,524	2,953	6,477
1928	1,684 (9)	20,630	16,157 (16)	3,587	2,712	6,299
1929	2,042 (10)	21,664	13,672 (6)	3,265	2,719	5,984
1930	1,553 (10)	20,143	12,118 (14)	3,151	2,369	5,520
1931	1,566 (10)	19,966	12,023 (5)	2,900	2,124	5,024
1932	1,395 (10)	17,905	10,394 (4)	2,542	1,787	4,329
1933	1,499 (9)	16,244	8,978 (14)	2,352	1,334	3,686
1934	1,511 (9)	16,367	8,379 (20)	2,281	1,302	3,583
1935	1,724 (12)	16,625	8,170 (21)	2,155	637	2,792
1936	1,945 (12)	17,555	8,276 (14)	2,194	582	2,776
1937	2,075 (12)	16,282	8,304 (22)	2,245	499	2,744
1938	2,086 (12)	16,355	8,809 (17)	2,252	422	2,674
1939	2,213 (12)	15,621	7,203 (72)	2,005	459	2,464
1940	2,634 (12)	A	6,260 (A)	2,424	1,476	3,900
1941	2,631 (12)	A	11,330 (1)	5,005	2,356	7,361
1942	2,816 (12)	A	10,958 (2)	4,225	2,352	6,577
1943	2,916 (12)	A	13,897 (12)	4,979	2,860	7,839
1944	3,675 (12)	A	16,100 (31)	5,485	2,785	8,270
1945	3,810 (12)	A	12,812 (26)	5,181	2,567	7,748
1946	4,261 (12)	A	9,513 (17)	4,635	2,426	7,061
1947	3,674 (11)	A	7,369 (109)	4,366	1,849	6,215
1948	3,799 (12)	A	7,588 (70)	4,802	1,913	6,715
1949	4,139 (12)	A	7,374 (43)	4,685	2,208	6,893
1950	14 (A)	A	6,511 (18)	4,664	2,302	6,966
1951	A (A)	A	5,826 (37)	3,878	2,101	5,979
1952	A (15)	A	5,282 (39)	3,414	1,579	4,993
1953	A (15)	A	5,064 (9)	3,293	1,622	4,915
1954	A (15)	A	5,132 (8)	2,948	1,030	3,978
1955	A (14)	A	4,673 (9)	2,810	587	3,397
1956	A (13)	A	5,394 (16)	3,255	573	3,828
1957	A (13)	A	5,749 (14)	3,676	773	4,449
1958	A (13)	A	5,160 (23)	3,634	674	4,308
1959	A (12)	A	4,450 (47)	3,418	677	4,095
A – Not recorded						

A view of the running in board on the Up platform in August 1963, looking towards Exmoor. The board survives and was recently acquired by the author. *Neil Parkhouse collection*

A variety of goods were delivered, comprising mainly coal, oil, seeds and fertiliser, with a fleet of lorries responsible for their distribution in GWR days under their Country Lorry Service scheme. The monthly 'Great Market' and bi-annual sheep fairs brought significant passenger and livestock traffic, the latter ensuring that the short cattle dock siding required some significant and complicated shunting manoeuvres. At its peak, the yard handled 600-700 wagons per month, making it the busiest for goods of the intermediate stations on the D&SR. The *1947 Appendix to the Service Time Table* stated that a re-railing ramp was kept in the goods yard.

The original signal box was located at the west end of the station, in front of the goods shed. It was of timber construction, square in shape and raised on wooden stilts (*see Vol. 1, page 76*). It was replaced circa 1901 by a brick-built box, located at the east end of the Down platform near to the station buildings. It has been reported that the signal box fire burned all year round, as it was apparently also used for cooking!

A more general view of the Up platform and running in board, illustrating how the line curved round to the right as it made its way towards Barnstaple direction. Taken on 1st October 1966, everything looks neat, tidy and in good order but, sadly, this was the last day of services.
The late Owen Mogg, courtesy Peter Triggs

A water tower was located on the Up side of the line, at the west end of the station near the rail entrance to the goods yard but set back from the Up loop. It was provided for storage and general supply purposes, feeding the station and the platform mounted water cranes, one at each end as was the norm, from which locomotives were replenished. The cast-iron columns supporting the tank were 20 feet 4 inches in height, whilst the tank itself measured 20 feet by 10 feet by 8 feet deep. The water capacity at a depth of 7 feet 6 inches was 9,375 gallons.

Typical staffing levels throughout the station's life comprised a station master, two signalmen each working one of the two shifts, one passenger and one goods porter, one passenger booking and one goods clerk, and a lorry driver; the latter carried out deliveries for Molland and Filleigh stations as well. Occasionally,

SOUTH MOLTON – GOODS TRAFFIC 1903-1959

Year	Coal/Coke charged/ forwarded (tons)	Other minerals (tons)	General merchandise forwarded (tons)	Coal/Coke charged/ received (tons)	Other minerals received (tons)	General merchandise received (tons)	Coal/Coke not charged forwarded/ received (tons)	Total goods tonnage	Total receipts (excl. not charged) £	Livestock wagons forwarded/ received	Total carted tonnage (incl. total goods tonnage)
1903	9	17	2,341	1,867	2,573	6,718	1,623	15,148	7,412	579	2,408
1913	0	924	2,805	2,080	4,008	7,443	1,814	19,074	9,331	601	2,647
1923	0	33	2,911	636	5,028	7,239	3,006	18,853	15,310	386	2,815
1924	9	40	2,037	711	5,440	7,759	3,630	19,626	14,353	549	2,807
1925	18	33	2,543	547	7,711	7,475	3,919	22,246	15,502	539	2,601
1926	33	32	2,496	632	6,043	7,133	2,936	19,305	14,020	519	2,491
1927	34	58	1,878	430	4,415	7,829	4,432	19,076	14,785	524	2,631
1928	18	11	1,853	447	4,244	7,828	3,953	18,354	14,331	531	2,760
1929	2	68	2,285	380	4,616	8,161	4,874	20,386	15,680	531	2,968
1930	11	50	1,410	512	4,871	8,140	4,715	19,709	14,628	569	2,644
1931	10	56	1,260	355	5,449	8,962	5,057	21,149	14,942	507	2,367
1932	0	44	1,090	630	4,681	8,572	4,838	19,855	13,576	320	2,611
1933	0	66	1,150	559	4,497	8,384	4,343	19,001	12,558	210	5,030
1934	11	118	786	692	4,721	9,048	3,867	19,243	12,784	256	5,208
1935	0	49	937	748	4,350	10,292	4,113	20,489	13,833	356	6,278
1936	16	62	1,149	742	3,722	11,053	4,334	21,078	14,779	380	7,801
1937	20	259	903	358	2,385	11,156	4,412	19,493	13,488	236	8,867
1938	5	119	715	297	2,555	10,286	4,830	18,807	13,681	152	8,151
1939	29	337	940	250	2,194	9,805	4,936	18,491	15,621	157	8,320
1940	7	241	1,635	841	1,918	9,425	5,487	19,554	Not recorded	496	Not recorded
1941	10	152	2,770	1,437	1,817	7,380	4,771	18,337	Not recorded	441	Not recorded
1942	0	309	7,127	1,143	2,133	6,656	3,212	20,580	Not recorded	387	Not recorded
1943	68	245	5,988	312	2,990	6,251	5,250	21,104	Not recorded	433	Not recorded
1944	162	162	4,924	124	2,866	6,220	5,399	19,857	Not recorded	453	Not recorded
1945	71	124	5,789	109	2,472	7,922	5,210	21,697	Not recorded	439	Not recorded
1946	48	103	4,056	109	3,693	7,880	5,589	21,478	Not recorded	470	Not recorded
1947	48	14	1,249	26	2,104	4,297	3,343	11,081	Not recorded	115	Not recorded
1948	35	53	1,462	102	1,766	5,724	5,029	14,171	Not recorded	410	Not recorded
1949	166	125	4,275	153	4,194	11,876	8,791	29,580	Not recorded	547	Not recorded
1950	31	65	1,634	54	4,320	13,120	9,371	28,595	Not recorded	626	Not recorded
1951	0	91	791	18	3,215	10,325	10,624	25,064	Not recorded	426	Not recorded
1952	0	115	677	0	3,094	8,272	9,276	21,434	Not recorded	499	Not recorded
1953	A	58	1,035	A	4,846	8,488	9,492	23,919	Not recorded	518	Not recorded
1954	A	49	215	A	3,661	8,523	8,468	20,916	Not recorded	352	Not recorded
1955	A	42	257	A	4,124	6,443	9,522	20,388	Not recorded	Not recorded	Not recorded
1956	A	106	165	A	4,332	5,334	8,150	18,087	Not recorded	49	Not recorded
1957	A	159	636	A	3,532	5,720	8,102	18,149	Not recorded	76	Not recorded
1958	A	33	200	A	6,311	3,626	7,767	17,937	Not recorded	114	Not recorded
1959	A	66	94	A	5,257	4,266	3,661	13,344	Not recorded	69	Not recorded
Zoned at Barnstaple 1st August 1947 to 1st June 1948											
Includes goods at Filleigh and Bishops Nympton & Molland from 1st June 1948											
A – Included in not charged											

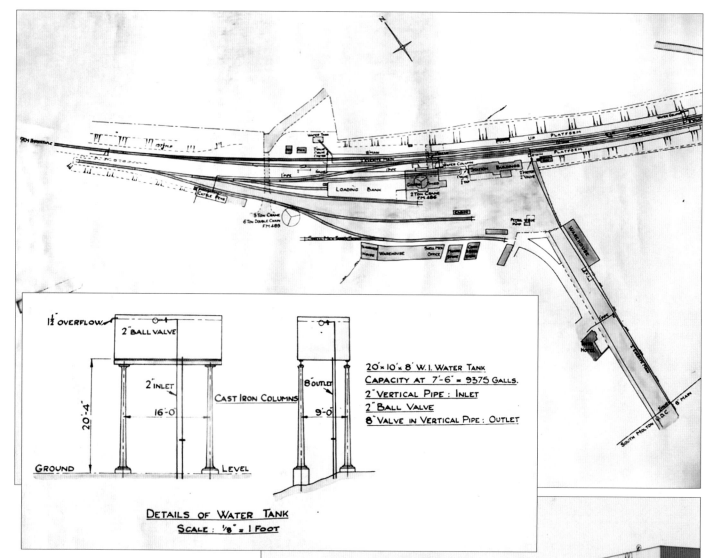

DETAILS OF WATER TANK
SCALE: ⅛" = 1 FOOT

20' × 10' × 8' W. I. Water Tank
Capacity at 7'-6" = 9375 Galls.
2" Vertical Pipe: Inlet
2" Ball Valve
8" Valve in Vertical Pipe: Outlet

the signalman would collect tickets and also help to load and unload parcels, which often included Harris sausages and Lyon's cakes. The public telephone was in the parcels office, with an alarm bell in the signal box as that was staffed for longer periods.

The ganger's trolley was diesel propelled and would reside, when not in use, on its own piece of track, set perpendicular to the running line, near the ganger's hut (Note: This is most likely the Abtus Babe referred to in Chapter 9, page 443).

The *IRS Handbook* also notes the existence of a narrow gauge line (600mm gauge) in use circa 1918 at the Hacche Sawmills (they refer to it as South Molton Sawmill), just to the north of the station. An 0-4-0 petrol engined 10hp locomotive manufactured by Baguley Cars was reportedly in use there.

Finally for South Molton, some receipts for the early years are set out in the table below:

Top: **A hand-drawn plan of South Molton circa 1936, showing some additional detail of the goods yard. The Shell-Mex siding (which also seems to have been used by the Anglo-American Oil Co.) and office were on the south side of the yard.** *Courtesy Wiltshire Records Office*

Above Centre Left: **The plan, top, was prepared in conjunction with the installation of the water tank, a drawing of which was also included.** *Courtesy Wiltshire Records Office*

Above: **Now preserved Collett 0-6-0 No. 3205 passes the water tank as it arrives at South Molton with the joint Plymouth Railway Circle/RCTS 'The Exmoor Ranger' rail tour on 27th March 1965.** *Stephen P. Derek*

Year	Passengers	Goods	Other	Total
1874	14,934	7,258	1,055	23,247
1899	10,870	7,805	1,687	20,362
1900	10,916	7,555	1,736	20,207

A fine view of No. 7306 departing South Molton with the 4.04pm Taunton to Barnstaple Junction service on 25th July 1964. Much of the relatively extensive (compared to other stations on the D&SR) goods yard can be seen in the right background, including a glimpse of the warehouses on the south side. The goods yard looks busy, with plenty of wagons to be seen, despite the fact that the withdrawal of goods services was just over a week away. The headshunt in the right foreground, at a lower level than the main line which was climbing at 1 in 60 out of the station, was the only means of accessing the sidings; it will feature in a dramatic story in Volume 3. Note the tubular metal posted bracket Up Home signal, the right arm of which permitted access to the Down platform for Up trains. This picture should be compared with that in Vol. 1, page 212, showing the North Devon Link Road (NDLR) under construction from a similar viewpoint. *Peter W. Gray*

LEFT: No. 6363 runs through the fields near Hacche Moor as it approaches South Molton with the 3.50pm train from Barnstaple Junction to Taunton on 25th July 1964. The view is looking west from Hacche Bridge, which was demolished when the NDLR was built in the 1980s. *Peter W. Gray*

BELOW: Looking in the opposite direction from Hacche Bridge on 3rd April 1961, No. 5369 of Bristol St Phillips Marsh shed was photographed heading west away from South Molton, just visible in the left distance, where a plume of white steam indicates that it had crossed with an Up train at the station. A strong north wind is whipping No. 5369's exhaust away to the south. The 'Mogul', which we have not seen before on the line, is likely to have been pressed in to service by Taunton shed after arriving from Bristol, to cover a temporary shortage of motive power. *Michael L. Roach*

Chapter 8

A Description of the Line and its Stations Part 3: South Molton to Barnstaple

Looking east back towards South Molton, a 'Mogul' climbs the near straight section of line by West Ford Farm with a six-coach Down train on Friday 3rd July 1953. The carriages are all in the early BR period crimson and cream livery and beneath the fourth vehicle is the bridge carrying the line over Ford Lane. The trackbed is now lost beneath the A361 NDLR and Ford Lane no longer exists. *Roger J, Sellick, courtesy National Railway Museum*

On leaving South Molton, the line initially continued on the 25 chain radius right-hand curve that ran through the station, passing above the goods headshunt and then straightening out for about a mile. It climbed initially at 1 in 60 up through Hacche Moor Cutting and passed under Hacche Bridge, which carried a minor road, Hacche Lane, over the line; this lane is now split in half by the A361 NDLR, with a short section between the Link Road and South Molton having been closed completely. The line emerged from the short cutting into open fields and then ran on to a low embankment, below which there were rolling fields as the countryside opened up.

The railway continued to climb, crossing over Ford Lane and then passing the Queen Anne-styled Snurridge House to the right and West Ford Farm (no longer in operation and with the buildings all converted for residential use) to the left. It then entered another cutting, passing under a stone bridge carrying the South Molton to Brayford road, the site of which is now hidden beneath North Aller

roundabout. Just before this point a speed restriction of 50mph was applied through to the viaduct ahead at Castle Hill. The cutting deepened after the bridge and began a left-hand curve of 34 chains radius, the line then dropping slightly (at 1 in 100) as it passed under the stone occupation bridge enabling the occupants of North Aller Farm to access their land on the north side of the railway.

Emerging out of the cutting just beyond this bridge, the rear of North Aller Farm was visible on the left-hand (south) side. The farm, a rented property belonging to the Castle Hill Estate (and now a bed & breakfast), was apparently built on the site of an earlier mansion. The line cut into the fields before being supported on an embankment as it turned on a broad sweeping curve to the north-west of 30 chains radius and commenced a climb, again at 1 in 60, for about half a mile.

The height of the embankment at this point was emphasised by the fields falling away below and Bremridge Wood first surrounded the line and then covered it as the rails burrowed beneath through

No. 6318 drifts through the cutting behind North Aller Farm with
what looks to be another six-coach Down train on 3rd July 1953.
Roger J, Sellick, courtesy National Railway Museum

A marked change of motive power here, as ex-London & South Western Railway 'T9' Class No. 30710 heads east towards South Molton through the fields of North Aller on 3rd July 1953, with a Taunton-bound train. The grazing sheep seem unimpressed by the Dugald Drummond-designed 'Greyhound' 4-4-0. Behind the rear carriage, the line can be seen curving round towards Castle Hill Tunnel, which burrowed beneath Bremridge Wood, covering the hill in the background. The A361 NDLR deviates away from the trackbed at the point of the cutting seen in the previous picture, to pass round the hill to the north, so this section of the route is still extant today, albeit the embankment is now lined with trees. The 'T9', built by Dübs & Co. at their Glasgow works for the L&SWR in 1899 as No. 710 and based at Exmouth Junction shed at the date of this view, was withdrawn from Salisbury shed in early 1959. *Roger J, Sellick, courtesy National Railway Museum*

Castle Hill Tunnel. The wood is the site of an Iron Age fort and formed part of the historic Bremridge Estate. A wing of Bremridge mansion house, dating from 1654 and situated to the east of the line as it swung almost due north towards the tunnel, still survives and is now Grade II* listed. However, prior to reaching the tunnel, on the right side of the line was a long disused small quarry, most likely used for ballast. The railway then straightened in the last few yards before reaching the southern portal or Taunton end of Castle Hill Tunnel. There was no cutting leading up to the tunnel, the terrain sloping down to the line on its western side and then dropping away to the east, so that it arrived at the Taunton-end portal on a ledge.

ABOVE: The northern approach to Castle Hill Tunnel, as photographed from a Barnstaple-bound train in February 1958. *James G. Tawse*

CASTLE HILL OR BREMRIDGE TUNNEL

Located between South Molton and Filleigh, and cut through the rock of hillside clothed by Bremridge Wood, Castle Hill Tunnel was locked away in the landscape. It was 321 yards long and straight, its bore appearing more spacious to the locomotive crew than that at Bathealton. The summit of this stretch of the railway was in the tunnel so as it emerged out of the northern or Barnstaple end, the line was initially on a falling gradient of 1 in 63. This changed then to 1 in 100 as it curved to the left, turning through almost ninety degrees over the next half mile on curves of 27 and 26 chains radius curves as it ran out of the tunnel cutting and then through the next deep cutting, still enveloped by the trees of Bremridge Wood, which again is part of the Castle Hill Estate.

The Ordnance Survey originally noted it as Bremridge Tunnel on their 1889 edition 25 inch map but later reverted to Castle Hill, the name used by the railway. The eastern portal of the tunnel was 199 miles and $35^3/_4$ chains from London and, similar to its counterpart at Bathealton, the south and north portals had no supporting walls. The entrances were built of local stone but there is evidence of red brick in parts on the portals and inside the tunnel, which may have been later repairs. The tunnel was lined with stone inside the southern entrance for about twenty yards. At the northern end, the stone lining extended for approximately forty yards, at which point the ceiling height lowers by a few inches. The stone lining then continued for approximately another sixty yards. Apart from two more short stretches of stone lining towards the southern portal, the remainder of the bore was cut out of solid rock and not lined. One suspects that the lining was not carried throughout to save costs but equally it would not have been necessary given the solidity of the rock through which it was cut. At various points inside were the usual refuges where platelayers and gangers could wait safely as a train passed by. Again some of these were neatly finished, whilst others were rough-hewn out of the rock.

ABOVE LEFT: The Taunton end or southern portal of Castle Hill Tunnel, almost hidden by trees circa 1953 but showing the short telegraph pole and the permanent way men's hut close to the entrance. *Roger J, Sellick, courtesy National Railway Museum*

ABOVE RIGHT: No photograph has yet been unearthed showing the northern portal when the line was still open, so this is a recent view of it. *Author*

With just a few yards to go before entering Castle Hill Tunnel No. 6363 is just about to step off Castle Hill Viaduct with the 12.20pm Ilfracombe to Taunton train on 29th August 1964. *Tim Stephens*

No. 7333 rumbles across Castle Hill Viaduct with a five-coach Wolverhampton to Ilfracombe train on Saturday 28th July 1962. *James G. Tawse*

CASTLE HILL OR FILLEIGH VIADUCT

Almost immediately on breaking out of this second cutting, Castle Hill or Filleigh Viaduct could be seen ahead, over which a speed restriction of 25mph was imposed. It was located just less than half a mile west of Castle Hill Tunnel and was exactly 200 miles from Paddington (via Bristol) – an appropriate landmark to represent such distance. Built on a gentle left-handed curve of 27 chains radius, it was constructed of stone and iron and was of a similar design to the Tone Viaduct. This six span structure, 232 yards in length, carried the line a maximum of 94 feet above the River Bray and the valley below. Views to the north and south of the line were spectacular; passengers looking north might perhaps have felt that they were looking somewhat intrusively into the hills as the valley narrowed but the more open aspect to the south had a more inviting feel.

Built between 1870 and 1872 to take a line of broad gauge rails, the viaduct comprised stone buttresses at either end, with five tapered stone piers on the valley floor, supporting six wrought iron, lattice girder spans. The piers towered up like factory chimneys from the valley floor, with some 7,000 tons of masonry being used in their construction. It has not so far been ascertained who supplied the 400 tons of ironwork used to build the main deck and in what form. Were the individual spans delivered complete or were they fabricated on site from pre-wrought parts? A photograph taken during construction (*Vol. 1, page 63*) shows one complete span in place and another on the valley floor but otherwise gives no clue. The same photograph appears to show that a crane was used to lift the spans in to place.

Once the spans were in position, as with the Tone Viaduct, the stonework of the piers was raised to track level either side, hiding the joins. However, unlike Tone, Castle Hill Viaduct retained these

extensions to the piers right up until closure and they were only removed during the subsequent dismantling of the spans. Castle Hill also had a walkway running the length of the viaduct beneath the trackbed, between the girders. In the *1900 Working Time Table*, the speed of all trains passing over the viaduct was, as for the Tone Viaduct, not to exceed 15mph, although this was increased to 25mph in later years.

The narrowing of the line to standard gauge in 1881 resulted in a repositioning of the rails on the viaducts. As described in Volume 1 (*Chapter 3, pages 88-89*), initially only one running rail was slewed over but this led to an imbalance of weight on the structure and a number of calculations were subsequently carried out. A letter dated 24th April 1883, from the GWR Engineer to Major General Hutchison, stated that the dead load on one of the spans of the viaducts was as follows:

	TONS
Two main girders and cross bracing	42
Cross girders	6
Parapet..	4
Permanent way.	10
Ballast	8
Total (about)	70

Today the stone built piers survive as a testament to Victorian engineering as they were incorporated into the A361 North Devon Link Road bridge. They needed increasing in height by the addition of about six feet of stonework, roughly equating to the height of the original pier extensions removed during the dismantling. The rebuilding of the viaduct for road use is illustrated in Volume 1, Chapter 5.

ABOVE: Taken on the same day as the previous picture, this view is looking up at the underside of the viaduct from the west side of the valley, with Bremridge Wood in the background. The walkway running beneath the main deck for the length of the iron spans can just be made out and the stone extensions on the top of each pier, hiding the joins between the spans, are also clearly shown.
James G. Tawse

ABOVE RIGHT: A view from a train passing over the viaduct and bound for Barnstaple Victoria Road in February 1958. The gentle left-hand curve of 27 chains radius is evident, as is the River Bray 94 feet below.
James G. Tawse

RIGHT: Looking back towards Castle Hill Tunnel from the same train. It is clear from these two pictures that the primary purpose of the stone extensions to the piers was to further support the bridge deck and in particular the parapet railings. It thus seems a little odd that, on the Tone Viaduct, they were dismantled.
James G. Tawse

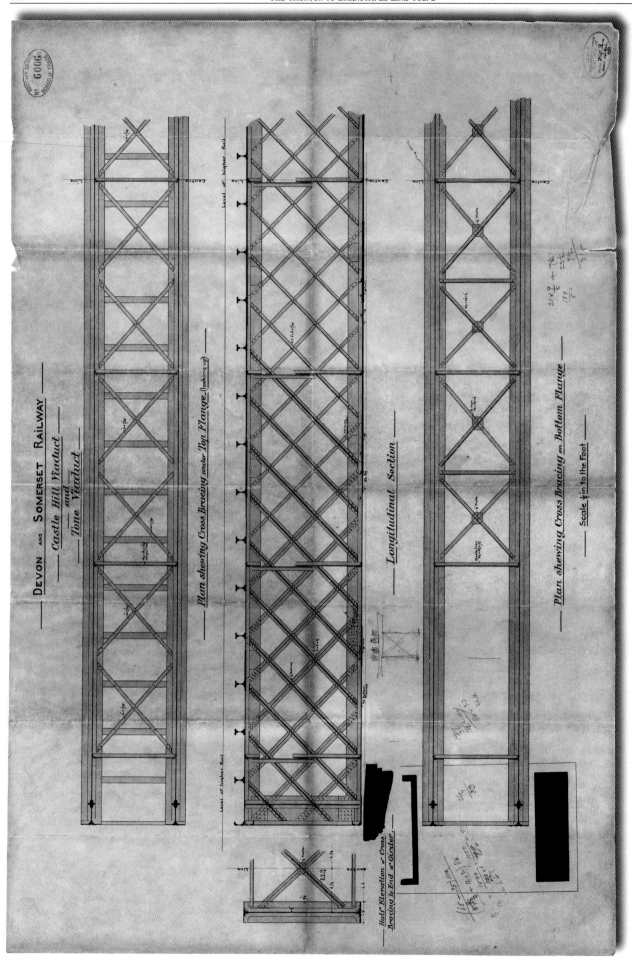

DEVON AND SOMERSET RAILWAY

Castle Hill Viaduct
and
Tone Viaduct

Plan shewing Cross Bracing under Top Flange (looking up)

Longitudinal Section

Plan shewing Cross Bracing on Bottom Flange

Scale ⅛ in to the Foot

Half Elevation of Cross Bracing to End of Girder

A plan of the lattice girders, indicating that their box girder assembly, with top and bottom flanges, was identical for both Castle Hill and Tone viaducts. The GWR Engineers Office Taunton stamp on the right is dated 14th April 1883, the drawings being produced in conjunction with the narrowing of the rails across from broad to standard gauge; as initially carried out, it moved the centre of gravity of trains passing over to one side and thus unbalanced the bridge decks. Note the additional pencil calculations and sketch. The workmen's walkway rested on the cross bracing of the bottom flange. *Courtesy the National Archives*

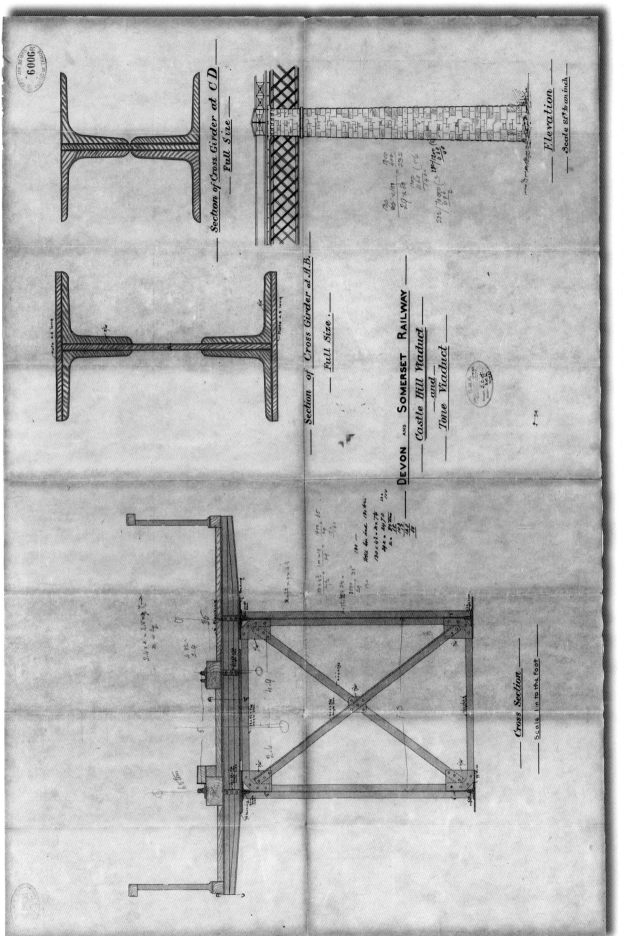

DEVON AND SOMERSET RAILWAY

Castle Hill Viaduct
and
Tone Viaduct

Section of Cross Girder at C D
Full Size

Section of Cross Girder at A.B.
Full Size.

Elevation
Scale 8ft to an inch

Cross Section
Scale 1 in to the Foot

A cross section of one of the box girders, showing how the gauge was narrowed by moving one set of rail inwards, on new baulk timbers. The drawing also clearly shows how this then unbalanced the bridge deck, with the track now sitting off to one side. The Engineers' Office clearly looked at whether the bridge could cope with this extra stress, hence all the additional calculations, but ultimately they had no choice but to close the line for a few days whilst the track across both viaducts was relaid in the centre of the deck. Also illustrated was one of the bridge piers, showing how the stone extensions at the top also supported the bridge deck. Note that neither drawing is reproduced to scale. *Courtesy the National Archives*

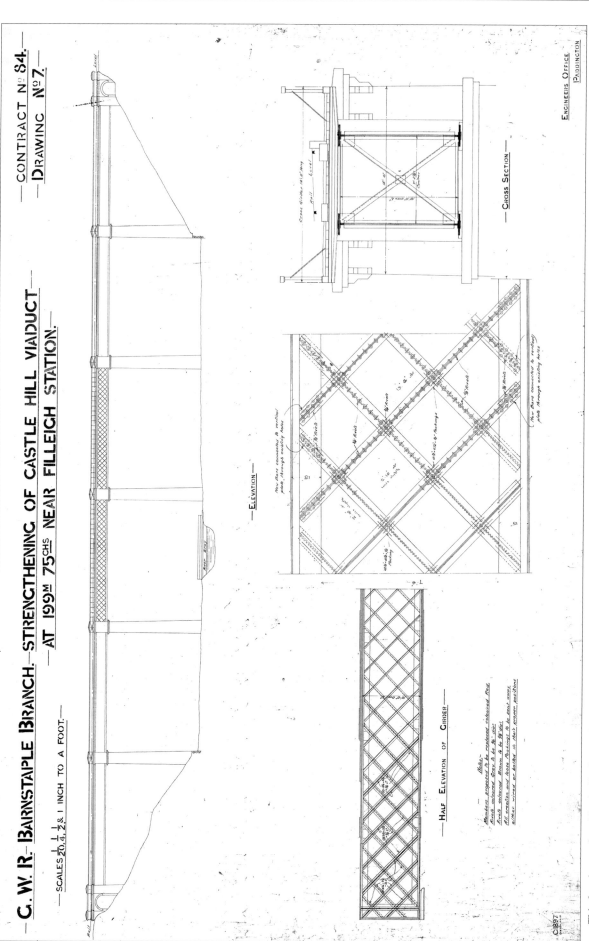

This drawing produced by the Engineers' Office, Paddington in 1897, gave a full side elevation of Castle Hill Viaduct and improvements that were necessary to strengthen it. Clearly the structure was not deemed strong enough to cope with the weight of traffic passing over it but with this additional work being carried out just sixteen years after the D&SR line was narrowed to standard gauge, the idea that it was acceptable to slew the rails to one side of the bridge deck in the first place looks short-sighted in the extreme. The cross section on the right also illustrates how the stone pier extensions provided additional support for the bridge deck. *Courtesy Mark Henshaw and Martin Tester*

RIGHT: The view northwards up the Bray Valley, taken from the deck of the bridge on 28th July 1962. The River Bray meanders down the valley, whilst to its right is a trackway leading from Shallowford to Embercome Lodge, visible in the centre distance. This picture should be compared with the similar view from the deck of the rebuilt bridge in 2010 (*Vol. 1, page 214*). *James G. Tawse*

BELOW: With an empty 6-wheeled milk tank wagon being returned to Torrington on the rear, the 6.20am Taunton to Ilfracombe train trundles over the viaduct on 28th July 1962. *James G. Tawse*

BOTTOM: The 9.20am Ilfracombe to Taunton train heads across on 17th August 1963. *Stephen P. Derek*

As the line curved off the viaduct, the parkland of the Castle Hill Estate lay off to the left-hand side. It then straightened and ran into a short cutting, climbing initially at 1 in 204 before dropping down at 1 in 120 towards Filleigh station. This straight section was about half a mile in length.

At the end of this, the line then curved to the right at 35 chains radius to head in to a cutting leading up to a high-arched, stone overbridge carrying Park Lane, a minor road between Shallowford and Proutworthy, over the railway. Through the arch, the line entered Filleigh station, about three quarters of a mile from the viaduct, where we arrived at 11.45am, still two minutes late.

Surrounded by spectacular scenery, No. 7303 drifts down the bank on the approach to Filleigh station with the Saturday's only 8.00am Wolverhampton (Low Level) to Ilfracombe train on 29th August 1964. The train has just entered the station loop, whilst Castle Hill Viaduct is out of sight beyond where the line dives into the trees in the distance. Note the fireman leaning out of the cab as he takes a short break from his firing duties. *Tim Stephens*

FILLEIGH (37 MILES 43 CHAINS)

Opened to Passengers ....1st November 1873
Opened to Goods ....11th November 1873
Closed to Goods ....3rd August 1964
Closed to Passengers ....3rd October 1966

Filleigh station was built on the continuing right-hand curve and was nearer the Castle Hill Estate of Lord Fortescue (on whose land it was situated) than Filleigh village and the station initially bore the name Castle Hill when the line opened (*see Vol. 1, Chap. 3*). The village lay about a mile away to the south and its population was recorded as 311 in 1864, 319 in 1901 and 209 by 1961. The station also served the nearby villages of East and West Buckland (and its school), which lay a mile and a half, and two miles away to the north and north-east respectively. Their 1864 populations were 151 and 321

people. The station's name was changed to Filleigh on 1st January 1881, to avoid confusion with Castle Hill station in west London, which had opened in 1871 (it subsequently became Castle Hill Ealing Dean, until 1898, when it was changed to West Ealing).

Filleigh was a single platform station from its opening in 1873 until 1937, at which time a number of improvements were carried out. The stone-built platform on the north side of the single line supported the modest station buildings, which comprised a one-storey structure with a central area and two wings either side. As elsewhere on the D&SR, the central part had the roof apex at right angles to the line, whilst the side wings were parallel to it. The main booking office, waiting room and toilet facilities were housed here. In the later period of the line, to the west of these buildings a pre-cast concrete provender shed was erected, along with another storage shed nearer the signal box but just back from the platform. The platform was originally 262 feet in length.

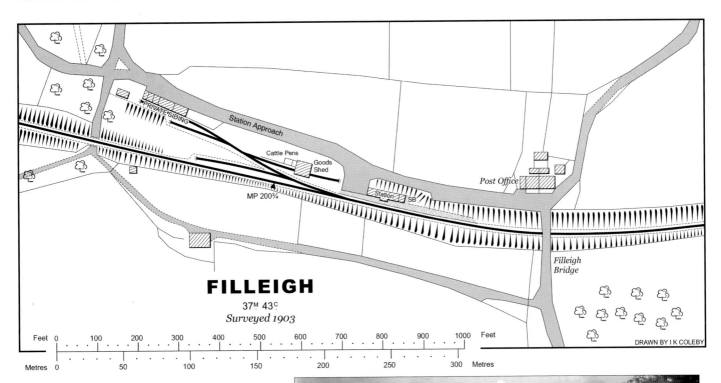

FILLEIGH

37ᴹ 43ᶜ

Surveyed 1903

Feet 0   100   200   300   400   500   600   700   800   900   1000   Feet

Metres 0   50   100   150   200   250   300   Metres

DRAWN BY I K COLEBY

The 1937 improvements included the provision of a passing loop, a new Down platform, the extension of the Up platform and an extra goods loop, brought into use on 15th December that year (and taken out of use on 20th December 1961). This loop ran parallel to the running line at the Barnstaple end of the station. Filleigh was the last station on the line to get a passing loop. It is also clear from photographs of the station buildings that the front of the waiting area was modified at some stage, probably in 1937. There was no waiting shelter provided on the Down side and no footbridge, so the line had to be crossed by the barrow crossing at the west end of

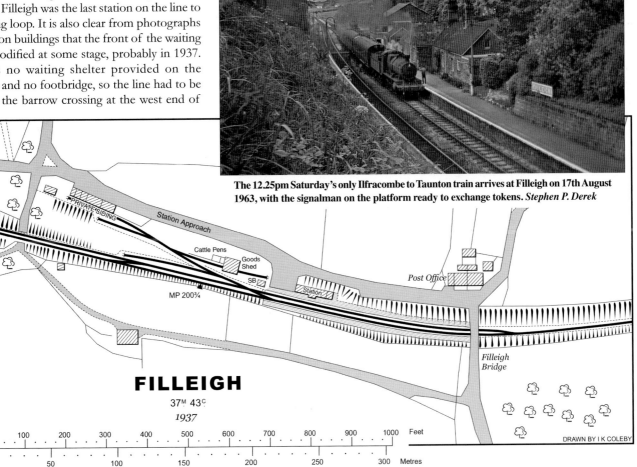

The 12.25pm Saturday's only Ilfracombe to Taunton train arrives at Filleigh on 17th August 1963, with the signalman on the platform ready to exchange tokens. *Stephen P. Derek*

FILLEIGH

37ᴹ 43ᶜ

1937

Feet 0   100   200   300   400   500   600   700   800   900   1000   Feet

Metres 0   50   100   150   200   250   300   Metres

DRAWN BY I K COLEBY

Moments after taking the picture on page 366, the photographer had turned around and crossed the lane over the bridge to take this view of No. 7303 coasting to a halt in the Down platform. *Tim Stephens*

the platforms. A retaining wall was built behind the Down platform to support the earthworks excavated behind it. In 1947, the loop lengths were stated in the *Appendix to the Service Time Table* as 885 feet Up and 747 feet Down. In addition, the bi-directional goods loop was 1,020 feet in length.

The goods yard was situated at the west end of the station and on the north side of the line. It comprised a 40 foot long, stone-built goods shed near the Up platform, which housed a 2-ton crane. Right at the back of the yard, at the end of a private siding, there was a stone-built stores building for the exclusive use of the Fortescue

ABOVE: No. 5336, missing its smokebox door numberplate, draws in with the 12.55pm Taunton to Ilfracombe train on 29th August 1964. The Taunton end of the station was in a cutting, which required retaining walls on either side, with the one bordering the rear of the Down platform being particularly substantial and frequently leaving it in shadow. *Tim Stephens*

RIGHT: A busy moment at Filleigh circa 1960, as No. 6343 draws in with a Taunton-bound service, crossing with a Down train. *Courtesy Roger Joanes*

As with most of the other intermediate stations on the line, brief moments of action were interspersed with long periods of quiet calm between trains and thus this view of Filleigh, looking west circa 1952, is much more representative and the normal state of affairs here. Note the bracket signal with subsidiary arms for the bi-directional goods loop, in the centre, and the goods yard.
Courtesy The Lens of Sutton Association

Estate. The goods yard had two main sidings located parallel to the running lines, the near one with ten wagon capacity and the adjacent line holding three wagons. The goods shed siding kicked back from the line leading to the private siding and had a total capacity for eight wagons – three to the rear of the shed alongside a 67 foot loading bank (which also had a carriage shoot at the end), two in the shed and three outside at the front, alongside cattle pens and another 58 foot long loading bank. Goods deliveries to this station included provisions for outlying areas such as Lynton and Parracombe.

The first signal box was a small facility within the main station building, which was all that was needed initially given the single line and simple goods yard. This box was replaced on 20th June 1937 by a 42-lever brick-built box (GWR type 12B), which was located at the west end of the station and just off the end of the platform on the Up side of the line.

As would be expected, the passenger receipts for this small station were modest, serving as it did a rural area and, as already indicated, situated some distance from the various villages it served. The pre-1923 highs in the 8,000s were never to be replicated and

FILLEIGH – PASSENGER, PARCELS & STAFF STATISTICS 1903-1958

Year	Payroll cost £ (& staff no's)		Total Receipts incl. goods £	Tickets issued (season tickets)		Passenger receipts £	Parcels etc receipts £	Total £ (incl. Parcels)
1903	125	(2)	2,101	8,200	(n/a)	661	248	909
1913	131	(2)	2,457	8,839	(n/a)	735	366	1,101
1923	472	(3)	4,310	8,201	(12)	1,162	844	2,006
1924	452	(3)	4,046	7,746	(10)	1,120	704	1,824
1925	439	(3)	3,541	7,795	(1)	994	659	1,653
1926	426	(3)	3,479	6,470	(0)	965	728	1,693
1927	418	(3)	3,839	6,403	(1)	943	700	1,643
1928	442	(3)	3,771	6,330	(1)	870	663	1,533
1929	440	(3)	3,745	6,270	(1)	882	604	1,486
1930	491	(3)	4,143	5,751	(1)	808	676	1,484
1931	454	(3)	3,698	5,233	(0)	711	596	1,307
1932	419	(3)	3,886	4,840	(0)	731	436	1,167
1933	415	(3)	4,038	4,566	(2)	776	304	1,080
1934	458	(3)	2,627	4,542	(0)	572	279	851
1935	502	(3)	3,384	4,495	(0)	676	355	1,031
1936	500	(3)	3,693	3,967	(0)	668	377	1,045
1937	509	(3)	3,648	3,926	(0)	727	245	972
1938	552	(3)	2,979	3,446	(6)	704	277	981
1940	590	(3)	A	3,105	(1)	678	471	1,149
1945	990	(3)	A	5,597	(0)	1,340	169	1,509
1950	B	(4)	A	2,656	(0)	864	159	1,023
1955	B	(3)	A	1,902	(0)	810	212	1,022
1958	B	(3)	A	2,525	(1)	926	337	1,263
A – Goods receipts not provided; B – Not recorded								

An undated view of Filleigh looking east. This picture is worth comparing with that in Vol. 1, page 138, because it shows that the front of the waiting area had been rebuilt at some stage, possibly when the Down loop and platform were added in 1937. The open fronted section of the waiting area seen in that view had been blocked up by the stone-built extension seen here between the wooden partition and the gabled wing of the station building. The brick-built chimney at the near end of the waiting room was also clearly not original and in fact looks quite new here, whilst the slates around it also look a different colour. The brick building just in view on the left was also a later addition but its function has not been ascertained. Note the Up Starting signal positioned 'wrong side' at the end of the Down platform on the right, where it could still be seen by the signalman. *Courtesy, The Lens of Sutton Association*

No. 7304 pauses at Filleigh with a four-coach Up train bound for Taunton on 9th July 1962. Note the substantial running in board mounted on the retaining wall on the Down side and also the steepness of the cutting side, hence the need for the retaining wall in the first place.
C.J. Gammell, courtesy Roger Joanes

An Up train glides in to Filleigh in 1960, with the signalman waiting on the platform to exchange tokens with the fireman. The Down platform was carved out of the cutting side, so the retaining wall behind ran its entire length. *E.T. Gill, courtesy Rob Blencowe*

even the 1945 Second World War peak only reached a figure akin to that achieved in 1930. The double digit season ticket sales of the early 1920s dropped to one and then none in 1926. Passenger numbers were actually swollen by pupils and staff arriving and departing from the nearby West Buckland school, further emphasising the general paucity of ticket sales, which averaged 40-50 a week through the 1950s.

Goods traffic was equally modest, although there was more coal arriving than at a number of the other smaller D&SR stations. Livestock wagons despatched from here averaged ten or twelve a month.

After leaving Filleigh, the line ran straight for a quarter of a mile, before gently sweeping left-handed and then straightening for a

FILLEIGH – GOODS TRAFFIC 1903-1959

Year	Coal/Coke charged/ forwarded (tons)	Other minerals (tons)	General merchandise forwarded (tons)	Coal/Coke charged/ received (tons)	Other minerals received (tons)	General merchandise received (tons)	Coal/Coke not charged forwarded/ received (tons)	Total goods tonnage	Total receipts (excl. not charged) £	Livestock wagons forwarded/ received	Total carted tonnage (incl. total goods tonnage)
1903	0	511	358	823	380	1,350	425	3,847	1,200	127	236
1913	0	235	126	979	302	1,419	183	3,244	1,356	186	249
1923	0	0	214	118	1,186	1,546	667	3,731	2,304	103	251
1924	38	28	256	95	791	1,567	809	3,584	2,222	117	275
1925	10	12	179	44	923	1,471	746	3,385	1,888	86	239
1926	0	64	157	35	583	1,386	462	2,687	1,786	109	229
1927	0	80	295	96	448	1,386	587	2,892	2,196	147	229
1928	0	0	364	106	541	1,429	538	2,978	2,238	135	170
1929	0	24	424	105	368	1,620	580	3,121	2,259	128	247
1930	0	32	393	177	584	1,660	421	3,267	2,659	182	188
1931	0	0	175	162	415	1,805	489	3,046	2,391	214	168
1932	0	6	821	144	790	1,614	516	3,891	2,719	92	224
1933	0	0	1,167	113	402	1,623	540	3,845	2,958	66	1,150
1934	9	0	340	155	329	1,442	548	2,823	1,776	65	1,105
1935	0	0	438	225	418	1,502	360	2,943	2,353	93	1,270
1936	10	0	573	168	424	1,706	1,235	4,116	2,848	135	1,657
1937	0	39	693	322	264	1,617	1,463	4,398	2,676	96	1,524
1938	0	28	445	274	243	1,261	1,428	3,679	1,998	51	1,265
1940	12	0	1,229	309	169	902	1,850	4,471	Not reported	140	Not reported
1945	73	0	1,658	18	170	399	2,802	5,120	Not reported	19	Not reported
1950	Zoned at Barnstaple from 1st August 1947, then zoned at South Molton from 1st June 1948. By 1958 zoned at Exeter										
1959	0	0	0	0	203	6	1892	2101	Not reported	0	Not reported

further half mile on a shallow embankment. The line initially dropped down at 1 in 60 but then levelled before another shallow gradient down of 1 in 1200. As it passed under the Filleigh to West Buckland road bridge at the 201³/₄ milepost, the line entered a shallow cutting and gently curved to the right at 30 chains radius. Emerging from the cutting, it slipped through fields on both sides, on a low embankment and passing by the occasional coppice as it gently weaved though this pleasant low-hilled countryside for one and a quarter miles. In this stretch it also passed over two further road bridges connecting West Buckland to the main A361 road and at milepost 203¹/₂, a 50mph speed restriction was imposed. Looking

ABOVE: No. 7304 arrives with a three-coach train from Barnstaple Junction to Taunton, which has an additional ex-GWR 'Fruit D' van tucked inside at the front for perishables traffic. The barrow crossing in the foreground was the only means of crossing the line here and on the right is a good view of the front of the 1937-built Filleigh Signal Box.
Paul Strong, Neil Parkhouse collection

RIGHT: A view of the goods shed and yard in the 1950s, with two cattle wagons standing in front of the livestock pens. The track layout of the yard is well shown, with the double compound access point in the right foreground and the private goods shed/store of the Fortescue Estate at the rear. *Roger Joanes collection*

FILLEIGH.
Station is on an Incline of 1 in 60, falling towards Swimbridge.

No vehicle must be detached and allowed to remain on the Main Line.

Before engines of Freight trains performing work are detached from their trains, the brake of the guard's van must be fully applied and sufficient wagon brakes put down and sprags used to prevent the train moving. Any wagons shunted on to the train must be immediately coupled up.

Guards of Freight trains must fully apply the hand-brake before leaving their vans.

Six sprags must be kept by the side of the line at the Barnstaple end of the Up and Down Goods Loop.

Up and Down Goods Loop Line.

The standard Regulations for signalling trains and engines by Permissive Block System over Goods Running Loop Lines and other Permissive Lines, as shown in the Book of Regulations for Train Signalling on Double and Single Lines, apply.

Auxiliary Electric Train Token Instrument.

An Auxiliary Electric Train Token Instrument, for the Filleigh-Swimbridge section, is fixed in a hut on the Down Side of the Main Line adjacent to the Down Main Advanced Starting Signal.

The Instrument is provided as an additional facility for the withdrawal of a Token by the Driver of a Down Freight train which has been sidetracked to the Up and Down Goods Loop Line. Telephone communication is provided between the Instrument and Signal Box.

When a Down Freight Train, which has been sidetracked, can proceed, and the Driver is not in possession of the Token for the Filleigh-Swimbridge Section, he must send his Fireman to the Auxiliary Token Instrument to obtain permission on the telephone to withdraw a token.

When the Signalman at Filleigh has obtained permission from Swimbridge for the train to proceed, both Signalmen must press in the plungers of their Token Instruments to permit the withdrawal of a Token from the Auxiliary Instrument.

A Token can be placed in the Auxiliary Instrument at any time, but one can only be withdrawn by co-operation between the Filleigh and Swimbridge Signalmen.

For instructions as to operation of Auxiliary Electric Train Token Instrument by Fireman see the General Appendix to the Rule Book.

straight ahead at this point, as the line turned to the right, passengers would have spotted to the left the distinctive dome shape of Hangman's Hill, to the south of Swimbridge village in the distance. Most of this section of the line was on the downgrade and about half a mile from Swimbridge it made a distinctive reverse 'S' bend as it swept around to the right at 26 chains radius. It then straightened and curved back to the left on a 22 chains radius before starting to climb at 1 in 60 for a quarter of a mile. At the end of this, as the line curved back to the left, Swimbridge station lay straight ahead, 204 miles from Paddington and 38³/₄ miles from Norton Fitzwarren. The village of Swimbridge was just visible a short walk away to the left or south of the station. The time was now 11.52am, still two minutes down.

No. 7326 heads east between Swimbridge and Filleigh on the evening of Saturday 6th July 1963, with the 7.18pm service from Barnstaple Junction to Taunton. This consisted of a rake of eight coaches that had previously been employed on a Down holiday express to Ilfracombe. However, the locomotive was labouring up the 1 in 60 gradient at a low speed and, according to the photographer, wallowing from side to side in an alarming manner. This was his last sighting of No. 7326, as it was withdrawn two months later. The eight coaches would have been close to the limit for a 'Mogul' (280 tons) and the timings of passenger trains on this line were based on a load of 230 tons.
Michael L. Roach

SWIMBRIDGE (40 MILES 69 CHAINS)

Opened to Passengers ....1st November 1873
Opened to Goods ....11th November 1873
Closed to Goods ....3rd August 1964
Closed to Passengers ....3rd October 1966

Swimbridge station was located a short walk up a hill to the north of the village, making it one of the closest to the community it served, the population of which was recorded as 1,532 in 1864 (Parliamentary Select Committee). The village is famous for its vicar, the Reverend Jack Russell ('The Sporting Parson'), who early in the

19th century first bred the terriers that still carry his name. Nearby Landkey had 699 people (1864 Parliamentary Select Committee).

When it first opened, the station comprised a single platform on the south of the line. The station building was of a different design to the others on the line, being a simple rectangular, single-storey, stone-built structure with two tall chimneys, one at either end. A goods shed and goods loop were provided at the time of opening but the loop was set back from the running line and was for shunting purposes only, as it ran through the shed.

The gap left between the running line and the loop was to prove fortuitous here, as there was just enough space to squeeze in a new running loop and platform when it was decided to make

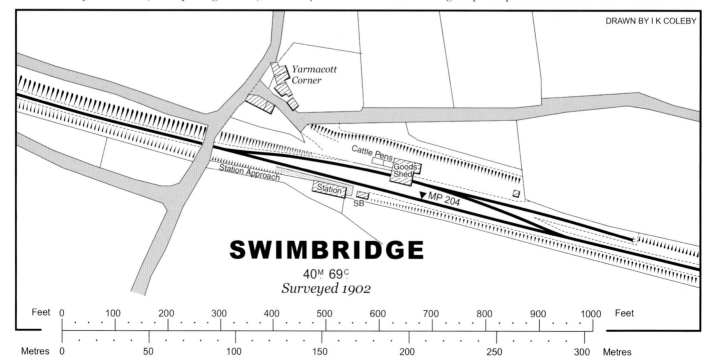

DRAWN BY I K COLEBY

Yarmacott Corner

Cattle Pens

Goods Shed

Station Approach

Station

SB

▼ MP 204

SWIMBRIDGE

40ᴹ 69ᶜ
Surveyed 1902

Feet 0   100   200   300   400   500   600   700   800   900   1000   Feet

Metres 0   50   100   150   200   250   300   Metres

Swimbridge looking east from the road bridge in the 1950s. The unusual profile of the Up platform is clear from this view, wide at this end to allow for the waiting shelter and then narrowing to clear the goods shed, beyond which it remained at the same width. The goods loop was also slewed northwards to make room for the waiting shelter, curving back beyond it to run through the goods shed. The simple, rather austere station building was in marked contrast to all of the others on the line and note too the non-standard GWR design signal box just beyond. *P.J. Garland, courtesy Roger Carpenter*

improvements to the station. Construction of the second, brick-built platform – on what became the Up side – and the Up passenger loop line began in 1903 and opened on 24th February 1904. The waiting shelter constructed on the new Up platform was built of brick and as a consequence was more substantial than other shelters on the line, with the exception of Dulverton, although it was timber and glass fronted. Once again there was no footbridge, so passengers had to traverse the line by means of the barrow crossing at the Barnstaple end of the station. One anomaly caused by the slightly restricted space in which the second platform had to be fitted was that it narrowed as it passed the goods shed and remained at this lesser width for the rest of its length.

The platforms were both 400 feet in length. The 1937 enhancements lengthened the loop line and improved the pointwork to allow faster

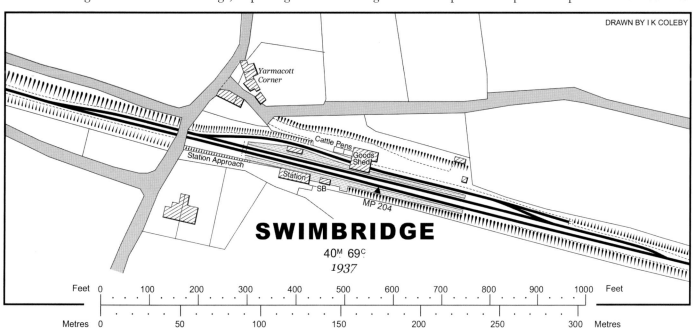

DRAWN BY I K COLEBY

SWIMBRIDGE

40ᴹ 69ᶜ
1937

Feet 0 100 200 300 400 500 600 700 800 900 1000 Feet

Metres 0 50 100 150 200 250 300 Metres

No. 6327 arrives at Swimbridge on 7h June 1963 at the head of an Up train bound for Taunton, with a selection of wagons on view in the tiny goods yard. Note too the 204 milepost on the Up platform and the rather large number of tiebars in the end of the goods shed wall, holding the building together. At the far end of the Down platform, the station master has a chat with the guard during the train's brief pause here for passengers. *David Johnson, courtesy Roger Carpenter*

Another example of the occasional variety in motive power that could be experienced on the line, as BR 'Standard' Class '3MT' 2-6-2T No. 82040 pulls in to the station on 27th June 1964, with the seven-coach 11.25am service from Taunton to Barnstaple Junction. The viewpoint provides good detail of the interior of the open fronted waiting alcove in the station building on the right and the wood and glass facia of the Up side shelter. Several wooden sprags can be seen lying between the tracks, which were used for pinning down or 'spragging' wagon brakes.

R.A. Lumber, courtesy Dave Mitchell

running in, at 40mph. In the *1947 Appendix to the Service Time Table*, the loop lengths were stated as 642 feet Up and 825 feet Down.

The 40-foot long, stone-built goods shed was located immediately behind the Up platform, with cattle pens and a goods platform dock of 55 feet alongside; the shed housed a 2-ton capacity crane. The goods loop extended into a short headshunt at the Taunton or east end of the station. There were no other sidings, so this was the extent of the yard here, which thus qualified as the most modest on the line. The wagon capacity was for just eleven wagons to the west of the goods shed, two in the shed and ten to the east, with a further four on the

SWIMBRIDGE – PASSENGER, PARCELS & STAFF STATISTICS 1903-1958						
Year	Payroll cost £ (& staff no's)	Total Receipts incl. goods £	Tickets issued (season tickets)	Passenger receipts £	Parcels etc receipts £	Total £ (incl. Parcels)
1903	167 (3)	1,559	7,572 (n/a)	325	138	463
1913	195 (3)	1,632	8,525 (n/a)	469	161	630
1923	487 (3)	2,901	8,666 (13)	556	101	657
1924	428 (3)	2,991	8,202 (4)	518	89	607
1925	511 (3)	2,779	7,407 (0)	467	68	535
1926	469 (3)	2,447	5,779 (0)	367	135	502
1927	452 (3)	3,083	5,992 (0)	346	173	519
1928	429 (3)	3,339	7,572 (0)	368	189	557
1929	463 (3)	3,431	6,841 (0)	340	179	519
1930	513 (3)	3,475	5,574 (0)	289	178	467
1931	415 (3)	3,452	6,136 (0)	291	125	416
1932	424 (3)	2,868	6,539 (0)	335	92	427
1933	445 (3)	3,092	6,313 (0)	377	163	540
1934	449 (3)	3,491	6,030 (0)	306	126	432
1935	461 (3)	4,965	6,010 (0)	327	200	527
1936	473 (3)	3,464	6,180 (3)	365	152	517
1937	501 (3)	2,587	6,172 (10)	346	74	420
1938	501 (3)	2,227	5,412 (4)	371	36	407
1940	578 (3)	A	3,223 (0)	431	75	506
1945	996 (3)	A	3,371 (0)	575	136	711
1950	B (3)	A	1,255 (0)	435	76	511
1955	B (4)	A	1,711 (0)	339	38	377
1958	B (4)	A	1,641 (11)	392	38	430
A – Goods receipts not provided; B – Not recorded						

All is peaceful and quiet in this undated view of Swimbridge, looking eastwards and showing the Up platform and its waiting shelter, both added in 1904, along with the goods shed and the loop line around the rear of the platform. The livestock pens, which stood on the loading dock at this end of the goods shed, can also just be seen.
Courtesy The Lens of Sutton Association

SWIMBRIDGE.

Station is on summit of Inclines of 1 in 60, falling towards Filleigh and Barnstaple.

No vehicle must be detached and allowed to remain on the Main Line.

Before engines of Freight trains performing work are detached from their trains, the brake of the guard's van must be fully applied, and sufficient wagon brakes put down and sprags used to prevent the train moving. Any wagons shunted on to the train must be immediately coupled up.

Guards of Freight trains must fully apply the hand-brake before leaving their vans.

Six sprags must be kept, 10 yards apart, by the side of the line between the facing points at the East end of the Loop.

SWIMBRIDGE – GOODS TRAFFIC 1903-1959

Year	Coal/Coke charged/ forwarded (tons)	Other minerals (tons)	General merchandise forwarded (tons)	Coal/Coke charged/ received (tons)	Other minerals received (tons)	General merchandise received (tons)	Coal/Coke not charged forwarded/ received (tons)	Total goods tonnage	Total receipts (excl. not charged) £	Livestock wagons forwarded/ received	Total carted tonnage (incl. total goods tonnage)
1903	0	0	491	583	213	1,447	30	2,764	1,096	12	369
1913	0	0	95	272	1,855	656	144	3,022	1,002	97	166
1923	0	0	304	17	1,198	1,134	787	3,440	2,244	17	352
1924	0	0	399	43	1,088	1,337	772	3,639	2,384	19	362
1925	0	4	324	182	443	1,288	689	2,930	2,244	15	347
1926	0	15	344	30	197	1,219	613	2,418	1,945	16	347
1927	0	12	573	0	345	1,314	1,100	3,344	2,564	14	347
1928	0	48	600	99	346	1,409	953	3,455	2,782	9	411
1929	53	252	610	108	249	1,391	892	3,555	2,912	29	415
1930	35	108	639	62	163	1,597	1,083	3,687	3,008	14	400
1931	74	9	661	24	88	1,700	1,181	3,737	3,086	12	417
1932	99	0	514	58	39	1,359	1,360	3,429	2,441	4	365
1933	8	0	636	18	177	1,395	895	3,129	2,552	1	577
1934	0	0	674	37	91	2,310	384	3,496	3,059	21	1,551
1935	0	0	826	9	75	4,592	428	5,930	4,438	26	4,122
1936	0	0	790	24	101	1,423	348	2,686	2,947	36	1,161
1937	0	0	405	10	84	1,035	518	2,052	2,167	16	825
1938	0	0	335	10	89	788	336	1,558	1,820	7	646
1940	0	0	173	0	60	875	294	1,402	Not recorded	0	Not recorded
1945	0	6	2547	8	61	1,089	163	3,874	Not recorded	4	Not recorded
1950	Zoned at Barnstaple from 1st August 1947; Zoned at Exeter by 1958										
1959	0	0	88	0	195	162	1,406	1,851	Not recorded	0	Not recorded

In contrast to the picture opposite, this view shows one of the brief but regular periods of action at the station, as No. 6372 arrives with the 2.24pm Barnstaple Junction to Taunton train, to cross with the corresponding 1.03pm Taunton to Barnstaple Junction service on 15th April 1963. No. 6372 is mirrored on the side of the leading carriage of the Down train, which had sister engine No. 6327 at the head. *Stephen P. Derek*

headshunt. Goods traffic comprised mainly coal and fertiliser being brought in, along with skins for a nearby tannery, with livestock heading out. Occasionally, cattle were loaded for transport on a Tuesday or a Friday, bound for Banbury market. Goods traffic peaked in 1935, showing a significant spike that stands out from all the other years at the station. This was particularly in general merchandise received and carted, and it would be interesting to know what caused this peak but the figures give no clue.

The signal box was located on the Down platform to the east of the station buildings. Its origins are uncertain but it was certainly in place by the early 1880s and may have been a B&ER box (*see pages 434-35*). It was enlarged in 1904 when the loop and Up platform were added.

Staff at Swimbridge comprised a station master, two signalmen (on shift) and a lad porter. Passenger numbers remained fairly constant right up until the Second World War but, bucking the trend seen elsewhere on the line, Swimbridge then saw a drop off in ticket sales through the 1940s and then a slump by the 1950s from which the figures never recovered. Season ticket sales were inconsistent to say the least, with peaks of 13, 10 and 11 in 1923, 1937 and 1958 respectively but none in most other years.

Leaving Swimbridge station the line immediately passed under the Brayford road bridge and into a cutting. Curving to the right, it then opened on to a long straight section of just under one mile, mainly on a series of downgrades, with several being at 1 in 60 but relatively short in length. The line was now on a low embankment and the countryside around was open fields. Coming off the embankment, it passed over the Harford road bridge before entering a cutting on a gentle left-hand curve and then under the first Goodleigh road bridge. Staying in this cutting, which hid the railway from the village of Landkey just to the south, the line then passed under the second Goodleigh road bridge. Emerging out of the cutting just beyond it, the line curved gently to the right, with views of Acland Woods ahead and to the right.

The hard work was now almost done, as this final two miles were virtually straight and downhill, mostly at 1 in 60 until just before Barnstaple East Junction. Halfway down this grade, the line passed under the Barnstaple to Goodleigh road bridge, about a mile out from Victoria Road station. Once beyond the bridge, the broad width of the Taw Estuary became apparent, stretching ahead in the far distance. The grades were shallow in the final stretch, being at 1 in 750 and 1 in 120 as the line approached the outskirts of Barnstaple. Noticeable in the distance was the imposing tower of Holy Trinity church, described by some as the tallest man-made structure in the town.

Despite now being very close to the terminus, there was no significant urban development to be seen, apart from a few council-style houses appearing on the right of the line in the near distance. To the left there were still fields, bisected by the out of use (but still virtually intact) East Loop line swerving away to the south to Barnstaple Junction. About a quarter of a mile further on, the West Loop came in and joined from the left; these two chords had met at Barnstaple South Junction, trapping a few acres of pasture in the triangle thus formed.

Beyond the junction of the West Loop, the line entered the throat of Victoria Road station. On the immediate left, the foundation stones just visible were all that remained of the old GWR engine shed (closed in January 1951) and beyond that was the site of the oil depot. To the right was Victoria Road's single platform and station buildings. As the train approached the station, the locomotive gave two sharp blasts on its whistle to forewarn the signalman. The Swimbridge/Barnstaple token would be handed to him before the train eased over a right-hand point and into the main arrivals platform, as opposed to the shorter bay on the right, coming to a halt some way short of the buffers and the station buildings. With the time at 11.58am, the two minute delay had not been made up but no one seemed to mind. The substantial goods shed was visible on the left side of the train and the yard was likely to be busy, with cattle wagons, covered vans and open wagons on view. On the occasion of our arrival, a goods train was in the process of being made up in the yard, with the familiar clanking of buffers. This was often again in the hands of a 'Mogul' engine or sometimes a Collett 0-6-0, which, having brought in the 11.05am trip working from Barnstaple Junction, would then shunt the yard prior to heading out with the 2.45am Up goods from Barnstaple.

A roadside view of the wooden passenger station buildings at Barnstaple GWR (it did not become Victoria Road until 1949) circa 1905. The horse-drawn vehicles pictured are a parcels delivery van on the left and a Landau 4-wheeled carriage on the right. *Courtesy The National Railway Museum*

BARNSTAPLE VICTORIA ROAD (44 MILES 58 CHAINS)

Opened to Passengers ....1st November 1873
Opened to Goods ....11th November 1873
Closed to Passengers ....13th June 1960
Closed to Goods ....5th March 1970

Barnstaple Victoria Road station was 207³/₄ miles from Paddington and 42¹/₂ miles from the junction at Norton Fitzwarren. Some trains terminated here, usually the last two of the day, but most went over to Barnstaple Junction on weekdays and beyond to Ilfracombe on summer Saturdays. If heading on to Barnstaple Junction, the locomotive had to run round its train at Victoria Road and then work tender first out of the station and round the West Curve. Occasionally, Up and Down trains were scheduled to cross with one another at Victoria Road. In the event of this, the Up train would usually arrive first, with the locomotive running around its train and then shunting it into the bay platform. This would clear the main platform for the Down train's arrival, upon which the Up train could take the token for the section to Swimbridge. Today, our next Up

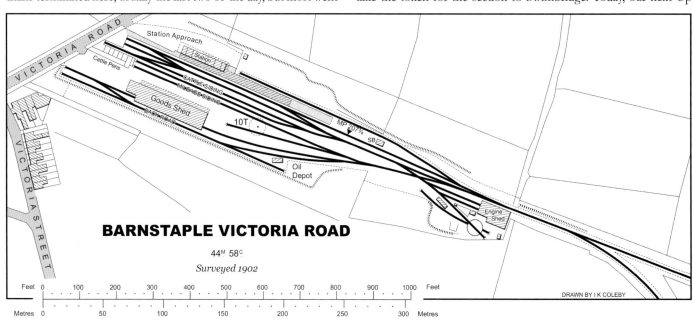

BARNSTAPLE VICTORIA ROAD

44ᴹ 58ᶜ

Surveyed 1902

Feet 0   100   200   300   400   500   600   700   800   900   1000 Feet

Metres 0   50   100   150   200   250   300   Metres

DRAWN BY I K COLEBY

'Bulldog' Class 4-4-0 No. 3360 *Launceston* uncouples ready to run round its train at Barnstaple GWR in summer 1926. We can be sure of the date thanks to the GWR 1926 Holiday Haunts poster on the end wall of the building, behind the engine's smokebox. *Launceston* had actually been renumbered in 1912, becoming No. 3348 but, along with other class members, continued to carry its old oval combined name and number plates on the cabsides. Following complaints to the GWR that passengers were apparently mistaking the places names of many locomotives for destinations, the Traffic Department asked if these could be removed from the numerous engines that carried them. A programme of removal commenced in the later 1920s and *Launceston* lost its distinctive oval plates in September 1930, when it presumably finally became No. 3348 but remained nameless for the rest of its career, which ended with withdrawal in November 1934. Their duties on the D&SR line were to be taken over by the Churchward 'Mogul' 2-6-0s that feature so prominently throughout these pages. The days of clerestory-roofed coaches were also coming to an end. *Courtesy The National Railway Museum*

train was the 1.11pm from Barnstaple Junction, arriving at Victoria Road at 1.16pm and departing at 1.22pm, so there was no need for any shunting manoeuvres to allow for a Down arrival.

The station was located to the east of the town and was therefore not centrally located. Thus in the early decades of the railway there was a requirement for passengers to walk or get the horse-bus service between the GWR station and the town, or indeed over to the L&SWR station on the other side of the river if they were travelling beyond Barnstaple. The location chosen was supposed to have been a temporary one, the intention being to build a more centrally located station near the clock tower (*see Vol. 1 Chap. 3*). In consequence, station buildings and a goods shed were constructed of timber, as it was expected that they would not be required for long.

The station comprised a single, stone-faced platform located on the north side of the line. Most arrivals and departures used this platform, primarily because of its run round facilities. However, subsequently, a shorter bay platform was also added on the north side, which could handle departures at busy times when trains crossed at Victoria Road. The original temporary station buildings only lasted from 1873 until 1876, being replaced by a long, single-storey, slatted-timber structure, with a slated gable roof. This was built at the west end of the platform and housed (from west or the Barnstaple end to east), a parcels office,

refreshment room (which was later used as a store and cycle room), the booking office, waiting room and ladies' toilet, gentlemen's toilet, station master's office and a porters' room with a store behind. All rooms were accessible from the platform only, with the exception of the booking hall, which had a door on the station forecourt side in the middle of the structure. The parcels office was entered from the forecourt by a gate next to the station building, thus allowing barrows ease of access. Horse traffic could also use this gate when required, horses being loaded at the end of the platform. The parcels office consisted of a counter and telephone, with a set of scales on the public side, whilst on the back wall was a label rack; parcels awaiting collection or delivery were stored in the area between the back wall and the counter. The refreshment room was run on a tenancy and consisted of a bar extending the full length of the room, tables and chairs. The booking office had two desks facing an open fireplace (which shared a chimney with the fireplace in the refreshment room next door) and conventional ticket racks positioned on the opposite wall, with a booking window looking out on to the general waiting room, this latter boasting a large table and chairs, and a time table board. The ladies' and gents' toilets were next door alongside each other, with the former on the road side. The station master's office had a desk, chair and cupboards, and the porters' room a table and

An overall view of the passenger and goods facilities at Barnstaple, looking from the signal box steps and taken by a Great Western Railway official photographer circa 1905, on the same occasion as the picture of the front of the station building on page 380. The long rake of wagons waiting to be dealt with in the Mileage siding on the left include a Bradbury private owner laden with coal and a pristine Pratts Spirit tank wagon, No. 1193. Further along nearer the goods shed, the 10-ton crane serving the siding can be seen. *Courtesy The National Railway Museum*

Taken on the same day as the previous picture but further along the platform showing more detail of the platform awning and the goods shed on the left. Closer up it can be seen that the goods shed awning did not extend over the Mileage siding but provided covered loading/unloading for road vehicles. A second Bradbury wagon can be seen partially hidden behind the GWR van on the left, whilst the rear of the horse-drawn parcels van seen in the picture on page 380 can just be made out in the station forecourt beyond the end of the bay. *Courtesy The National Railway Museum*

chairs. There was a store room at the back of the porters room for cleaning equipment.

The main platform was 570 feet in length when built. The bay platform was originally 270 feet but authority to extend this to 375 feet was given in June 1910; this presumably meant extending the main platform as well. Another authority dated January 1924 specified a further platform extension but the details are unclear and there is no evidence that any work was ever carried out.

Along the front of the station building on the platform side was a flat-roofed canopy supported by a number of timber posts set back from the platform edge. A further canopy was later added, with a curved corrugated iron roof on twin wooden post supports, running from the Taunton end of the main station building for around 200 feet along the bay and main platforms, providing additional cover for both. On the forecourt side, behind the station there was an extensive access area for horse-drawn coaches in the early days and cars and buses latterly. There was a slim protective wooden canopy over the main entrance on this side of the station building, running for about half of its length.

The original signal box was replaced in 1910, by a new larger cabin with a 36-lever frame. On a similar site just off the platform at the east end, thus affording the signalman a good view of the station area, goods yard and locomotive yard, it was probably constructed alongside the first box. The new box had a brick base and a timber top half, classified as a GWR Type 3 by the Signalling Record Society. Beyond the signal box was a ground-mounted water crane.

The temporary wooden goods shed lasted until 1876, when a contract to build a new facility, along with other improvements at the station, was concluded. The new shed was a substantial stone-built construction with a gabled, slated roof and was of a different design to the 'standard' 40 foot and 60 foot sheds built elsewhere on the D&SR. Still standing but now converted for use as a Baptist church, based on rough on-site measurements it is approximately 130 feet long and 33 feet wide. There were five access doorways for collections and deliveries, measuring 10 feet each in width and of a similar height, with access from the mileage yard side of the shed. A stone built office attached at the far (Barnstaple) end of the main building measured around 22 feet by 22 feet, again having with a gabled slated roof. Adjoining the original stone extension is a further brick-built extension measuring around 10 feet square, which has a sloping, slate roof. The rail access doorways at either end were around 10 feet wide and a similar height. The canopy which provided protection to those using the access doors still remains. It extends to about 7 feet beyond the shed and is supported by eighteen wooden posts.

The goods shed was served by a single track running right through it. This siding could hold up to thirty wagons along its full length (ten in the shed, fifteen in front and five behind). As mentioned above, there was a canopy which ran the length of the northern side of the shed, providing a little cover on the road delivery/collection side. The platform inside was provided with four hand cranes each of 35-cwt capacity, which were located between each of the five bays. The two bays at the west end of the shed were for town centre traffic, whilst

A panoramic view of the station and goods yard at Victoria Road circa 1958. On the far left are first the back road (alongside the low grass bank) and the siding running into and through the shed. The wagons in the left foreground are standing on the short crane road in front of the goods shed, the 10-ton crane that featured in the 1905 view having been replaced in the late 1920s by the 6-ton crane seen here. This short rake includes three oil tank wagons serving the petroleum depot behind the photographer on his left. To the right of the crane is the Mileage siding, the nearest wagon in which is loaded with a farm tractor, followed by the carriage siding, the middle and cattle dock siding, the run round line and finally the platform line. In the left background is the tower of Holy Trinity church. *R.J. Sellick, courtesy National Railway Museum*

A useful panorama of the east end of the station, which probably dates from the 1930s, showing the diamond crossover serving the locomotive shed. The train of non-gangwayed ex-L&SWR coaching stock is apparently departing running tender-first, so may in fact be about to be shunted in to the bay. It is under the control of the lattice Starting signal to the left of the train and adjacent to that is the Bay Starting signal, which has 'BAY' painted on its arm. Beyond the signals is the water storage tank which supplied the tank next to the shed, which had recently been dismantled, with just a part of the brick base still remaining. The coaling stage alongside was also possibly redundant by this time. *Arthur Sellick, courtesy National Railway Museum*

On 28th February 1953, an unidentified Class '22XX' 0-6-0 is seen in the cattle dock siding, preparing to depart with a mixed Up goods to Taunton. A 'Mogul' 2-6-0 stands at the platform with a Down train, having just run round the stock prior to hauling it round to Barnstaple Junction. A small pile of parcels have been unloaded on to the platform. *R.J. Sellick courtesy, National Railway Museum*

Barnstaple Victoria Road station, looking east from the buffer stops in October 1952, with a fine display of posters and advertising signs still displayed on the end wall. The locomotive shed in the middle distance had closed nearly two years earlier. *P.J. Garland, courtesy Roger Carpenter*

the remaining three were for general merchandise, such as bales of wool. Heavy ironwork was occasionally unloaded in the shed using the cranes to facilitate handling. The goods office was located at the west end of the structure but built in to the main shed. This office consisted of a public lobby, with separate offices for the chief clerk and his staff, and there was a communicating door between the office and the goods deck. Alongside that was a lock-up and nearby

a desk used by the foreman, whilst beyond the shed and just inside the goods yard entrance was a mess room/toilet, weighbridge and petrol pump. At the east end of the building adjacent to the wall there was, for some years, a smaller, rectangular corrugated iron shed, which was a warehouse for Lyon's Tea and is understood to have been built between 1926 and 1930. Railway wagons serving it were unloaded using a bridging board into the shed, where the cartons

Photographed from the same position in 1956, apart from the posters and advertisements, the main change had been the demolition of the engine shed. In the distance, what looks to be a Southern 'Mogul' shunts the goods yard. *Mowat Collection, courtesy Brunel University*

of tea were stored awaiting local deliveries. This was undertaken using a Lyon's Tea lorry, which was loaded from an opening on the east (long) side of the shed.

There was originally a 10-ton crane which served the mileage siding in the yard but this was replaced between 1929 and 1938 by one of 6-ton capacity. The mileage siding was a common feature to most larger goods yards and was so named as it was where wagons were stored for goods that were loaded or unloaded by the customers themselves, so they just paid a cartage or mileage charge to the railway. The capacity of the mileage siding was noted as seventeen wagons to the crane and then another five beyond that to the points, although other records show a total capacity for twenty-five wagons. The livestock pens, which could take three or four wagons, were situated at the west end of the goods yard, at the end of the third line across from the passenger platform. Behind the pens was a shed for storing sawdust brought here from local timber merchants, to spread on the floor of the cattle wagons and soak up some of the mess produced by the animals. The end-loading dock incorporated a carriage shoot and was at the buffer stops end of the middle (run-round) line, sandwiched between the platform line and the cattle dock. In the days of gas-lit coaching stock, a cordon wagon was usually located at these buffer stops and used to replenish the gas in the carriages (*see Vol. 1, page 135*). Between the cattle dock line and the mileage siding was the carriage siding, which could hold four bogie coaches. However, it was often used for goods wagon storage and was recorded as having a capacity for twenty-one wagons. The remaining sidings comprised the short mileage yard siding near the goods shed, which could take eleven wagons, and the back road behind the shed (capacity fourteen wagons), with its kick-back line running to the fuel depot (capacity six wagons). The back

Top Right: A Taunton-bound train arrives at Victoria Road from Barnstaple Junction in June 1960, hence the tender-first working. The locomotive will run round the carriages in order to complete the main part of its journey smokebox leading. The impending closure of Victoria Road removed the need for these wasteful additional manoeuvres, as trains then ran directly to Barnstaple Junction over the East Curve. Note the large number of parcels on the platform.

Centre: On the same day, No. 6372 runs round its train having arrived from Taunton. The goods yard remained busy.

Right: Now coupled up to the other end of its three coach train, No. 6372 prepares to depart on the final leg of its journey, tender-first round to Barnstaple Junction. *All Peter Barnfield*

Following on from the bottom picture on the previous page, No. 6372 disappears into the distance round the West Curve as it heads towards Barnstaple Junction. In the left foreground is the 1910-built Barnstaple Signal Box, whilst the vacant land on the right of the tracks between the two lighting poles is the site of the demolished locomotive shed and yard. *Peter Barnfield*

No. 6309 was photographed in the act of running round its train on 6th June 1960, which on this occasion comprised an ex-GWR two-coach 'B-set'. We have not seen this particular 'Mogul' before and it was clearly some way from home, as it carries a Swindon shed 83C shedplate on its smokebox door. Note the National Benzole sign in the centre background, marking the site of the oil depot. *John Spencer Gilks*

In the first of two views illustrating how Up and Down trains were crossed at Victoria Road, No. 6372 stands at the platform in the early part of 1960, having just brought in a train from Taunton, comprising a two-coach 'B-set', plus a parcels coach and three vans. The locomotive will shortly uncouple to run round its train and, on this occasion, will draw the stock back out of platform and then shunt it into the bay platform. The group on the platform look to be military personnel, mostly in uniform and wearing forage caps but a couple are in 'civvies'. They were probably waiting for the next Up train, perhaps taking them to Norton Fitzwarren, where there was a large REME military vehicle depot close to the station. The angle of this photograph allows a view up the line towards Swimbridge in the right distance, with the junction for the West Curve just visible beyond the bracket signal. With closure to passengers imminent and no doubt having been mooted for some time, essential maintenance had lapsed and both the station awning and the platform canopy beyond were starting to sag in places quite noticeably. *E.T. Gill, courtesy Rob Blencowe*

road had a set of crossover points in the early years (believed to be up to the 1920s) but these were removed and the capacity of the back road was then recorded (circa 1940s) as twenty-seven wagons. There was a fouling point board between the necks of the short mileage siding and the shed road, whilst the *1947 Appendix to the Service Time Table* stated that a re-railing ramp was retained in the lamp room.

At the eastern end of the station and to the south side of the running line was a two-road, wooden engine shed with a gabled slated roof, opened at the request of the B&ER when the line opened through to Barnstaple. Originally built to house broad gauge engines, it measured approximately 85 feet by 40 feet and always contained two lines, both in broad gauge days and after the D&SR was narrowed to standard gauge in 1881. Both lines terminated inside the shed, which was constructed of slatted timber on all four sides, resting on a 2 foot high brick plinth. The slated, gabled roof was punctuated by eight smoke ventilation chimneys and there were two wooden doors at the entrance, with a glazed section above each; a ventilator was positioned in the centre of each of these glazed sections and there was also a grill in the gable at the front end of the shed. Finally, there were five glazed windows on the rail side of the building, two single windows

BARNSTAPLE – PASSENGER, PARCELS & STAFF STATISTICS 1903-1957						
Year	Payroll cost £ (& staff no's)	Total Receipts incl. goods £	Tickets issued (season tickets)	Passenger receipts £	Parcels etc receipts £	Total £ (incl. Parcels)
1903	2,261 (35)	23,219	32,987 (n/a)	5,579	3,449	9,028
1913	2,195 (28)	27,549	26,824 (n/a)	5,265	3,462	8,727
1923	5,821 (33)	48,563	28,089 (32)	10,819	2,562	13,381
1924	5,171 (33)	48,485	25,427 (21)	10,482	2,321	12,803
1925	5,285 (33)	52,020	26,694 (12)	10,768	2,360	13,128
1926	4,814 (36)	50,944	25,494 (41)	11,571	2,901	14,472
1927	5,383 (35)	54,772	23,336 (25)	10,628	2,871	13,499
1928	5,429 (37)	59,494	24,211 (37)	10,923	2,937	13,860
1929	5,513 (38)	59,696	22,405 (17)	10,622	2,964	13,586
1930	5,531 (38)	56,729	20,388 (35)	9,764	3,308	13,072
1931	5,447 (38)	53,432	17,983 (40)	8,897	2,932	11,829
1932	5,274 (37)	47,190	16,536 (31)	7,912	2,688	10,600
1933	5,722 (37)	47,125	15,715 (78)	7,820	3,325	11,145
1934	5,834 (37)	50,557	15,357 (70)	7,642	3,260	10,902
1935	7,026 (38)	52,571	17,611 (62)	7,817	1,791	9,608
1936	6,490 (39)	55,938	15,956 (106)	8,132	1,833	9,965
1937	6,759 (38)	55,506	14,788 (151)	8,380	1,566	9,946
1938	6,533 (38)	51,165	13,131 (146)	8,052	1,444	9,496
1939	6,430 (38)	49,747	11,134 (72)	6,937	1,641	8,578
1940	7,114 (38)	Not recorded	10,986 (19)	8,051	2,203	10,254
1941	8,021 (39)	Not recorded	18,841 (3)	15,552	3,270	18,822
1942	8,283 (39)	Not recorded	14,224 (3)	9,400	2,571	11,971
1943	9,406 (39)	Not recorded	16,980 (9)	10,148	2,814	12,962
1944	11,477 (39)	Not recorded	19,548 (8)	11,091	2,496	13,587
1945	11,422 (39)	Not recorded	18,565 (89)	11,200	3,180	14,380
1946	11,666 (39)	Not recorded	14,873 (127)	10,988	3,674	14,662
1947	12,533 *(43)	Not recorded	12,316 (115)	10,288	4,121	14,409
1948	14,055 †(43)	Not recorded	11,870 (61)	10,918	4,554	15,472
1949	14,212 (43)	Not recorded	12,029 (36)	11,006	4,510	15,516
1950	(47)	Not recorded	10,230 (44)	9,686	4,688	14,374
1951	Not recorded (56)	Not recorded	9,301 (4)	8,761	6,497	15,258
1952	(56)	Not recorded	9,624 (4)	8,755	7,183	15,938
1953	(56)	Not recorded	9,669 (1)	9,505	5,523	15,028
1954	(53)	Not recorded	10,704 (0)	9,397	3,449	12,846
1955	(56)	Not recorded	9,593 (0)	8,646	2,577	11,223
1956	(58)	Not recorded	12,034 (0)	10,150	2,623	12,773
1957	(56)	Not recorded	12,925 (0)	11,480	3,046	14,526

All reporting transferred to the Southern Region from 1st February 1958
* Includes East Anstey, Bishops Nympton & Molland, Filleigh and Swimbridge from 1st August 1947
† Includes East Anstey and Swimbridge only from 1st June 1948

With No. 6372 having shunted its Down train into the bay on the left, the main platform was now clear for the arrival from Barnstaple Junction of the next Up working. Working tender-first via the West Curve, the 2-6-0 will be able to run round its train here and then head off to Taunton smokebox leading. Once in the platform, the route was clear for No. 6372 to depart from the bay with its train and head tender-first round to Barnstaple Junction. It is not surprising that the station was closed and all services diverted to the Junction station in order that the railway could divest itself of this cumbersome and inefficient method of operation. Note the remains of the oil depot on the right and the tatty metal Victoria Road sign tacked on beneath the main nameboard just eleven years earlier on the left.
E.T. Gill, courtesy Rob Blencowe

RIGHT: On 6th June 1960 and having run round its train, the 10.15am from Taunton to Ilfracombe, No. 6309's fireman climbs down from the footplate in order to couple the engine back up to its coaches. It will work tender-first round to Barnstaple Junction but will then hand the train over to another locomotive which will be facing the right way to take it on 'over the hill' to Ilfracombe. No. 6309 will be coaled and watered on the ex-L&SWR shed at the Junction. Note the porter loading a number of sizeable parcels in to the leading vehicle. *John Spencer Gilks*

BELOW: Class '63XX' No. 6343 stands outside the twin-road wooden engine shed at Barnstaple on the 10th June 1935, awaiting its next turn of duty. The engine has a full tender, so had recently been coaled at the stage out of sight on the right. *W.A. Camwell, courtesy Stephenson Locomotive Society*

Above: Class '45XX' No. 5503 replenishes its tanks from the water crane alongside the signal box on 28th July 1951, whilst the coaches of its train stand at the platform. The 'B' in a white circle on the bufferbeam was for the benefit of the Norton Fitzwarren Junction signalman, indicating it as a Barnstaple line train; Minehead workings carried an 'M' disc. *R.J. Sellick courtesy, National Railway Museum*

Left: The 9.25am Saturday's only Ilfracombe to Cardiff service leaves Victoria Road behind 2-6-0 No. 7311 on 19th September 1953. In the foreground are the remains of the locomotive shed, which had closed less than three years earlier, with the timber superstructure having been dismantled, leaving only the low brick walls which had formed its base and the concrete filled inspection pits. Another engine can be made out in the left background shunting the goods yard. *Hugh Davies collection*

of twelve panes each and three doubles of twenty-four panes. The offices and mess room for locomen were contained in a smaller wooden building attached to the south wall of the shed. A 1920s photograph (*page 437*) also shows a single-storey building adjacent, with a square, brick-built 25 foot chimney, which most likely housed a sand drying plant. Just in front of the shed and a little to the right was a water tower mounted on a brick base. A 42-feet turntable was located on the south side of the shed and a timber coal stage on the road leading to it completed the facilities.

The turntable had originally been provided at Wiveliscombe in 1871 but was transferred to Barnstaple when the line opened throughout in 1873. It could take 'Bulldog' Class 4-4-0s and Collett '22XX' Class 0-6-0s but was too short for the larger Class '43XX' Churchward 'Moguls', so these were usually turned at Barnstaple Junction shed on the larger turntable there. The *Summer 1939 Service Time Table* did make reference to the fact that '*if engines require turning they must run around the triangle*' but this was only relevant in the summer period, when the triangle was in use, whilst such manoeuvres would have

BARNSTAPLE – GOODS TRAFFIC 1903-1957

Year	Coal/Coke charged/ forwarded (tons)	Other minerals (tons)	General merchandise forwarded (tons)	Coal/Coke charged/ received (tons)	Other minerals received (tons)	General merchandise received (tons)	Coal/Coke not charged forwarded/ received (tons)	Total goods tonnage	Total receipts (excl. not charged) £	Livestock wagons forwarded/ received	Total carted tonnage (incl. total goods tonnage)
1903	12	1,120	6,369	877	3,113	11,290	322	23,103	14,191	576	5,172
1913	3	1,355	8,176	185	1,937	15,312	867	27,835	18,822	688	6,917
1923	23	423	4,019	199	2,291	19,419	5,471	31,845	35,182	622	6,974
1924	0	556	3,991	308	3,952	20,928	5,394	35,129	35,682	642	7,371
1925	20	439	4,184	123	4,298	23,373	3,991	36,428	38,892	659	7,787
1926	20	535	3,709	738	3,454	22,613	3,436	34,505	36,372	618	7,405
1927	40	518	5,813	249	3,362	22,704	4,191	36,877	41,223	643	8,062
1928	58	701	6,310	238	2,513	24,739	3,401	37,960	45,634	685	8,277
1929	18	805	5,774	247	3,207	25,849	4,240	40,140	46,110	722	9,026
1930	25	1,134	5,247	245	3,374	25,488	4,211	39,724	43,657	752	8,361
1931	0	539	4,466	249	3,857	25,943	3,856	38,910	41,603	570	8,239
1932	0	881	3,397	281	3,236	23,695	3,145	34,635	36,590	282	7,526
1933	11	825	3,717	216	2,848	23,562	2,306	33,485	35,980	166	8,033
1934	0	1,049	3,525	311	3,305	25,468	2,399	36,057	39,655	257	9,244
1935	67	1,291	4,122	341	3,034	27,656	2,722	39,233	42,963	332	11,548
1936	34	1,481	3,992	433	3,522	32,060	2,807	44,329	45,973	418	17,364
1937	19	1,336	4,362	301	3,383	30,501	3,583	43,485	45,560	358	16,953
1938	10	1,185	3,659	75	2,761	28,031	3,649	39,370	41,669	266	15,247
1939	0	1,600	3,424	297	2,414	29,793	3,340	40,868	41,169	231	Not recorded
1940	9	1,552	5,829	804	1,997	34,840	3,241	48,272	Not recorded	706	Not recorded
1941	168	952	8,751	1,702	3,914	45,226	3,333	64,046	Not recorded	601	Not recorded
1942	0	1,350	11,835	829	4,355	42,368	1,215	61,952	Not recorded	511	Not recorded
1943	0	1,031	15,386	692	3,960	51,007	724	72,800	Not recorded	595	Not recorded
1944	0	791	18,077	26	2,685	49,553	1,690	72,822	Not recorded	597	Not recorded
1945	53	733	16,015	0	2,963	46,157	1,461	67,382	Not recorded	842	Not recorded
1946	9	925	8,793	11	1,628	44,419	801	56,586	Not recorded	1,185	Not recorded
1947	0	638	9,911	44	2,043	46,412	4,920	63,968	Not recorded	813	Not recorded
1948	33	802	6,232	19	2,724	46,803	4,841	61,454	Not recorded	913	Not recorded
1949	32	818	6,028	11	1,640	42,922	938	52,389	Not recorded	666	Not recorded
1950	0	902	4,297	19	2,277	46,471	6,760	60,726	Not recorded	1,228	Not recorded
1951	0	1,227	6,399	0	10,247	70,317	36,542	124,727	Not recorded	1,597	Not recorded
1952	0	2,432	4,880	0	8,531	69,113	31,024	115,980	Not recorded	1,412	Not recorded
1953	A	2,780	4,593	A	11,969	72,314	31,377	123,033	Not recorded	1,512	Not recorded
1954	A	2,163	5,167	A	9,549	66,118	19,551	102,548	Not recorded	1,444	Not recorded
1955	A	7,775	4,126	A	13,807	52,805	24,325	102,838	Not recorded	672	Not recorded
1956	A	7,021	3,849	A	16,322	48,697	20,854	96,743	Not recorded	746	Not recorded
1957	A	8,580	4,453	A	17,714	38,986	17,224	86,957	Not recorded	554	Not recorded

A – See Coal/Coke Not Charged/Forwarded
Includes East Anstey, Bishops Nympton & Molland, Filleigh, South Molton and Swimbridge from 1st August 1947
Includes Swimbridge only from 1st June 1948
Barnstaple Junction included from 1st November 1950
Transferred to Southern Region from 1st February 1958

ceased after that year anyway when the East Loop was closed.

The water tower comprised a square cast-iron tank supported on a tall brick-built plinth. Water was supplied by a larger concrete tank located on the bank on the north side of the running line, opposite the shed. The timber-built open coaling stage was raised a few feet off the ground but still required some back-breaking manual effort with a shovel to get the coal into the locomotive tenders. A water crane was situated between the shed lines and just in front of the building, supplementing the crane on the platform. The water tower was dismantled prior to the shed's closure, probably in the early 1930s, but the concrete tank remained, as it supplied water to the rest of the station. The sand drying plant seems to have been demolished at the same time.

Barnstaple did not have a shed code, being classed as a sub-shed to Taunton (coded TN in GWR days) and also by BR (who re-coded it 83B). It did have an allocation of locomotives and these for selected years will be given in Volume 3. The shed closed on 1st January 1951, with locomotive servicing thereafter being carried out at Barnstaple

Junction (72E). The shed sidings were removed in July 1953, along with the crossover into the yard, the turntable and locomotive pits were filled in and the site left desolate. Barnstaple Junction shed was closed on 6th September 1964, with diesels and diesel multiple units being the normal and final motive power for the line in its last two years of operation.

Between the engine shed complex and the goods yard was an oil depot operated by Shell-Mex, BP and National Benzole (the *1926 Kelly's Trade Directory for Devon* makes reference to the Anglo-American Oil Company at Barnstaple in addition to Shell and BP). The depot comprised a mix of sundry buildings constructed of corrugated iron along with other sheds, and included a garage, offices, and underground and overground storage tanks. The depot was reached by a kick-back spur running from the back road behind the goods shed, whilst road access was through the goods yard and across the access lines to the back siding. There were also facilities for Pratts Oils in the 1920s and 1930s (later replaced by Esso) but these were located at the west end of the station, on the other side of Victoria

This photograph, probably taken circa 1930, provides a rare glimpse of the rail-served petrol store on the south-east side of the yard. *Kelly's Trade Directory* for 1926 shows the Anglo American Oil Company at Barnstaple as well as separate entries for Shell and BP. The supply of Pratts Spirit, shown on the sign in the background, was generally handled by the Anglo-American Co. and had been for many years since the late 19th century. The tank wagon is interesting; fleet No. 632, it is lettered 'MOTOR 'R O P' SPIRIT' on the end of the tank, which stood for Russian Oil Products, which company was formed in 1925 to distribute petrol imported from Russia. ROP were taken over by Regent Oil in 1948. No. 6394, along with fireman Frank Clement and driver Fred Beer, have paused from shunting operations on the back road (where they assembled the Up Bristol goods) to have their picture taken, along with shunters Len Gregory and Taffy Wilkins, guard Jack Parkman and one other unknown.
Courtesy National Railway Museum

Road itself. Indeed, today (2017), the filling station on that site is still an Esso facility.

Post-war, Esso had the largest petrol depot at the station, under the management of Charles Lancey for many years. The tank wagons placed on the back siding were discharged via an underground pipe direct to the storage tanks. There were also three discharge tanks located just down the embankment below the back road, which were used by Rullaman and Gorman. The Rullaman tanks were the first two nearest the road and held tractor vaporising oil and paraffin, whilst

Gormans used the third tank for paraffin for farmers. Occasional wagon loads were received in the yard to top up the tanks. In the 1950s, the local distribution of fuel was in company-owned lorries, such as an Austin KV with a 1,000 gallon tank and a cradle on the back for delivering lubricating oil (driven by Frank Crook), or the Leyland Comet with a tank capacity of 1,500 gallons (driven by Stan Cann). These were supplemented by a 1,200 gallon Dennis lorry (driven by Bill Handford) and a Commer van used for maintenance (driven by Eddie McDonald). The vehicles were painted a light orange colour

No. 7337 about to depart with a three-coach train for Taunton in 1960. The low angle serves to illustrate the join where the 1910 brick-faced extension abutted the original stone-faced platform. Running along the face are the water pipes carrying the station supply. Note the spot of hand shunting under way on the far left, not an easy operation to replicate in model form! *Courtesy Rob Blencowe*

that was referred to officially as 'ochre'.

The Barnstaple Branch Railway, the spur line to Barnstaple Junction opened on 1st June 1887, allowing trains to run from Taunton through to Ilfracombe via the L&SWR route. However, it branched off the D&SR from Barnstaple GWR in the Up direction, which therefore required trains to arrive at the station, the locomotive to run round its train and then depart back in the direction from which it came for a short distance to access the spur. This practice, as inefficient as it may seem, lasted until Victoria Road was closed, although a more direct route was also in operation for some of the station's existence.

The more direct route was brought in to use in 1905, when the East Loop, a chord line about a quarter of a mile in length, was built and opened between East Junction, 46 chains outside of the GWR terminus towards Swimbridge, to join the spur line to Barnstaple Junction opened in 1887, at what became South Junction. This enabled trains to avoid the GWR terminus and run directly around the East Loop, thereby removing the need for locomotives to run round their carriages before proceeding to Barnstaple Junction and beyond. The lines now formed a triangle and the first section of the original spur became the West Loop. Two new signal boxes were also provided to control the passage of trains through the new connection, Barnstaple East Junction Signal Box and Barnstaple South Junction Signal Box.

The East Loop was only opened for through summer services, the opening and closing dates (usually the duration of the summer time table) being notified by special notice each year (*see Appendix 15*). This would result in an interesting manoeuvre when

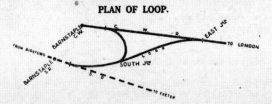

BARNSTAPLE.

Direct Junction Loop Line between East and South Junction Signal Boxes.

This Loop Line, the diagram of which is shewn below, is opened for the summer service traffic to provide a direct connection to Barnstaple Junction Southern Railway and the Ilfracombe line.

The date of opening and closing will be announced each year by special notice.

The instructions on page 104 must be observed :

PLAN OF LOOP.

Trains from Taunton to Barnstaple Junction—Ilfracombe which pass over the Loop must be formed in the following order : engine, vehicles for Ilfracombe, other vehicles for Barnstaple Junction, vehicles for Barnstaple G.W.

Such trains must come to a stand clear ahead of the points at Barnstaple South Junction. Station Master, Barnstaple, will arrange for an engine, accompanied by a Traffic Department man, to be waiting at the South Junction Down Home Signal. On arrival of the train, the Traffic Department man will divide it, pilot the local engine to the rear of the Barnstaple portion, and couple it on and send the Ilfracombe portion forward, after attaching tail lamp. He will then place a tail-lamp on the Barnstaple portion, and accompany it as Guard to the G.W. Station.

Station Master, Taunton, to instruct his Staff, when the Barnstaple Branch trains are being dealt with at Taunton, that the passengers and luggage for Barnstaple G.W. or for stations on the Southern Railway system, respectively, must be placed in the proper portion of the trains, and thoroughly to examine the trains, in order to ascertain that the passengers are in their proper compartments. The Station Masters at Norton Fitzwarren and on the Barnstaple Branch must also pay particular attention to this and see that everything possible is done to place the passengers and stow the luggage in the proper portions of the train, and if a vehicle is attached en route Barnstaple must at once be advised.

Trains from Ilfracombe to Taunton via the Loop, which attach a Barnstaple G.W. portion at East Junction, must come to a stand clear ahead of the points at Barnstaple East Junction. The coaches from Barnstaple G.W. will be propelled to East Junction Up Home Signal, and after the Ilfracombe train has stopped they will be attached to it, after which the train will proceed to Taunton. While the Barnstaple G.W. portion is being propelled, a man provided with a horn must ride in the leading compartment and keep a sharp look-out.

Admitting Freight trains into Yard.

When a Freight train has to be admitted into the Goods Yard owing to the platform line being occupied, the train must be met at the Home Signal by the Shunter or other competent man, who must pilot the train past the Home Signal under the authority of the Signalman.

Wheel Stops in Oil Sidings.

A wheel stop is fixed at the Locomotive Shed end of the back road used as Oil Sidings.

The wheel stop must be kept padlocked except when the Sidings are being shunted, and the key kept in the Signal Box.

Care must be taken when shunting the back road that wagons are not pushed against the wheel stop.

Level Crossing in Goods Yard to Oil Depots.

The level crossing leading to the Oil Companies' depots is largely used by road vehicles, and the Shunter must keep a sharp look-out before shunting over the level crossing.

Passenger Train Stock for Ilfracombe Branch.

No coaches with lower centre-step boards will be accepted at Barnstaple for working over the Southern line to Ilfracombe.

L. & N. E. Co.'s coaching stock 59 feet long (63 ft. 7 ins. over buffers) and 9 feet wide may be worked to Ilfracombe via Barnstaple.

A last look at Victoria Road in the early 1960s, after passenger traffic had ceased. By now in use solely as a goods depot, sacks of agricultural goods are stacked on the platform beneath the canopy. The yard was still busy, with much of the town's goods traffic now concentrated here and rationalisation of the track layout had not yet commenced. This began with the removal of the two sidings to the right of the run round loop in 1966.
Courtesy,
The Lens of Sutton Association

through workings to Ilfracombe had coaches for the GWR station. In the Up direction, the train from Ilfracombe would traverse the East Loop and then, once it was clear of the points, stop on the Swimbridge side of Barnstaple East Junction. The coaches to be collected would already have been propelled by an engine out of the GWR station up to the Barnstaple East Junction Home signal to await the arrival of the Up train, so they could then be attached to it with minimal delay. A railwayman was required to ride in the leading compartment of the GWR coaches when they were being propelled and he was provided with a horn so he could sound a warning if required. Once the Taunton-bound train had departed with its increased load, the shunting engine would run light back to the GWR station.

The East Loop was closed in 1939, although it remained intact for a time and may have seen occasional use by special workings during the war. However, at some stage a short section of rails were lifted near to East Junction preventing its use.

In 1948, all parcels traffic ('smalls') for the area was concentrated at Victoria Road. After the war, goods traffic increased considerably and in 1951 reached a peak of 124,727 tons, the equivalent of thirty-five 10-ton wagons a day. Cattle and livestock transshipment suffered a decline in the years before the Second World War but peaked in 1951 at 1,597 wagons, remaining in excess of 1,000 wagons a year until 1955, when decline set in for the final time.

With Nationalisation the station's Barnstaple GWR name became redundant, with the result that, on 26th September 1949, it was changed to Barnstaple Victoria Road, distinguishing it from the two former Southern stations, Barnstaple Town and Barnstaple Junction. The Victoria Road suffix, added to the existing Barnstaple station nameboard at the end of the platform in the form of a metal sheet below it, looked rather temporary but remained to the end.

The station had a staff averaging just under forty for the last four decades of its life, up a little from earlier years when it was nearer to thirty. The payroll averaged out at around 12% of total receipts up until the Second World War, after which the latter were not recorded.

Passenger tickets peaked in the early years of the 20th century, dropping from just under 33,000 in 1903 to under 27,000 in 1913. A slight climb up to just over 28,000 in 1923 served only to precede a steady drop from thereon, down to a little over 11,000 in 1939. War-time saw a peak just over 19,500 in 1944 but the decline began again in 1946, to a low of 9,300 in 1951, although a recovery to nearly 13,000 had been made by 1957, the last year for which figures are available. Season tickets issued peaked at 151 in 1937 and there were only 19 by 1940, just 4 by 1951 and none from 1954.

To complete our description of the line, it is now appropriate to take the brief journey over to Barnstaple Junction, a distance of 1 mile and 61 chains, via the line referred to in Volume I as the Barnstaple Branch Railway (page 89).

Leaving Victoria Road at 12.05pm (having run round the train smartly to cut the turn round time by two minutes from the allotted nine), the train again passed by the site of the locomotive shed on the right. We then branched off to the right, on to the embankment carrying the West Loop, which was rising on a shallow gradient at this point of 1 in 117 towards South Junction. There was a 10mph speed restriction imposed on the West Loop between Victoria Road and Barnstaple South Loop Junction Signal Box, which eased then from South Loop Junction to the Taw Bridge to 40mph.

The out of use (at the date of our journey) East Loop joined from the left at South Loop Junction and as the line straightened off the chord it continued to climb but at 1 in 100. The East Loop would be brought back in to operation in June 1960 (at which time it also

officially became known as the East Loop), after the closure of Barnstaple Victoria Road station to passengers, services then working directly to Barnstaple Junction instead.

The line then entered a cutting and after about a quarter of a mile, ran beneath the red brick arch carrying the A361 Taunton to Barnstaple main road over the line. This part of the town is the suburb of Newport and the A361 at this point is named Landkey Road. Continuing straight for about another quarter of a mile, the line then started to curve towards the right on a broad bend that turned the railway through ninety degrees, taking it around the south-eastern edge of the town. Still in the cutting, the line then passed under two further, similar red brick bridges in close succession, carrying Rumsam Road and the A377 Tawton Road respectively, before emerging in to the Taw Valley proper, on the level. Passing Barnstaple Girls Grammar School on the right before leaving Newport behind, the line traversed an embankment for about 200 yards alongside Rock Park. It then dropped at 1 in 70 to approach a typical Southern Region lattice bracket signal, just ahead of the Taw River and the iron girder bridge which crossed it. Looking to the right once on the bridge, the tower of Holy Trinity church was again the prominent landmark but other parts of the town also came into view in the distance. To the left, the Taw River came winding its way northwards through the broad valley, whilst the hill on the east bank of the river towards Bishops Tawton provided a scenic backdrop.

The West Loop as seen from the 'Exmoor Ranger' rail tour heading round to Barnstaple Junction on 27th March 1965. Note the embankment was still devoid of tree growth. *The late Owen Mogg, courtesy Peter Triggs*

The Saturday's only Wolverhampton to Ilfracombe train, with No. 7306 in charge on 27th June 1964, has just come off the East Loop and is about to pass under the first of the bridges in the suburb of Newport, carrying Landkey Road, the main A361 Taunton to Barnstaple road. South Loop Junction can be seen immediately behind the train but Barnstaple South Loop Junction signal box had been demolished by the time this photograph was taken and reduced to a ground frame, the tiny cabin housing which can be seen just to the right of the last carriage. In the background, the Forches Estate is spreading along the lower slopes of the hill overlooking the railway. *R.A. Lumber, Dave Mitchell collection*

ABOVE: No. 6327 crosses the Taw River on 27th July 1962 with the 4.15pm Taunton to Barnstaple Junction service. The lattice posted Southern Railway bracket signal mentioned in the text can be seen in the right background and note the 30mph speed restriction sign for Up trains at the far end of the bridge. *James G. Tawse*

LEFT & BELOW LEFT: Side views of the viaduct in 2011 and 2008. *Author*

TAW BRIDGE

Located 1 mile and 10 chains from Victoria Road station on the route to Barnstaple Junction, the bridge, which still survives today carrying a foot and cyclepath, comprises a five-span, wrought iron structure 119 yards in length. This is made up of two spans of 85 feet, two of 55 feet and one of $71^1/2$ feet. The bridge is supported on 5 foot diameter cast iron pillars, which it is believed were cast at Rafarel's Iron Foundry in the town. Some indication of the method of construction is given in the contract, signed between the contractors Messrs Meekin & Co. and the GWR, for the building of the Barnstaple Branch Railway extension from Victoria Road to Barnstaple Junction in 1885.

The abutments were built of brick on concrete foundations, which carried down to rock granite strings and were finished at the top by a course of granite to support the floor of the bridge. Cornish granite beds were set in cement to carry each girder, whilst the pilasters were built parallel to the line and surmounted by granite caps.

The superstructure was supported on four pairs of cast iron cylinders, carried down to rock, excavated, cleared and filled with concrete (consideration had to be given to possible flooding and damage to the concrete). Care was taken with regard to the workforce when under construction, as each cylinder was filled with gratings and hatchways and it was stated that there should be *'proper attendance to danger to workmen'*. The concrete fill was flush with the underside of the casting for

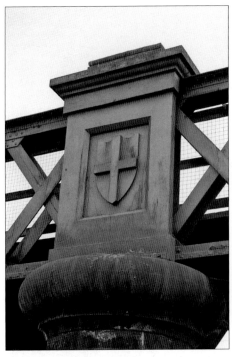

the roller path. All roller paths, along with girders, cross-girders and timber flooring, were delivered to Barnstaple in trucks and it was the responsibility of the contractor to convey the material to the site.

The girders were cast by iron founders Messrs E. Finch & Co. Limited of Chepstow. Liverpool-based Edward Finch had built the Brunel-designed tubular bridge carrying the South Wales Railway over the River Wye at Chepstow in 1851-52. Afterwards, he remained in the town and established a substantial bridge and ship building business on the banks of the Wye, which was taken over by the Government in 1917. The viaduct over the Taw River is today a rare surviving example of the company's bridges and having found another use since the closure of the railway, it is heartening to report that a refurbishment of it was completed just before Christmas 2016.

Once off the viaduct, the former L&SWR route to Barnstaple could be seen straight ahead, coming in from left to right. The line from Victoria Road was supported on a short embankment as it turned to the right to converge with and then join its Southern Region neighbour, just outside of Barnstaple Junction station. This lay immediately ahead, with a sheer rock face looming over it on the western or left-hand side, acting almost as a protective backdrop, with the expansive goods yard and engine shed facilities to the right, beyond which in the distance could be seen the town centre. Meandering across the pointwork at the station entrance, on this occasion our train pulls in to Platform 2, the main Down platform, but often Platform 3, the other side of this island platform, was used instead. As our locomotive came to a halt, now on time at 12.10pm, its journey was completed. It would shortly be uncoupled from its coaches and would then be released and taken to the shed for servicing, coaling, watering and turning. The stock would next be shunted to a carriage siding or placed in Platform 1 in preparation for its return journey; on this day, the stock was shunted to work back to Taunton on the 2.25pm departure. Passengers wishing to go on to Torrington or Ilfracombe would generally change trains to depart from here, except on summer Saturdays, when some Taunton trains worked through to Ilfracombe often with a GWR/ Western Region engine and occasionally with a Southern pilot as well.

Top Left: Cast-iron detail on one of the joining sections between girders at the top of one of the piers.

Top Centre: The red brick and granite support stones covered in ivy in 2011.

Top Right: The underside of the bridge, showing the wrought iron cross supports and the cast-iron piers.

Above: Although at the time (2011) looking a little the worse for wear and in need of a repaint, the bridge found a secondary role carrying the Tarka Trail footpath and cycleway over the Taw River.

Left: A close-up of one of the cast-iron support piers, which are filled with concrete.
All author

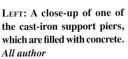

ABOVE & RIGHT: Various detail views of the newly refurbished and repainted bridge in early 2017. *All author*

RIGHT: The E. Finch & Co. Ltd cast-iron builder's plate. *Courtesy Melvyn Lovell*

No. 6372 alongside Platform 1 at Barnstaple Junction on 13th September 1961, as its three-coach train is made ready for the journey back to Taunton. The 'Mogul' had brought its train in to Platform 3, out of sight on the other side of the island on the left, and had then uncoupled and gone on to the shed to turn on the turntable, before reversing in to Platform 1. Meanwhile, the Ivatt Class '2MT' 2-6-2T seen on the rear of the train here on station pilot duties, collected the stock from Platform 3 and then shunted it in to Platform 1 to be coupled up to No. 6372's tender. *Derek Joanes*

CHAPTER 9

SIGNALLING

THE BROAD GAUGE ERA

There is little recorded about the early signalling on the line but common practice at the time had lines operating without block instruments or the interlocking of points and signals. However, the Inspectors' reports on the D&SR indicated that on the first section to Wiveliscombe, the absolute block system would be in operation. Furthermore, the extension on to Barnstaple had references to the interlocking of signals and points. A brick lodge at Watchet Junction, off the main line near Norton Fitzwarren, which opened in 1862 for West Somerset Railway traffic only, was also used for the D&SR when this opened in 1871 to Wiveliscombe. Policemen, who worked hand capstans located at the points to switch them, were based at the lodge. It was general practice at the time for these 'Bobbies' to be dressed in a smart uniform along with a high top hat to complete the outfit.

Generally, signalling was basic and spartan in the broad gauge era and there were two components to it at this time, namely disc and crossbar signals, which gave the absolute 'stop' instruction, and flags. Operationally, the signals were turned to danger when a station was blocked due to the presence of a train or shunting operations taking place. The signal was placed at 'Stop' to prevent a train from proceeding and was then kept at that indication for a specified time interval after the train had passed. On railways lacking any connection between point operation and signalling there was a potential for mishaps, as signals could be showing clear when points were not properly set. The signals were also sited where they could be seen and easily worked by the policeman but not necessarily where the train was to stop.

The signals themselves were complex structures, based on Brunel's original design with some modification. A tall wooden post (usually 40 to 60 feet in height) supported a metal rod which had the signal disc (usually about 4 feet in diameter) on top and the crossbar (usually 8 feet long and 1 foot deep) just beneath it. The arms of the crossbar would usually have downward or upward projecting ends to indicate the signal's relevance to Down or Up trains; also, some signals were bi-directional and the projecting ends reflected this. The disc and

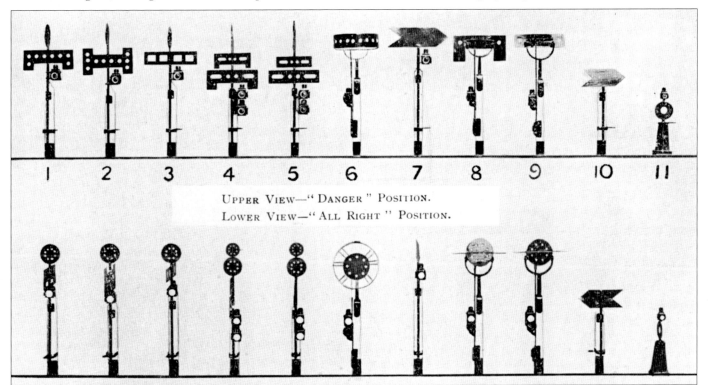

A diagram from the March 1908 issue of the *Great Western Railway Magazine*, illustrating the range of broad gauge signals: 1 & 3 are typical GWR disc and crossbar signals, for Up and Down lines respectively; 2 was in general use to control trains passing over level crossings; 4 & 5 are branch line junction signals, Down and Up respectively; 6 was known as a tambourine or drum signal and there was apparently only one in use, controlling trains entering Windsor station; 7 was of a type noted as being in use on the Forest of Dean Branch, so may have a design specifically for use on goods only lines; 8 & 9 are the B&ER style main line Down and Up signals respectively; 10 was one of the earliest types of signals, used with the time interval system, the arm being kept at 'stop' for a prescribed length of time after a train had passed; 11 is a capstan indicating the position of the points to which it was attached. This latter would be operated by hand lever and when it was rotated to move the points, the disc on top rotated with it to provide an indication of how they were set. These examples are shown with lamps, a safety improvement that was added as signalling developed. *Neil Parkhouse collection*

crossbar were set at 90 degrees to one another and when the disc faced the traffic this meant 'All Right' or proceed. To operate the signal, the policeman used a lever to rotate the metal rod, which would then in turn rotate the ensemble at the top. The original Brunel signal design had the whole post rotating, arguably an even more cumbersome arrangement. Whilst there is photographic evidence of a disc and crossbar signal at Milverton in the early years of the line (*see Vol. 1, page 58*), precious few photographs of signals at other locations exist but this method of signalling applied throughout the length of the line in the broad gauge era. Indeed, an extract from the *Great Western Railway Magazine* in 1908 stated that the B&ER also employed the revolving disc type signals '*One of those the writer remembers at Barnstaple station when that company worked the Devon & Somerset line*'.

The power of the Board of Trade, which regulated the railways at the time, increased when Parliament passed the 1873 Regulation of Railways Act. This required that all new lines were properly signalled with interlocked levers. In addition, on single lines trains were to move under the block system, with telegraphic communications between signal boxes, along with either the train staff, or train staff and ticket arrangements, as described below. However, existing lines did not fall under the 1873 Act, so the Board of Trade could only enforce the rules for new works on existing lines and these only got upgraded when required. That was until the passing of the 1889 Regulation of Railways Act, whereby the Board of Trade could insist on all remaining lines being upgraded. By 1885, most single lines of the GWR network were worked by train staff and ticket, in conjunction with block telegraph, and the D&SR was no exception, as will be explained.

OPERATION OF DISC AND CROSSBAR SIGNALS

When the crossbar was visible, it was the signal to 'Stop'. The red flag on the flagstaff by day and the red light at dusk or at night was also the danger or stop signal and had to be shown in every instance of the line being obstructed and also for three minutes after the passage of an engine or train in the same direction along the line.

The green flag on the flagstaff by day and the green light by night was a caution signal to slacken speed and had to be shown after three minutes and up until ten minutes had elapsed since the passing of the previous engine or train, or in any case where it may have been proper to recommend a reduced speed.

When the disc was shown in full (after the crossbar had been rotated through 90 degrees so as not to be visible), it indicated 'All Right'. The white light at night also implied 'All Right'.

The disc had always to be reversed, so as not to be seen along the railway, and the crossbar shown whenever the danger signal was indicated upon the flagstaff, whether by red flag or red light. Consequently, the full disc could only be seen when the line was perfectly clear and no engine or train had passed for three minutes previously.

THE DIFFICULTIES IMPOSED BY SINGLE LINE WORKING

Before discussing matters that are specific to the D&SR, it is appropriate to outline the basic method of operating on a single branch line in the B&ER and early GWR eras. The focus is clearly on safety, as would be expected and as can be seen from the development of train operations outlined below.

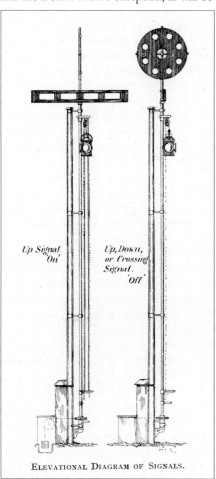

Up Signal 'On'.   Up, Down, or Crossing Signal, 'Off'.

ELEVATIONAL DIAGRAM OF SIGNALS.

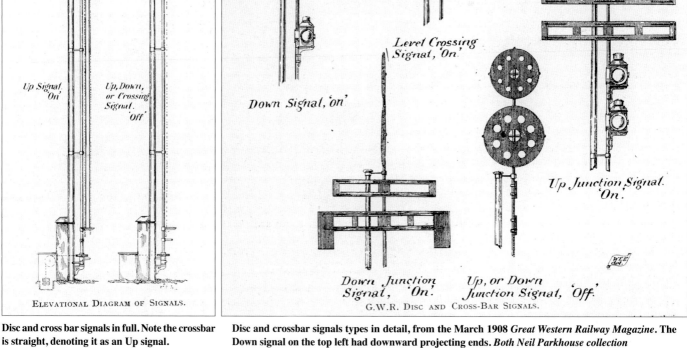

Down Signal, 'on'   Level Crossing Signal, 'On'   Up Junction Signal, 'On'.

Down Junction Signal, 'On'.   Up, or Down Junction Signal, 'Off'.

G.W.R. DISC AND CROSS-BAR SIGNALS.

Disc and cross bar signals in full. Note the crossbar is straight, denoting it as an Up signal.

Disc and crossbar signals types in detail, from the March 1908 *Great Western Railway Magazine*. The Down signal on the top left had downward projecting ends. *Both Neil Parkhouse collection*

THE TRAIN STAFF METHOD OF OPERATION

Given the length of the D&SR, once the line had opened through to Barnstaple, it was never going to be possible for it to operate with just one train working Up and Down a single line, with the driver in possession of the train staff. The railways developed a system of operation to enable more than one train to move on a single track line of any length. This worked on the basis of some form of 'pass' or authority to allow the train to proceed from one signal box to the next, to ensure that only one train had access to that particular section. This system was designed to ensure the safety of the train and its occupants as it traversed that length of track, although it did, of course, rely on the diligence of the persons involved. In the early days of the D&SR's operation, this authority was still provided in the form of a train staff, with additional developments that followed its introduction. The use of a staff did not require block working, staff working in fact being developed before it was introduced.

The staff was a piece of wood about 18 inches in length and coming in a variety of distinguishing shapes, such as round, triangular, square or octagonal. The names of the two connecting stations for which the staff was relevant were initially painted directly on it but later they were engraved on a brass plate (because the paint rubbed off over time) which was fixed to the staff. Sometimes the engraved names on the plate were filled with wax. In addition, the staff was also painted an obvious colour, such as blue or red, for ease of identification. The staffs on adjacent sections would be a different colour and a different shape to avoid confusion on hand-over and use.

To enable a train to proceed into the next section, the signalman would need to be in possession of the relevant staff to hand out and it would be kept in the signal box when not in use. In advance of any train movement, the signalman would seek 'line clear' permission from the next signal box. Once this was given to the departure box signalman, he would then give the relevant staff to the train driver, so he could proceed into the next section. Communication between signalmen was by telegraph in the early days of this new procedure (the telegraph also being used for general day-to-day matters on the line as well as signalling). The telegraph message was usually transmitted to an apparatus with a single needle, which would deflect as the message was received; the number of deflections one way or the other would determine the appropriate letters of the alphabet to spell out the particular message. Whilst the telegraph would notify the departure of a train, it would not and could not display a continuous 'line clear' message. However, it did enable a 'line clear' acceptance to be transmitted.

On occasion, the telegraph system could lead to confusion and messages could take time in sending, especially with inexperienced operators as the tapping of letters and interpretation of the needle deflections was quite a skill. An improved means of communication was needed and this resulted in the development of a system of bell codes to enable signalmen in adjacent boxes to communicate more effectively. However, transmission by bell code was only possible once additional line wires were installed and the system was also dependent on block instruments or electric train staff instruments being installed, which was a development beyond the use of just a train staff.

Once the signalman had received 'line clear', he could then pass the staff to the driver. He, in turn, had to be sure he was receiving the correct staff for the next section and had to have it in his possession as he proceeded into it, once the signals had been set to clear. With only one staff for each section and both signalman and driver being sure that it was the right one, there could never be two trains in the same section at any point in time. However, there was an inherent problem with this method of operation. Trains had to be balanced; that is, for every Up train, there had to be a Down train in turn (and *vice versa*) so that the staff could be returned ready for the next Up working. This, of course, was not always practicable, if the case of late running or an engine failure, even if the time table had balanced workings.

The unbalanced train-working dilemma was resolved by introducing the train staff and ticket system, in conjunction with what was known as 'block working'. The 'block' is a length of line between the section signal of one signal box (often the Starting signal) and the outermost Home signal of the next box. Rules were developed such that only one train could be allowed in the block section at any one time and the train staff and ticket system facilitated this. Initially, the block instruments were independent of the signals and reliance was placed on the signalman. Later developments had the signal levers connected electrically to the indicators of the block instruments for added safety, with less reliance being placed on the signalman.

Train staff and ticket operation worked by means of a key attached to the staff, which unlocked a secure box held in the signal box containing paper tickets. These tickets allowed the signalman to authorise the driver to proceed through a single line section without him actually carrying the relevant staff. If two trains were to proceed

Extract from the *GWR Telegraph Appendix*, effective from 1st January 1905, showing the interpretation of the needle deflections required to transmit a letter. To this was added further strokes to confirm full stops, etc. The recipient's response of '*I understand, go-ahead*' was usually transmitted by sending one letter back (commonly '**Q**').

Example of a standard GWR train staff ticket, from *GWR Regulations for Train Signalling* on Double and Single Lines (1936).

Examples of GWR train staff tickets; ABOVE: Front and rear of a semi-circular South Molton to Barnstaple ticket coloured dark green; RIGHT: A circular buff-coloured ticket for Barnstaple South Junction to Barnstaple East Junction (the East Loop). *Courtesy Chris Osment*

train that was running to time on schedule, so as to not allow the late running train to create more problems or delays. With adequate notice, the signalmen would have reacted accordingly and, as appropriate, written one more ticket or passed the staff over earlier. However, if the signalman did not get sufficient notice and time, the staff could end up in the wrong location, as it would have proceeded along the section too soon. On this basis, no train could enter that section until the staff had come back on a return working. If there was no immediate return working, then the staff had to travel from one end of the section to the other end by alternative means. In isolated sections on the D&SR, for example, this may have had practical problems, given the lack of roads or their poor quality in the 19th century when the staff and ticket method was employed on the line.

along the single line in the same direction before the passage of another working in the opposite direction, the first driver would receive a ticket on which the signalman would write out the details of his train. In addition, the driver would also be shown the relevant staff, so that he could ensure it was the correct one and be assured that there was no opposite working in the section. However, the signalman would retain the staff. The first train would then proceed into the block section and once it had cleared, confirmation of that would be passed back to the signalman at the departure signal box by his opposite number in the arrival box. On receipt of this notification, the signalman would then be in a position to release the next train to follow the first. The driver of this second train would then receive the train staff and take that with him (assuming that this was the last train before a return working). Any number of trains could therefore proceed in one direction, each taking a ticket but only the last train would carry the train staff. Space separation between following trains was enforced by block working and this was an absolute requirement for the use of the staff and ticket method of operation.

Whilst relatively simple to operate and allowing trains to proceed one after the other in the same direction with no need for balanced workings, the staff and ticket system still fell down if there were alterations caused by late running or special trains were added, resulting in the staff being at the wrong end of the section. In the case of a late running train, the signalman might decide to change passing places to keep the

CONTROL OF THE LAST STOP SIGNAL

By the early 20th century, it was felt by railway management that it was desirable to have the semaphore signals electrically connected to the indicators of the block instruments, especially on double lines, giving interdependence of signals and the block telegraph. With this system, the lever for the signal permitting entry into a section was locked at 'danger', until the signalman in the advance box had given the release by 'line clear' and the lock electrically withdrawn by the block instrument at the signal box. It also enabled locking the signal at 'danger' until the train had passed through the section. The GWR invested in Automatic Train Control (ATC), which intervened if a driver passed a Distant signal at caution. On single lines, the electrical release of section signals was only embarked on after the Abermule accident on the Cambrian Railways in 1921. Despite this, only a handful of single lines had this safety feature added until the mid 1950s and even by the time of closure, few on the D&SR were so fitted (as denoted by an arrow in the post on the signalling diagram).

RIGHT: The 'head' of an electric train staff instrument, now preserved at Kidderminster Railway Museum.

FAR RIGHT: Diagram of an Electric Train Staff instrument from *GWR Regulations for Train Signalling on Double and Single Lines (1936)*.

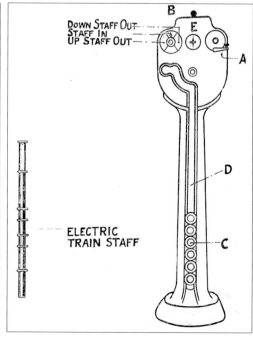

DEVELOPMENTS USING ELECTRICAL EQUIPMENT TO FACILITATE TRAIN MOVEMENTS

Further innovation in respect of this system of railway operation led to the development of the electric train token (ETT) system, developed by Edward Tyer circa 1874 and patented in 1878. Tokens exist in a variety of forms, the two we are most concerned with here being staffs and tablets. They are very similar in their basic principles but different in their use, and both the electric train staff (ETS) and the ETT systems were adopted by the D&SR over its life, as described below. The introduction of the ETS system, which gave greater flexibility to train running, was devised by L&NWR employees and patented by Webb & Thompson in 1888. Initially, the Board of Trade questioned whether this mechanism was a method of block working. However, once it was agreed as such at a meeting on 22nd July 1890, the GWR adopted it, with the first ETS being operational in October 1891 at Dawlish. The ETS system, which was introduced to the D&SR in 1893, worked in the following manner.

A Webb & Thompson instrument installed in one signal box was connected to another machine in the adjacent signal box. The staff was an iron tube, usually 2 feet long and weighing about 3½ lbs. On its shaft at the centre were a series of four raised rings, with a fifth at the end and it was the spacing between the centre rings and the end ring which ensured that staffs only matched the corresponding grooves of instruments to which they belonged. With this arrangement it was impossible for the wrong staff to be inserted into the staff instrument. At the other end of it was a marker indicating the names of the two stations at either end of the section to which each staff belonged. Whilst more flexible in use than the wooden versions that preceded it, the electric train staffs were more cumbersome and thus exchange speeds barely changed. Wooden staffs had to be exchanged at less than 10mph and it was the same with the ETS. Indeed, GWR Regulations stipulated that this exchange should be carried out at speeds of less than 10mph (*GWR Regulation 36*), until they developed an exchanger to allow staff exchange at 15mph.

Whilst a step in the right direction, the electric staff was still not ideal and the development of the ETT system resulted in a more practicable token to handle. The modes of operation of the ETS and ETT systems are similar, so the section below outlines the operational aspects of the latter in detail. The ETT is sometimes referred to as the Electric Key Token, which is indeed what it is, but this nomenclature was never adopted by the GWR even though Tyer & Company called it this for worldwide marketing purposes and other railways did so too. From the 1960s, it has been referred to as Electric Token (ET) or Electric Token Block (ETB).

THE ELECTRIC TRAIN TOKEN METHOD OF OPERATION

The first tokens for the ETT system were made of cast-iron and were smaller in size to the ETS but only a little lighter. However, a lighter, smaller version, about 8 inches long, weighing about 8oz and (usually) made of aluminium, was subsequently developed and used from the 1920s onwards, and this token was much more practicable to handle and exchange.

The train token arrangement was invented by two employees of the GWR, Messrs Jacobs and Insell, in 1912, with the rights passing to Tyers thereafter. It was adopted by the D&SR firstly between Dulverton and East Anstey in 1928, and then throughout the line in 1937, replacing the large ETS system that had been in use for more than forty years. This was part of a number of D&SR line improvements described elsewhere and included the introduction of automatic token exchange apparatus (Whitaker Apparatus), which facilitated faster running on the branch.

The ETT system involved an instrument located in one signal box, being electrically connected to a similar instrument at the other end of the relevant single line section in another signal box. The two instruments, associated components and connected wiring would form the token circuit. Under this system (and ETS before it), a block bell would also be present in each signal box to call attention and for communication.

The tokens were held in a magazine within the instrument itself (see illustration below), each instrument containing a number of tokens for use. The instrument had an electrically operated lock, a plunger and an indicator needle. Whilst similar to that for the ETS system, the ETT instrument was smaller and more compact. The token, once removed from the instrument, could also be clipped into a holder, complete with a metal arm and large hoop at the end, to facilitate manual exchanges between signalmen and firemen at slow speed or to and from fixed token collection and delivery posts near the signal box. By the time the D&SR received the ETT in 1937, the token housing had an aluminium body with a hoop made out of tubular steel.

Operationally the ETT system worked as follows. The signalman at the sending box would call for the attention of the receiving box

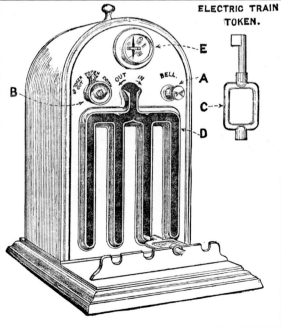

ELECTRIC TRAIN TOKEN.

FAR LEFT: Also at Kidderminster Railway Museum is this typical electric train token instrument, with tokens in the storage magazine which radiates down from the central point.

LEFT: Diagrammatic representation of the ETT apparatus, from *GWR Regulations for Train Signalling on Double and Single Lines (1936).*

signalman by using the plunger on the instrument. This would ring a bell (one beat) in the receiving signalman's box. He would then respond to the sending signalman (replying with one beat), who would in turn ring the bell to ask for 'line clear' (specifying the type of train by bell code). If the line was clear and he could receive the train, the receiving signalman would repeat the code back to confirm acceptance and he would keep the plunger in his ETT instrument depressed. The sending signalman would then be aware of this as the needle on the ETT instrument in his box would be deflected. The sending signalman would then be able to lift the token from the magazine and engage it in the electric lock. With the receiving signalman keeping the plunger depressed it freed the lock in the sending instrument, so the token could be rotated 180 degrees and taken out of it. The signalman would then hand the released token to the driver, which enabled the train to proceed through the section.

Within the instrument itself there was a barrel which contained a number of electrical contacts (the commutator). There was also a polarised relay. As the token key was rotated in the lock some of the contacts on the commutator were made and some broken, the circuits being arranged so that the withdrawal of a token changed the polarity of the current transmitted. With the instruments 'out of phase' because the token was 'out', the polarised relay would not

Above: Electric train tokens from the D&SR line, for the sections between Barnstaple Junction A and Swimbridge, and Venn Cross and Wiveliscombe.
Amyas Crump collection; Courtesy Chris Osment

Below: Examples of occupation release key plungers from the D&SR line.
Courtesy Blue Anchor Museum, West Somerset Railway

send a releasing current to the lock. In consequence, once a token was withdrawn from either instrument it was impossible to obtain another token until the original token had been returned to the instrument at the other end of the section having been carried by the train. On exceptional occasions, if the train failed to proceed, release was obtained by putting the token back into the instrument from which it was withdrawn. As long as the right token was used for the right section and the circuit completed, then a number of trains could proceed in the same direction without significant problems but with only one train in the section at a time.

Where shunting operations required a train to enter the block section, requiring the permission of the next signalman but with the train not proceeding as far as the next signal box, the token needed to be withdrawn and given to the driver for the shunt. This token was then replaced in the same instrument after shunting and a 'cancelled' signal sent to the other box; the section was then clear. A train token could also be used to release levers at intermediate ground frames.

When, during the course of a week's operations, train movements were unbalanced, then the tokens had to be 'rebalanced' from time to time and surplus tokens were transported independently. As this was defined as a 'high security' job, one of the Signal & Telegraph (S&T) staff would have the responsibility for carrying and delivering the surplus tokens to the box that had the shortage, usually by travelling on a normal service train. The delivering instrument would need to be unlocked to extract the tokens and again this was an S&T responsibility, as they would have the only key. The quantity of tokens transferred by the S&T staff would always be an even number and it is understood that each signal box on the D&SR initially had twenty tokens.

The token configurations were in different colours, as shown in the table below; along with an alphabetical designation, they indicated the position of the notch orientation at the 'business end' of the token.

ETT COLOURS (AND RELEVANT ALPHABETICAL DESIGNATION) IN 1963	
Section	**Colour**
Milverton to Wiveliscombe	Green (C)
Wiveliscombe to Venn Cross	Red (A)
Venn Cross to Morebath Junction	Yellow (D)
Morebath Junction to Dulverton	Red (A)
Dulverton to East Anstey	Blue (B)
East Anstey to Bishops Nympton and Molland	Green (C)
Bishops Nympton and Molland to South Molton	Yellow (D)
South Molton to Filleigh	Red (A)
Filleigh to Swimbridge	Light Blue [Blue] (B)
Swimbridge to Barnstaple Junction A box	Green (C)

THE BARNSTAPLE BRANCH IN THE 1800S

When the Barnstaple Branch opened – based on information obtained from the service time table of the 1880s – it operated the train staff and ticket system. Colonel Yolland's report of 9th June 1871 on the opening of the line stated '[there is] *single line working by train staff, in the mode described in the regulations of the Board of Trade in conjunction with and in addition to the Block System of Telegraph*'. There were initially seven staff sections: Norton Fitzwarren to Wiveliscombe, Wiveliscombe to Morebath, Morebath to Dulverton, Dulverton to East Anstey, East Anstey to Bishop's Nympton, Bishop's Nympton to South Molton and South Molton to Barnstaple. A notice was issued on 1st July 1881 by Mr J. Campfield, Superintendent at Exeter, which stated that, from 4th July, Milverton would also become a staff station, making eight sections. In a further notice issued on 26th June 1884, with the advent of the Exe Valley line, Morebath Junction also became a staff station, thus making nine sections.

Where a train was not booked to stop at a staff station or junction, the timetable was usually annotated with 'CS', indicating that it must run through slowly to permit the exchange of the train tickets or staff.

As mentioned earlier, each staff was of a particular distinctive shape and colour for each section of the line. The table below, taken from the service time table, shows the post-1885 coding of the wooden train staff and the relevant tickets. As far as can be established, these shapes and colours were always the same (with two exceptions noted).

SECTION	FORM OF STAFF & TICKETS	COLOUR OF TICKET
Norton Fitzwarren to Milverton	Round	Red (until end of 1885, thereafter Blue)
Milverton to Wiveliscombe	Triangular	White
Wiveliscombe to Morebath	Semi-circular	Green
Morebath to Morebath Junction	Oblong*	Blue
Morebath Junction to Dulverton	Round	White
Dulverton to East Anstey	Triangular	Drab (Chocolate)
East Anstey to Bishop's Nympton & Molland	Square	Yellow
Bishop's Nympton & Molland to South Molton	Round	White
South Molton to Barnstaple	Square	Green
Barnstaple GW to Junction	Oblong	Blue (the 1893 STT post ETS refers to this staff and ticket being round in form and red in colour. This section continued to be operated by staff)
* This Staff was used between Morebath and Dulverton prior to the introduction of the additional Staff Station at Morebath Junction (and described as "flat" rather than oblong).		

Electric Train Staff was introduced to the line in October 1893, by reference to service time tables of that period. At this time, Venn Cross, Filleigh and Swimbridge were added as staff stations so the full list then became: Norton Fitzwarren, Milverton, Wiveliscombe, Venn Cross, Morebath, Morebath Junction, Dulverton, East Anstey, Bishops Nympton & Molland, South Molton, Filleigh, Swimbridge and Barnstaple. The service time table stated that the crossing stations were those referred to above but excluded Venn Cross, Filleigh and Swimbridge because, although they were now staff stations, they had yet to have passing loops installed. Trains (two goods or a passenger and a goods) could pass at these three non-crossing locations, on the understanding that the passenger train was always kept on the running line and that if it had to stop at the station, it was stopped at the platform. Accordingly, a goods train would be set-back into the relevant goods yard to enable the other train to pass.

SIGNAL BOX DAILY OPENING AND CLOSING TIMES

None of the signal boxes on the D&SR were provided with a switch, so all were usually opened in accordance with the passage of the first train and closed after the clearance of the last train out of the signalman's section. There were two broad exceptions to this: Firstly, in the early days of the Venn Cross, Filleigh and Swimbridge signal boxes and, secondly, during the Second World War.

The table below shows the opening and closing times from the *June 1893 Service Time Table*.

In regards to the second exception, during the years of the Second World War, the boxes between Milverton and Morebath Junction were noted in the service time table as '*open continuously*'. This was presumably to allow access to and diversions off the main line down the Exe Valley route in the case of an emergency.

There were very rarely any regular time tabled Sunday trains but in GWR days the boxes would be open '*as required*'. For example, in the 1890s, the Down Chippenham/Bristol goods departed late on a Saturday night and travelled to Taunton in the early hours of Sunday morning. Leaving Taunton West Depot circa 5.00am early on the relevant Sunday mornings, it would traverse the line and arrive at Barnstaple circa 8.30am (as for weekdays). There was no Sunday return goods and also no early Monday morning Down goods if the Sunday Down service ran.

Also, in the period from 1936 to 1939, there were a limited number of Sunday trains. For example, in 1939, the 11.00am Ilfracombe Up train (11.42am departure from Barnstaple Junction) would avoid Barnstaple GWR station and arrive at Taunton at 1.05pm, with the final service passing through Barnstaple at 5.22pm to reach Taunton by 6.40pm. Thus the box at Wiveliscombe, for example, would be open for about six hours.

SIGNAL BOX DIAGRAMS AND RELATED INFORMATION

No research volume of this nature would be complete without the representation of signal box diagrams and a related summary of the various boxes built on the line. Nearly all of the boxes on the line were rebuilt or repositioned at various times. The diagrammatic representations set out below are with the courtesy of the Signalling Record Society (SRS) and broadly cover the diagrams that would have applied from the late 1930s until rationalisation of the line in the early 1960s. The classification of boxes referred to below (*e.g.* GWR type 7B) is used by the SRS as a shorthand description of boxes and was not used by the GWR or signal manufacturers. Track diagrams generally showing the development of station layouts, goods yards and general improvements, and ultimately the decline are covered in the preceding three chapters. Earlier period signal box diagrams have proved hard to come by but reference should be made to the detailed 2-chain survey in Volume 1 (*Chap. 3, pp 100-129*), which shows the track layouts of the stations and junctions in the 1880s.

By way of explanation, the details recorded below have been taken

SIGNAL BOX	TIMES CLOSED/OPENED, WEEKDAYS	TIMES CLOSED (SATURDAYS)/OPENED (MONDAYS)	REVISED BLOCK TELEGRAPH CIRCUIT WHEN BOX IS CLOSED
Venn Cross*	8.00pm and 7.30am	8.00pm and 7.30am	Wiveliscombe and Morebath
Filleigh *	9.10pm and 7.20am	9.10pm (Sat) and 7.30am (Mon)	South Molton and Barnstaple
Swimbridge*	9.30pm and 7.15am	9.30pm (Sat) and 7.15am (Mon)	South Molton and Barnstaple
* There is no reference to these boxes' opening/closing times prior to this date and it is therefore likely this is the first period they were brought into use. By July 1893, the closing times on weekdays of all three boxes became 8.00pm, whilst opening times were 7.30am at all three (and no change to the weekend arrangements as shown above). By October 1893, it was only Venn Cross box of the three that closed (other than with the last train), closing at 8.00pm and opening at 7.30am. In practice what this meant was that only the Bristol Down and Up goods would pass through Venn Cross prior to and after these opening/closing times. A curiosity is that these boxes were brought into use ahead of the locations becoming staff stations, which occurred when electric train staff was introduced in October (per the service time table). However, it may be that ETS came in to operation during the summer period but after the July time table was printed. The actual dates of introduction have not yet been established in research.			

from a number of sources and some information is incomplete. Where possible, a signal box's position (platform location and distance from London to the centre of the box) has been noted, along with dates of opening and closing, their size, type and construction. Details are also provided of the locking frame types (this is a technical area and further reference can be made to the Signalling Study Group's *A Guide to Mechanical Locking Frames*). What is covered here is the distance between the centre of one lever and its neighbour (shown in inches), the method of locking, the manufacturer and number of levers, along with the date of any changes. There were many different manufacturers of locking frames but the GWR fabricated their own from the 1880s. The designs all fulfilled the same purpose, that of locking the levers in the frame so that conflicting routes could not be set up, signals could only be lowered once the correct route had been set and the route could not be changed unless the signal lever had been restored to normal. Where reference is made to points or signals in the text that also relate to an SRS diagram, then it is the lever number that is designated in the text, *i.e.* No. 7. That number also appears next to the relevant point or signal on the diagram.

Locking frames on the D&SR broadly fell into four categories:

• the GWR Stud. Each lever directly drove one or more curved blades. Slings around a tier of blades had studs operating in slots and notches on the blades. This design was manufactured between 1892 and 1908. The lever pitch was 4 inches or $5^1/_4$ inches

• the GWR Double Twist (DbTw). The 'twist' is the method of driving the initial and final movements of the locking. The DbTw was a modification of the earlier Single Twist (SgTw) design, to effect both initial locking and final releasing by including two twists in the twist bar driven by the lever. The lever pitch was $5^1/_4$ inches

• the GWR Vertical Tappet 3 (VT3). The VT3 had three locking bars and was developed from the 4 inch horizontal tappet frame

but was only used with less than sixty levers. It was manufactured between 1908 and 1926.

• the GWR Vertical Tappet 5 (VT5). The VT5 had five locking bars in each locking channel and a cam plate which drove vertical tappets. The VT5 was manufactured between 1926 and 1966. The lever pitch was 4 inches. The tappet was a long flat bar $1^{15}/_{16}$ inches wide and $^3/_8$ inch thick, and was connected to each lever below the operating floor. All tappets were arranged parallel to one another and passed through trays containing a number of smaller 'locking' bars arranged at right angles to the tappet. These had shaped pieces of steel or non-ferrous castings (locks) connected to one another. It was the combination of the shape and position of the locks that coincided with the ports in the tappet bars that would enable locking and unlocking when the requisite levers were pulled. This way a signal, a Home signal for instance, could only be pulled into the 'off' position if all levers had been pulled in the correct order to set the points for the 'road', which then enabled the relevant signals to be pulled in their correct order. In such circumstances, the Distant signal (for the Home signal) would be the last signal to be pulled 'off' (assuming it was not a fixed Distant signal).

Norton Fitzwarren

It is important to start with the signal box at Norton Fitzwarren, as this is where the line commenced but it also highlights how the track layout changed over the years and how complex the junction (post-1936) was for the D&SR and WSR.

Despite the fact that the WSR opened in 1862, the first signal box was not opened until 1870 at Watchet Junction, replacing the police lodge there. The box was a Saxby & Farmer type SF2A and was in use before the station at Norton Fitzwarren was opened on 1st August 1873. The Saxby & Farmer box was located adjacent to

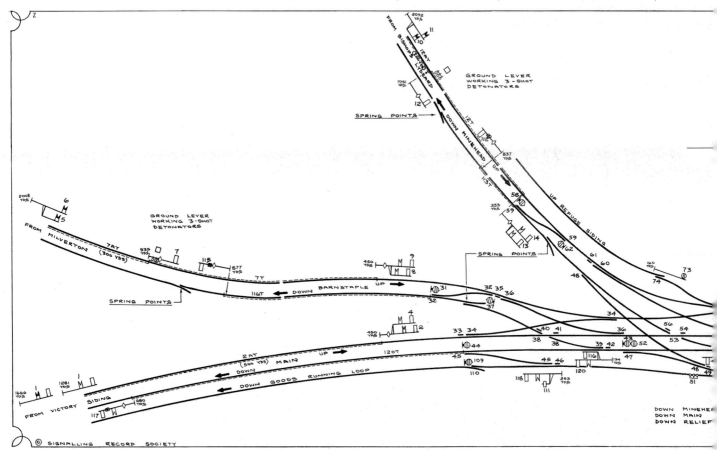

A circa 1931 view from the footbridge showing the 1891 GWR Type 3 Norton Fitzwarren Signal Box, the layout of the junction (with the Barnstaple Branch in the centre of the three double lines) and the original Saxby & Farmer signal box in the middle distance. Note the structure of the bracket signal and location of the two branch Starting signals. The pronounced vertical gap between the signals on the doll post was to facilitate visibility, given the station footbridge's location just in front of it and from which the photograph was taken. In the 'V' between the Up Main and Down Barnstaple lines, an unusual four-sided milepost can just be made out. *E. Wallis Collection, courtesy Kevin Robertson*

NORTON FITZWARREN JUNCTION —

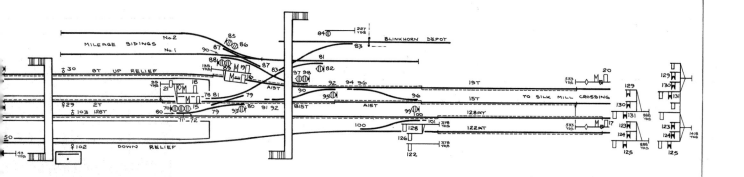

Norton Fitzwarren station, looking towards Taunton in the 1920s. The 1891-built type 3 signal box on the right and the view also graphically illustrates the proximity of the footbridge to the bracket signal, the upper arm of which is visible from a distance, whilst the lower arm could be seen by the driver of a train standing at the Down platform. *E. Wallis Collection, courtesy Kevin Robertson*

and between the Watchet and Barnstaple branches, broadly at the site where these lines diverged from one another. At that time, the Watchet Branch diverged to the right off the main line just to the west of Norton Fitzwarren, curving away to the north. Within a few yards of its start, the Barnstaple line branched off to the left to head almost due west. The 1870s box had eighteen levers prior to being converted to a ground frame. It was originally opened for the Watchet Branch and was then extended when the Barnstaple line opened but was relegated to ground frame status when the second Norton Fitzwarren Signal Box was built and opened circa 1891. The original box, although low to the ground, afforded clear views of both branches and the main line.

The replacement was a GW type 3 box sited in a different location at the west end of the Down platform, alongside the main line and close to the junction for the Minehead and Barnstaple branches. The date of this change is uncertain but it is understood that it was in place by 1891. This box initially had thirty-five levers, extended to fifty in 1923 (it can be speculated that this was because the old Saxby & Farmer ground frame was finally taken out of use at this time but this has not been officially confirmed). The new box had an HT (horizontal tappet) 3-bar frame with $5^1/4$ inch centres.

This second type 3 box was replaced in 1932, by a much larger GWR type 31 box opened on 14th February. The new box was

required as a direct result of quadrupling the main line from Taunton to Norton Fitzwarren and the consequential resignalling. It measured 41 feet in length by 12 feet in width, the floor level was elevated to 11 feet and it was located 165 miles and 10 chains from London. The lever frame was extended in 1936 in readiness for the 1937 extensive track remodelling in the area, which included a realignment of the junctions for both the Minehead and Barnstaple branches. The box was originally built with eighty-nine levers but a further forty-two were added when the layout was extended in 1936, bringing the total to 131, with the box being substantially enlarged at the same time to accommodate this. It contained a VT 5-bar frame with 4 inch centres, whilst the double line block instruments were originally of the GWR's 'Spagnoletti' pattern (so named after the telegraph designer) and later, in BR days, a WR '1947' needle block, 3-position instrument.

By 1932, the improvements at Norton Fitzwarren were completed and this led to a quadrupling of the line down from Taunton and facilitated train movements through the area, especially when there were additional trains on summer Saturdays. However, there were still constraints with the junction at Norton Fitzwarren. The Minehead Branch was double tracked to Bishops Lydeard, brought in to use on 8th June 1936. Subsequent work resulted in the Barnstaple Branch having its own independent connection to the main line, the junction being moved a few yards west of the Minehead junction.

Norton Fitzwarren in late 1931, before quadrupling of the lines between here and Taunton. The new box, opened on 14th February 1932, is being constructed alongside the Down loop line, on the left. The island platforms conversant with the quadrupling had also yet to be built; they were sited where the photographer was standing, running towards the new box. The arms on the bracket signal in the centre foreground had been lowered from their original height on the posts to improve sighting under the public footbridge, behind the photographer. Note the siding signal to the left, with its distinctive ringed arm (and missing a finial on top of the doll post); this siding was replaced by the Down Relief line and a platform. *E. Wallis Collection, courtesy Kevin Robertson*

Norton Fitzwarren Signal Box in the late 1950s. This GWR type 31 box, seen under construction in the previous picture, was enlarged to the size seen here in 1937, with the provision of three additional 'sections', which also doubled the number of windows in the ground floor locking room from three to six. *Courtesy, The Lens of Sutton Association*

cabin, became curiously isolated from the lines it used to control. It was still redundant and *in situ* in 1950 but had been removed by 1961 (perhaps following the late 1950s resignalling of the junction but this is again speculation).

Following the 1937 track layout and signalling changes, there were few other alterations for some years. The wooden square post semaphore signals were replaced by metal round post semaphores in 1959. The double track section to Milverton remained in operation until closure in 1966 but the points leading from the branch to the Up Main line (lever No. 36, along with No. 34, the facing point from the Up Main line to the Up Relief line) were taken out of use on 30th August 1964. Signals No. 8 (Home bracket off the branch) and No. 114 (Down Main bracket Starting) were taken out of use at the same time. Norton Fitzwarren station closed on 30th October 1961 and the signal box was closed on 1st March 1970, ahead of the Minehead Branch closing the following January, at which time the branch single line was extended to Silk Mill Signal Box.

At the same time, the line was doubled to Milverton (to produce the layout illustrated in the signal box diagram on the previous pages), this being operational from 7th February 1937. From then onwards, the Barnstaple Branch was independently accessible from both the Down relief and main lines, rather than off the Minehead Branch. Correspondingly, Up trains could enter the Up Relief or Main lines *en route* to Taunton. With the double track to Milverton, Down trains could then leave Norton Fitzwarren without having to wait for an Up train to clear the Milverton section like they had had to previously. With the realignment of the Barnstaple Branch junction in 1937, the Saxby & Farmer box, now an out of use ground frame

Given the nature of the junction at Norton Fitzwarren, that is the acuteness of their divergence off the main line, the trackwork on the Minehead and Barnstaple branches was adapted to permit higher speeds and smoother running at the points. The usually fixed angle in the 'V' of the common crossing was replaced by two moveable point ends, which were locked by their own facing point locks (No's 38, 40 and 41). When the junction facing points were reversed, the point ends also moved to provide a continuous ride through the junction. In GWR parlance they were known as 'moveable elbows'.

MILVERTON

The original box, of timber construction (*see Vol. 1, pp56-58*), opened with the line in 1871 and was replaced in 1903 by a GWR type 7B box. This first cabin was located close to the road bridge at the east end of the Down platform. The later box was positioned a little way to the west, next to the station buildings but still towards the Taunton end of the Down platform (at 169 miles and 48 chains). Measuring 21 feet by 12 feet, it was elevated at 8 feet. The first frame in the new box, a double twist with $5^1/4$ inch centres, had twenty-one levers but this was replaced by a VT 5-bar frame with 4 inch centres and thirty-seven levers on 29th November 1936. At this time, a new trailing crossover was installed at the Taunton end, replacing the single to double line facing turnout for Down trains, as part of the improvements associated with the new double track section to Norton Fitzwarren, signal renewals and alterations. Electric train staff was used on the section to Norton Fitzwarren until 7th February 1937, ending when the double track section was brought into use (see the signal box diagram right). A Spagnoletti block instrument was then installed for the double track section and the electric train token was introduced to Wiveliscombe on 19th May 1937, replacing the electric train staff previously in use on that section. Between Milverton and Norton Fitzwarren (over 4 miles) was operated as one section, so if there was a train on the Up line between those two locations, it was not possible to lower the Up Starting signal at Milverton until the 'line clear' release was given by Norton Fitzwarren,

after the first train had cleared the section. This was a common form of block control on double lines.

The Whitaker token exchange apparatus posts were located on the Taunton side of the bridge, with the delivery apparatus on the

PAGE LEFT: **Milverton Down platform on 13th July 1963, showing the signal box, main station building and goods shed. In 1945, the signal box, like most on the line, was open continuously while services were running *i.e* from before the first train until receiving train-out-of-section after the last working had passed. In 1964, the last year of steam, that would have constituted nearly thirteen hour days Monday to Thursday, and longer on Fridays and Saturdays.** *Author's collection*

RIGHT: **The Down Intermediate Starting signal (No. 33) at Milverton on the last day, 1st October 1966. The post is lattice steel construction, which was rare on the GWR, although there was another at Barnstaple Victoria Road (see page 437). They were more common on the Southern, so the original GWR signal may have been second-hand and replaced after Nationalisation.** *Michael L. Roach*

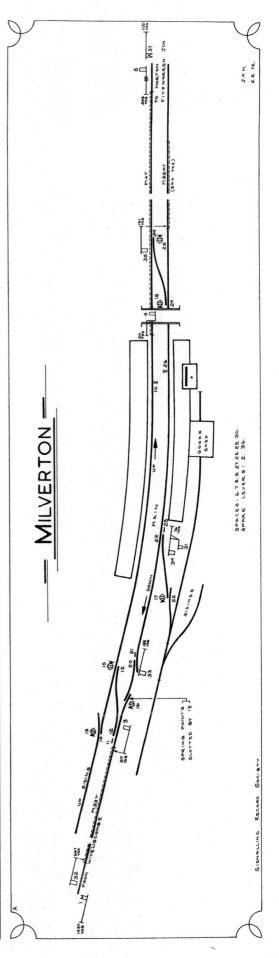

MILVERTON

A general view of the station for the road bridge circa 1960, showing the east end of the signal box and the steps leading up to it. The signalman stands on the Up platform with the staff for the next section, as No. 6372 drifts in with a three-coach train for Taunton. *Michael Hale*

A close-up front view of Milverton Signal Box on the final day of operation. The line of fir trees were on the road embankment leading up to the bridge over the railway line. *Michael L. Roach*

Down line and receiving apparatus on the Up line. They were virtually opposite one another but a short distance from the station, necessitating a walk for the signalman but avoiding any danger to passengers waiting on the platform, should the token bounce off at the time of exchange. The signalman had access to the apparatus by way of a set of steps down from the road, to avoid the need to walk alongside the track under the bridge.

It is likely that the short back siding in the goods yard was taken out of use near the end of the Second World War (Cooke notes it as '*removed late 1944*') but all sidings, including the Up refuge siding, were otherwise taken out of use on 8th May 1964, with the relevant levers bolted. The station retained Up and Down platforms and running lines along with the double line section to Norton Fitzwarren until closure. The box was officially closed on Monday 3rd October 1966, the last trains running, as was the case with so many line closures where there were no longer any Sunday workings, on Saturday 1st October.

Signalling notes show that the Up Starting signal (No. 4) was renewed on 5th April 1957, whilst the Down Starting signal (No's 31 & 34), which was a square post bracket with a Shunt signal, was renewed as a metal round post signal and disc as late as 26th April 1961. Curiously, the Down Intermediate Starting signal (No. 33) was for a period of time a lattice iron structure. There was an Advanced Starting signal (No. 32) a further 479 yards down from the Intermediate Starter (667 yards from the signal box), which was positioned on the right-hand side of the track for ease of vision.

WIVELISCOMBE

In the late 1870s early 1880s, Wiveliscombe was a staff station with Norton Fitzwarren in the east (7 miles distant) and Morebath in the west (8 miles away). When Milverton was provided with a passing loop circa 1880, that then became the easterly staff station. In 1893, Venn Cross was added as a staff station in the west (before it got its new signal box and passing loop in 1905). The original operation was with train staff and ticket, later changed to ETS in 1893.

The original 1871 box was a stone-built structure located at the Barnstaple end of the Up platform, containing a locking mechanism manufactured by Easterbrook. The frame initially had eight levers but this was extended to thirteen in 1880 and fourteen in 1904. This box was decommissioned in 1906 and the upper floor subsequently removed, being replaced – Cooke quotes a possible date of 20th June – by an all-wooden GWR type 27C signal box. The new structure measured 21 feet by 9 feet and was elevated to 8 feet. When built, it was located just off the Taunton end of the Up platform (at 172 miles and 42 chains) for a brief period. However, the Up platform was extended past the box in 1907, which remained in its location and thus thereafter became platform mounted. There was a stud locking frame with $5^1/_4$ inch centres and twenty-four levers. Single line operation was improved by use of the electric train staff system from October 1893 until 19th May 1937, after which the electric train token system operated to Venn Cross with effect from 20th May 1937 (the same date that the section from Wiveliscombe to Milverton was converted). With the extension of the loop lines by 88 yards in the period 7th to 20th September 1939 and the provision of trap points, a new

signal box diagram was provided. In addition, the Up Home signal was moved from 177 yards to 294 yards on the Down side of the line, along with the Down Starting signal, which was moved 80 yards further out, and the Up Advanced Starting signal was then brought into use. The automatic token exchange apparatus on the Up side was renewed. The trap points added on each loop enabled simultaneous running into the station from both directions but this was on the condition that both trains were brought to or nearly brought to a stand at the Home signal. These signals would then be pulled off when the signalman was satisfied that each train was under control. There were additional spring catch points installed on the Down loop, to stop any vehicles that may have run away back down the 1

Wiveliscombe Signal Box was at the Taunton end of the Up platform but the rural background is deceptive, as the bushes behind it are hiding the goods yard sidings. It was in need of a coat of paint but, with closure imminent, this never happened. *Michael L. Roach*

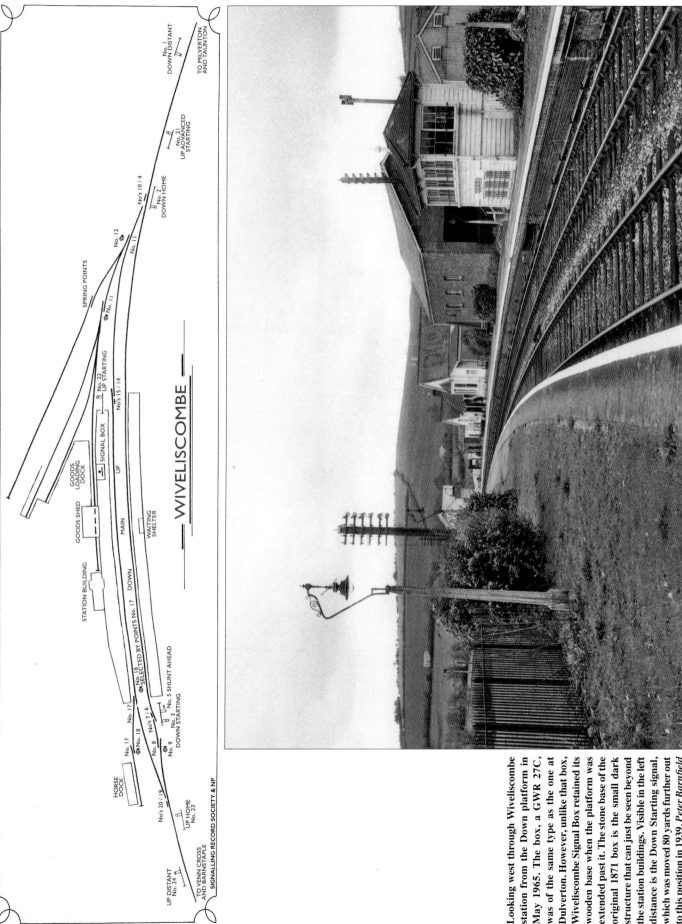

No. 1
DOWN DISTANT

TO MILVERTON
AND TAUNTON

No. 2
UP ADVANCED
STARTING

No's 10 / 4

No. 2
DOWN HOME

No. 12

No. 11

SPRING POINTS

No. 11

No. 22
UP STARTING

No's 15 / 14

SIGNAL BOX

GOODS
LOADING
DOCK

UP

GOODS SHED

MAIN

STATION BUILDING

WAITING
SHELTER

WIVELISCOMBE

DOWN

No. 16
SELECTED BY POINTS No. 17

No. 5 SHUNT AHEAD

No. 17

No's 7 / 6

No. 3
DOWN STARTING

No. 17

No. 18

No. 8

No. 9

HORSE
DOCK

No's 20 / 19

UP HOME
No. 23

UP DISTANT
No. 24

TO VENN CROSS
AND BARNSTAPLE

SIGNALLING RECORD SOCIETY & NP

Looking west through Wiveliscombe station from the Down platform in May 1965. The box, a GWR 27C, was of the same type as the one at Dulverton. However, unlike that box, Wiveliscombe Signal Box retained its wooden base when the platform was extended past it. The stone base of the original 1871 box is the small dark structure that can just be seen beyond the station buildings. Visible in the left distance is the Down Starting signal, which was moved 80 yards further out to this position in 1939. *Peter Barnfield*

in 58 gradient from the Bathealton Tunnel direction.

The Whitaker automatic token exchange apparatus (with both receiving and delivery arms) was 75 yards away on the Taunton side of the box on the Down side and 168 yards on the Taunton side of the box on the Up side. The final improvement occurred in June 1958, when the Up Starting signal was renewed.

Rationalisation began with the horse dock siding and its connection to the Up line, which were taken out of use on 19th May 1964, along with the associated disc signals and the Down Shunt-Ahead signal.

The middle goods yard siding was also taken out of use at this time, leaving just the goods shed siding, the two other sidings in the yard and the passing loop still in use. The box was closed with the line on 3rd October 1966.

Henry G. Elliott, who was a lay-reader, was one of the signalmen during the 1950s, along with William Screech, who was also a Justice of the Peace. The box was opened between 4.40am and 9.55pm, about $17^1/_4$ hours on weekdays (longer on summer Saturdays) and it could not be switched out.

A close up of Venn Cross Signal Box on 13th July 1963, which stood near the Barnstaple end of the Down platform. The steps up to the box were at the far end, where the steps and pathway down the cutting side from the station building met the platform. The locking room floor was below platform level and was accessed by the door at this end, which had steps leading down to it guarded by a short length of railing to prevent passengers falling in to the aperture. The county boundary between Devon and Somerset passed beneath the photographer's feet. *Michael L. Roach*

VENN CROSS

The track layout in the early period (1873-1905) was very basic. There was no passing loop and just one Down direction facing point off the running line leading to the siding. Venn Cross became a staff station in 1893 dividing up the Wiveliscombe to Morebath section. Given the basic layout there was no need for a signal box in the early days, until it became a staff station. It is therefore likely the first box operated from before 1893 (research indicating 1897 is believed to be wrong – see table of signal box opening/closing times on page 407). This box was replaced in early 1905 by a GWR type 7B box, measuring 25 feet in length by 12 feet, elevated to 8 feet. This new box (located at 177 miles and 28 chains) had a stud locking frame with $5^1/_4$ inch centres and twenty-nine levers (twenty-two were initially operational with seven spares). The new box was added to operate the more complex layout (primarily the passing loop and additional connections into the goods yard) which became operational in February 1905, albeit passed by the BoT in July 1905.

The Down Starting signal (No. 27) immediately at the end of the platform was abolished on 15th March 1937, with the lever becoming a spare. At the same time, the Up and Down Distants (No's 1 and 29) and Down Advanced Starting (No. 25) signals were renewed, so that they could be operated to facilitate the faster through running of trains

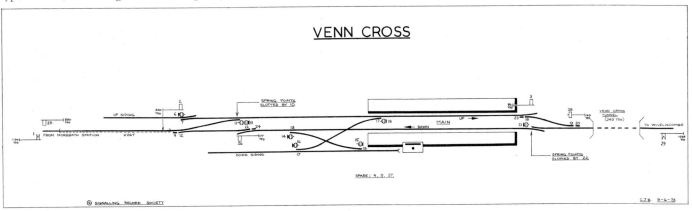

VENN CROSS

ABOVE: No. 7333 departs Venn Cross with the 11.19am to Taunton on 21st July 1961, past the unique centrally-pivoted Home signal at the east end of the station. Note the protective boarding around it at the base of the cutting. *Michael J. Fox, courtesy Rail Archive Stephenson*

LEFT: Another view of the signal. The spectacle glass was, most unusually, mounted on the post below the arm, so that it could be seen from the footplate of a locomotive still in the tunnel. The centrally pivoted wooden arm was also a rarity on the GWR; it allowed the post to be placed nearer the track, which also aided sighting from inside the tunnel. *Michael L. Roach*

using the Whitaker token exchange apparatus. The ETS was replaced by ETT on 6th June 1937 for the section west to Morebath Junction.

There were amendments in association with Morebath Signal Box's closure on 31st May 1963, as the ETT section from Venn Cross was extended to Morebath Junction with effect from 2nd June. In the two month period 24th April to 24th June 1964, all sidings including the

Venn Cross Signal Box from the Up platform. Note the obvious falling gradient in the Up direction, hence the slotted spring catch points on the Down line at the tunnel end (No. 22 on the diagram). The picture was taken after the closure of the goods yard and removal of all the track associated with it. However, the indent part way along the platform had been provided to allow for 'overhang' when using the crossover into the goods yard. *Courtesy Jim Elson*

refuge siding and associated connections and signals were taken out of use, leaving just the passing loop in place. On 29th April 1964, the ETT section was extended to Dulverton with the recovery of Morebath Junction box and extended again on to East Anstey with the closure of Dulverton box on 31st July 1966. Venn Cross Signal Box closed on 3 October 1966.

There was an unusual Home signal on the right bank of the cutting, just outside the tunnel, about 100 yards off the end of the platform. Essentially, it pivoted in the centre with its spectacle plates connected to the signal arm and half way down the short post. Its location permitted the signal to be visible through the straight tunnel for the driver of a Down train, with right-hand drive being standard on the GWR.

MOREBATH

The first box opened in 1876, at the time the passing loop was added. It was largely of timber construction but was built in to the ramp at the west end of the Down platform, so was mounted on a part stone/part timber base. The box also had a hipped, slated roof and measured 12 feet by 10 feet. It is likely that Morebath became a train staff station at this time but it certainly was by 1877, as shown in the service time table.

The original cabin was replaced by a GWR type 12A box opened on 6th June 1937, following further track (and platform) improvements. It was sited on the stone platform, just to the west of the original box but immediately before the start of the wooden platform extension. It measured 21 feet by 12 feet, being elevated to 8 feet and was located

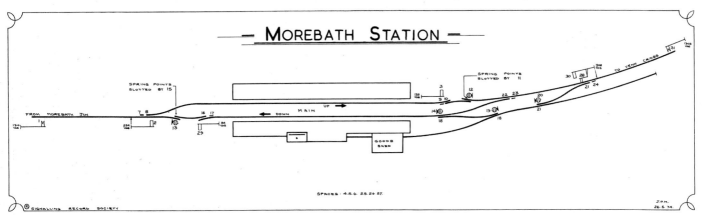

These rather cruel enlargements show contrasting aspects of the 1876 box at Morebath, looking west, left and east, right; both were taken circa 1906. The view left also shows the Down Starting and Up Home signals, the token apparatus and the parapet of the road bridge which the platforms were later to be extended across. *Both courtesy The Lens of Sutton Association*

at 180 miles and 74 chains. It had a timber upper on a brick base and a slate gable roof. The box had a VT 5-bar frame with 4 inch centres and thirty-one levers. There was electric train token operation from the opening of the new box.

The Up Home signal (No. 2) was renewed (and re-sited on the Up side of the line) in May 1958. The box was closed on 31st May 1963, after which time the loop, goods yard, signals and all points were secured out of use, leaving only a single line (the Down line) operational. This also necessitated extending the single line section from Venn Cross to Morebath Junction, as from 2nd June 1963.

No. 7333 departs westwards from Morebath in June 1963. The view provides useful detail of the rear of the GW type 12A box provided here in 1937, which also had a small window facing out on to the station approach. The platform extensions meant that the Down Starting and Up Home signals had to be repositioned slightly further away from the box. Note the token exchange apparatus by the telegraph pole to the left of the Starting signal. *Peter Barnfield*

RIGHT: A view of Morebath Junction Signal Box, a GWR Type 3, as No. 6372 runs through with the 5.55pm Taunton to Barnstaple train on 30th July 1963. Note that the arm of the Down side token exchange apparatus is extended out with token attached, ready for an automatic exchange with the speeding Down train.
Stephen P. Derek

Below Right: Morebath Junction Up Home bracket signal, with arms for the D&SR, left, and the Exe Valley, right.
Courtesy
The Lens of Sutton Association

MOREBATH JUNCTION

The box originally opened on 3rd July 1884, just ahead of the northern section of the Exe Valley line from Tiverton, which itself opened on 1st August 1884. Located at 182 miles and 25 chains, it was a GWR type 3 box. Fitted in 1922 with a nineteen lever stud frame with 5¼ inch centres, this was replaced in 1937 by a McKenzie & Holland frame with 4 inch centres and twenty-three levers, with 5-bar VT locking (which was most likely a GWR modification to the frame). Whilst it was originally train staff and ticket operation to Bampton on the Exe Valley line, this was replaced in August 1957 by electric train token operation. On the D&SR, train staff and ticket was originally used, followed by electric train staff to Morebath and Dulverton, which was replaced by electric train token in 1937. The loop lines were also lengthened at this time.

The box was shut on 29th April 1964, approximately six months after the Exe Valley line closed and the passing loop

was taken out of use, leaving only the Up line operational. Just prior to this, in May 1963, the block section to Morebath was extended on to Venn Cross as a result of Morebath Signal Box closing.

In the forty-four years after the signal box opened, it was all that existed at this otherwise isolated location, until the single platform Morebath Junction Halt was opened a little way to the west in 1928. However, the box remained a staff section throughout its life, the provision of the halt not impacting on this because trains could only cross at the loop and even this was restricted for certain longer trains until the loops were extended in 1937. Also, Exe Valley trains could be held on the branch to allow a D&SR line service to pass or proceed ahead of it.

From 1890, Morebath Junction box was understood to have been worked by a Mrs Towns, the only signal cabin at that time to be operated by a woman. Her employment is understood to have lasted until 1913, a total period of twenty-three years.

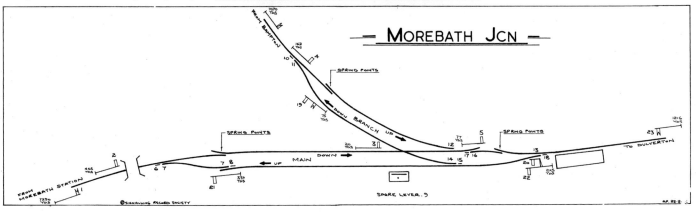

LEFT: An early 1960s view looking east along the platform at Morebath Junction Halt towards the junction, showing the bracket Home signal, with the box in the centre distance. The D&SR line heads east between the box and the evergreen trees, whilst the Exe Valley line can be seen curving off to the right.
Courtesy The Lens of Sutton Association

CENTRE BELOW: Enlarged from an old picture postcard view (*which appears in full in Vol. 1, page 18*), to date, this is the only glimpse we have of the box believed to have been built at Dulverton for the opening of the Exe Valley line in 1884, which was replaced in 1904.
Neil Parkhouse collection

DULVERTON

Dulverton was a staff and ticket station when the line first opened and recent research strongly suggests the existence of an early signal box here, which would make sense given that the station was a crossing point. The circa 1884 2-chain extract of Dulverton, below, shows a 'Cabin' just beyond the Barnstaple end of the Up platform (highlighted by an oval) and a 'Cabin' on the Down side at the Taunton end; this latter is the box shown in the accompanying enlargement from a circa 1900 view. The situation of the first cabin would be right for the station as originally opened, whilst the position of the

cabin at the east end really only makes sense if it was built for the opening of the Exe Valley line in 1884, when the passing loops were lengthened and the siding running in front of the box was added. Otherwise it would have been situated some distance from railway. This now believed to be second box had twenty levers and as the picture shows, had a brick base and chimney, with a timber upper storey and a gabled slate roof, whilst nothing has been discovered to date about this presumed first cabin.

The 1884 cabin was replaced in 1904 by a timber box measuring 29 feet by 10 feet, elevated to 8 feet 6 inches, which had a thirty-seven

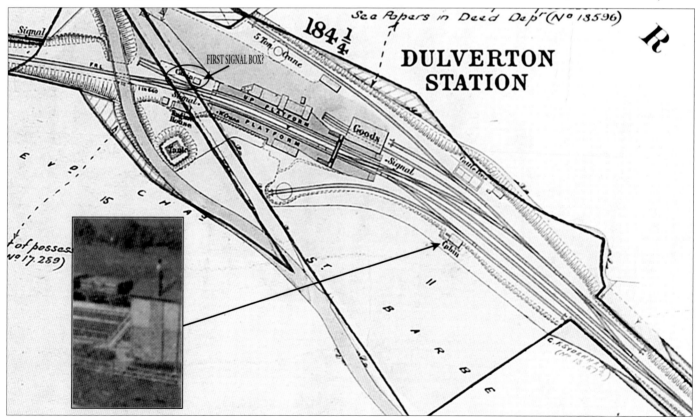

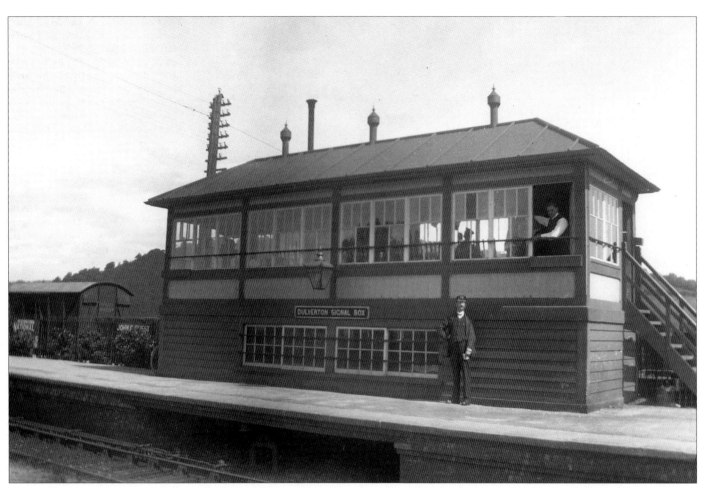

A frontal view of the 1910 signal box at Dulverton, in August 1923. The box was substantially reconstructed in the 1950s, presumably because many of the timbers had rotted, with the base rebuilt in red brick whilst the wooden panelling of the upper storey was replaced by horizontal planks. The roof was also slated, which it clearly was not at the date of this view. Note the position of the platform lamp hung off the centre upright and also the GWR's standard practice of the words 'Signal Box' being part of the name. *E. Wallis Collection, courtesy Kevin Robertson*

lever frame. However, it only lasted until 1910, when it was dismantled and relocated to Bilston, near Wolverhampton. The replacement box was opened on 6th January 1910 and was an all-wooden type 27C box, which measured 33 feet 6 inches by 9 feet 8 inches and elevated to 9 feet. Its frame was VT 3-bar with 4 inch centres and fifty-four levers. The 1910 box was mounted on the eastern end of the Up platform, beyond the goods shed and located at 184 miles and 16 chains. Later in its life (during the late 1950s but precise date unknown) the timber base of the box was replaced in red brick, as can be seen in the photographs; presumably the timbers at the base had rotted. Dulverton held the distinction of being the largest signal box on the line.

There was an auxiliary token apparatus off the end of the Down platform at the foot of the Down Starting signal (No. 6) in a small hut, this being provided from 7th June 1928. It is believed that the section between Dulverton and East Anstey was the first on the line to be converted to electric train token, ahead of the majority of the route just under ten years later. A Ganger's Occupation Key (GOK) system and control instruments were provided from 18th September 1933, covering the Dulverton to Barnstaple section.

The Down Main was slewed and locking alterations carried out

The box as rebuilt in the 1950s with a brick base. An Exe Valley line service stands in front, with the driver in the front compartment as No. 1442 waits to propel it away on 30th July 1963. *Stephen P. Derek*

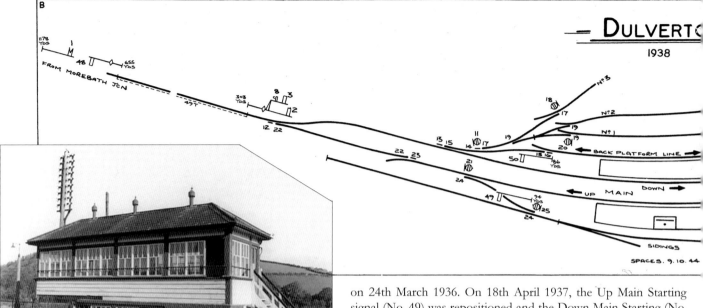

Front, rear and east end elevations of Dulverton Signal Box after closure. The nameboard had been removed. *Courtesy Chris Nelder/ Martin Bird*

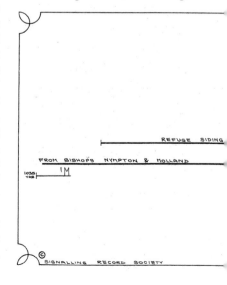

on 24th March 1936. On 18th April 1937, the Up Main Starting signal (No. 49) was repositioned and the Down Main Starting (No. 6) and Down Main Distant (No. 1) signals renewed. This preceded the lengthening of the loops and further signal renewals, and the provision of automatic token exchange apparatus on 11th May 1937. It will be noted that the Up Distant signal, located at 1,347 yards from the signal box was operational (No. 54).

Originally operated by train staff and ticket, ETS was used until 1937 for the section eastwards to Morebath Junction, after which electric train tokens were employed.

In December 1957, the Up Home signal (No's 51,52 & 53) which was on a wooden bracket, was reduced to a single wooden post signal and thus access to the Exe Valley platform line from the Barnstaple end for Up trains working through the back platform ceased. Shunting still continued from the west end and the back platform was used for arrivals and departures from the Exe Valley until that service ceased in October 1963. It should be noted that the bay (back) platform had a signal (No. 4) half way down the platform, by the footbridge, to protect the connections to the Down side goods yard. The Exe Valley locomotive would normally stop at this signal on arrival and only proceed beyond it to replenish water. The bay platform Starting signal (No. 5) was in its expected location at the Barnstaple end of the platform.

The track was rationalised on 20th April 1964, when the goods loop, coal siding, horse dock siding, goods shed road and headshunt siding leading from the goods shed siding were recovered and related signalling taken out of use. On 29th April 1964, the electric train token section was extended to Venn Cross with the closure of Morebath Junction Signal Box. Further track rationalising took place on 13th October 1964, when the back road, crane road and Up siding (behind the goods shed) were taken out of use, the associated signalling was removed and the levers bolted. The box was closed on 31st July 1966, so the extended section then ran from Venn Cross to East Anstey.

Throughout the life of the station most of the signals were wooden square-post but latterly the Up Main Starting (No. 49) signal

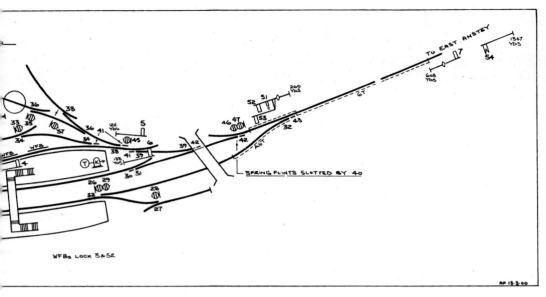

was replaced by a metal round post design, this most likely being one of the 1957 changes referred to above. This signal was also repositioned nearer the Up line by 5 yards (with the headshunt out of use) on 13th October 1964. The auxiliary token equipment was also recovered on this date.

East Anstey

The first box here was provided in 1876, when a new crossing loop was installed. The engineer's plan (see Vol. 1, page 83 but note that this plan is effectively upside down) shows it to have been located just off the Taunton end of the Down platform and approximately 12 feet by 10 feet in size. It was replaced at a date that has yet to be definitely established. Reference has been made to it opening circa 1901 but evidence below potentially points to an earlier date. The new box was located towards the west end of the Down platform, near the goods shed, at 188 miles and 1 chain. It was a GWR type 5 box and measured 19 feet 9 inches by 12 feet. The original frame had seventeen levers with $5^{1}/_{4}$ inch centres but this was replaced by a twenty-nine lever 5-bar VT frame with 4 inch centres in April 1937. Train staff and ticket was in operation until 1893, then electric train staff until 1937, when it was replaced

from 20th June that year by electric train token on the section to Bishops Nympton & Molland in the westerly direction. It is believed that the electric key token was provided on the section to Dulverton from 1928 – probably linked to the fitting of the auxiliary token equipment between East Anstey and Dulverton, which became operational at this time.

A Down Main Advanced Starting signal (No. 26) was provided from 4th May 1927. The Up refuge siding at the Barnstaple end, along with a trap point on the Up and a replacement catch point on the Down line at the Taunton end, were added from 11th April 1937. The Up and Down Distant signals (No's 1 and 29) were repositioned and the Down Main Starting signal (No. 27) had a bracket added at this time, to facilitate access to the goods yard (No. 19).

No. 7337 stands alongside East Anstey Signal Box with 1.15pm service from Taunton to Barnstaple on 30th July 1963. *Stephen P. Derek*

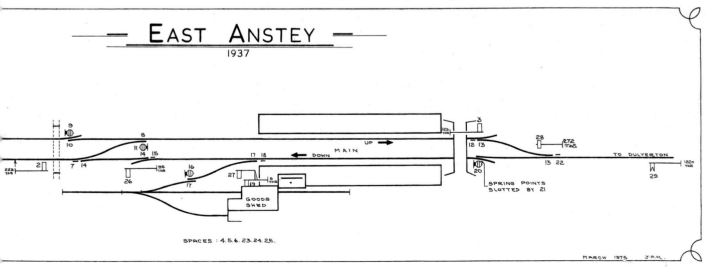

Looking west along the Down platform, showing the steps and entrance door elevation of the GWR type 5 signal box opened here at a so far unascertained date between 1897 and 1901. Ubiquitous No. 7337 pulls in with the seven-coach 8.35am Ilfracombe to Manchester Saturdays only train on 7th July 1962. Just beyond the box is the tubular post Down Starting signal provided in November 1960, replacing the previous wooden-posted bracket. As seen previously at Swimbridge, there are wooden spragging blocks between the tracks, used for pinning down wagon brakes. *Peter W. Gray*

The Down Home signal (No. 28) was renewed in November 1957. In November 1960, the Down Starting signal, a wooden post bracket (No's 27 and 19) was renewed as a straight tubular metal post/metal arm signal, along with a disc for access to the sidings.

All sidings were taken out of use on 16th March 1964 and associated discs removed with the levers being made spare. The passing loop was retained until closure, with the point (No. 8) being retained as a catch point. The box closed with the line on 3rd October 1966.

In the *May 1897 Service Time Table*, it was noted that the catch points were located on the Up line at 178 yards west of East Anstey Signal Box but the July edition noted they were just 92 yards west of the box. It seems unlikely that the catch points were moved at this time (and what would have been a substantial distance). It is more likely this reflects the move of the signal box 86 yards westwards and thus indicates that the new box may have been built and opened around June/July 1897, well before the circa 1901 date above.

Bishops Nympton & Molland

The station ceased to be called just Molland from 1st March 1876. The first signal box, provided in 1876 when the crossing loop was added, at the same time as that at East Anstey and probably of a similar – albeit unknown – design, measured 12 feet by 10 feet. It was closed in 1902, being replaced by a new box of timber construction, measuring 15 feet 6 inches by 11 feet, to a height of 7 feet, with seventeen levers and $5^{1}/_{4}$ inch centres, located at 193 miles and 4 chains. This cabin was in turn replaced by a GWR Type 12B box on 20th June 1937, located at the east end of the Down platform, positioned on the platform ramp at 193 miles. It measured 23 feet by 12 feet 1 inch and was elevated to 8 feet. The frame was a VT 5-bar with 4 inch centres and thirty levers. Train control was originally by train staff and ticket, then electric train staff from 1893, before electric train token was introduced in 1937.

The Up Starting signal at East Anstey, just off the end of the Up platform, is included here partly as being representative of a GWR wooden-arm type. Photographed on 1st October 1966, the wooden post has been strengthened with a bolted on stiffener, perhaps because of rot. The falling gradient down the cutting necessitated catch points on the Up loop (No's 12 & 13) and another set just out of sight on the right on the Down loop (No's 20 & 21). *Michael L. Roach*

The bracket Down Starting signals (No's 26 and 28) were renewed on 18th May 1961. The refuge siding and associated catch point were taken out of use on 8th March 1964, at which time the Up Main point (No. 8) was converted to a spring point. The goods sidings were taken out on 18th August 1965, leaving only the passing loop. The box closed with the line on 3rd October 1966.

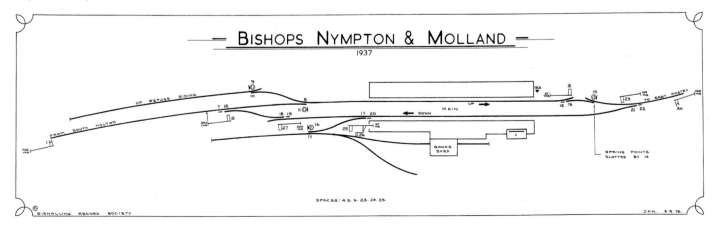

A view from the rear carriage of a departing Up train of the signal box and station buildings at Bishops Nympton & Molland on 15th August 1964. In the centre far distance, it can just be seen that the Up Home signal is still 'off'; it would be returned to danger once the train had departed and the signalman was able to walk back over the boarded crossing to his box, having completed the token exchange. *Edwin Wilmshurst*

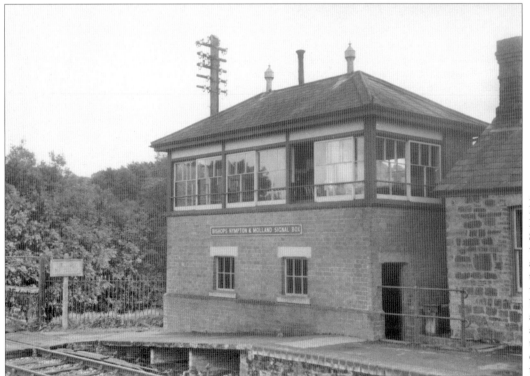

A front three-quarters close-up of Bishops Nympton & Molland Signal Box on the last day of operation, Saturday 1st October 1966. The box was in a cramped location, squeezed alongside the ramp at the east end of the Down platform, in between the east wing of the station buildings and the bridge over the lane between Hilltown and Bridgheyne. Consequently, it had an internal staircase, accessed from the doorway seen here, which was down a couple of steps and also led in to the locking room. *Michael L. Roach*

The signalman waits patiently with the token for the section to East Anstey as Taunton-bound 'Mogul' No. 6340 glides into the Up platform on 7th July 1962. The token is in an automatic-exchanger pouch, despite the manual hand-over, as it could be hung up on the locomotive, or the Whitaker apparatus may have been used at the next station if the train was not to stop there; on this occasion, it was most likely the former. There is much detail of the station to be studied here, from the climbing roses growing under the station nameboard on the Down platform to the Up side waiting room. The photographer took another picture here as the train departed, which features as the frontispiece on page 236. *Peter W. Gray*

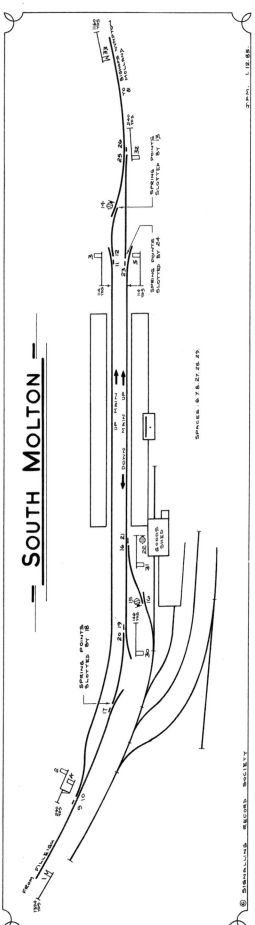

SOUTH MOLTON

The original timber box from the broad gauge era was located alongside the goods shed at the west end of the Down platform. It comprised a small timber cabin, possibly no more than around 6 feet square, perched around 10 feet up on top of a wooden frame, with three small windows, one each facing in the Up and Down directions, and forwards (*see Vol. 1 page 76*). It was built against the wall of the goods

ABOVE: The interior of South Molton Signal Box in the evening of the last day of operation. The signalman is believed to be Mr W. Mitchell. Despite this being the final shift, there was pride in the job and everything was still polished and tidy. Note the telephones on the wall in the background and the token instruments. *Gordon Bray*

BELOW: The Down line here – uniquely on the D&SR – was signalled for bi-directional operation. No. 7326 runs in to the Down platform with the up 11.15am Saturdays only Ilfracombe to Wolverhampton Low Level train, which on this occasion was loaded to five coaches. Note that two of the lampposts carry BR(WR) totems, the only station on the line to get them. *Stephen P. Derek*

No. 7337 heads away from South Molton with a Down train on 8th June 1963. The locomotive is just passing the Down Main Advanced Starting signal (No. 30), on a metal round post, which had been added in 1937. The third carriage is adjacent to the tubular metal posted Down Main Starting signal (No. 31), which had replaced the GWR wooden posted bracket signal previously in use here (see page 344) in 1958. A new ground disc signal (No. 22) for access to the goods yard was added at the same time, which can just be seen in the shadow to the right of the signal post. Also in view here are the trap points (No. 16) and the ground disc signal (No. 15) protecting the exit from the goods yard. *R.A. Lumber, courtesy of Dave Mitchell*

The South Molton signalman holds the token he has just exchanged with the driver of No. 7326 of Taunton shed (83B), which is again standing at the Down platform with an Up train for Taunton in the early 1960s. The picture was taken a few moments after the one on page 347. *Gordon Bray*

shed and was presumably raised up to improve visibility. It is noted as being replaced in or around 1901 by a GWR Type 7A box. However, it is difficult to believe that the original box shown in the 1873 photograph survived untouched until 1901, as it does not look to be anywhere near large enough to control the layout at South Molton and neither would the visibility from it have been good enough as services increased. It would seem likely, therefore, that the 1873 box was rebuilt or replaced at some date prior to 1901 but this is all supposition until definitive proof is unearthed.

The box provided in 1901 measured 21 feet by 12 feet, elevated to 8 feet and originally had a sixteen lever frame but this was replaced by a VT 5-bar frame with 4 inch centres and thirty-three levers on 20th April 1937. The box was located on the east end of the station buildings, on the Down platform at 197 miles and 29 chains.

Originally operated by train staff and ticket, then electric train staff from 1893, the electric train token was in use at South Molton from 20th June 1937. The loop was extended on 10th November 1907 and, from 2nd May 1928, the Down platform was signalled for the passage of trains in the Up direction, to facilitate loading and unloading of passengers and parcels given the lack of a footbridge. Although no other stations on the line had footbridges, apart from Dulverton, this bi-directional signalling of the platform line nearest the station buildings was unique to South Molton. The resignalling saw the Up-to-Down Main Home signal (No. 4) and Up Main Starting signal (No. 5) on the Down line added at this time.

From 18th September 1933, the Gangers' Occupation Key system was introduced throughout the section from Bishops Nympton & Molland and on to Barnstaple. In April 1937, there were signal renewals, with the loop further extended at both ends, at which time the new locking frame was provided, as above. On 5th July 1937, the Down Main Advanced Starting signal (No. 30) was added, along with trap and spring points near that signal's location towards the exit of the Down loop. The bracket signal (No's 22 and 31) was renewed as a tubular metal straight-post signal in April 1958, with an associated disc. The Up Home bracket signals (No's 2 and 4) were increased in height to 24 feet 9 inches and repositioned on the opposite side of the line (the Up side) on 14th May 1961.

The sidings were taken out of use and levers bolted in September 1964, with the sidings being recovered on 3rd February 1965, leaving just a passing loop. With the closure of Filleigh Signal Box, the single line electric token section was extended from South Molton to Swimbridge on 6th September 1964. The token colour for South Molton to Filleigh was red, with light blue being the Filleigh to Swimbridge colour but, with rationalisation, the colour of the extended section token was red. The box closed on 3rd October 1966.

FILLEIGH

As mentioned previously, Filleigh station was named Castle Hill until 1st January 1881. The original box, housed in the station buildings at platform level, was only required to operate a simple goods siding arrangement, because in the early years there was no passing loop. Filleigh was not a staff and ticket station when the line opened, the section then running through to Barnstaple from South Molton. However, it became a staff station in 1893, at which time electric train staff operation took over until 1937, when ETT was used.

Few signalling changes took place in the early years but the Up Distant signal was repositioned 692 yards further out and reduced in height by 9 feet from 27th December 1927. The original signal box was replaced by a GWR Type 12D box opened on 20th June 1937, at the time of major track improvements. It was unique, the only box listed as a 12D on the GWR system, and measured 27 feet 2 inches by 12 feet 2 inches, elevated to 8 feet. It had a VT 5-bar frame, with 4 inch centres and forty-four levers, and was the second largest box on the line. It was located off the end of the Up platform at the Barnstaple end, at 200 miles and 56 chains. With electric train token operation from 1937, an auxiliary electric token machine was installed at the Down Main Advanced Starting signal (No. 5). Points No's 33

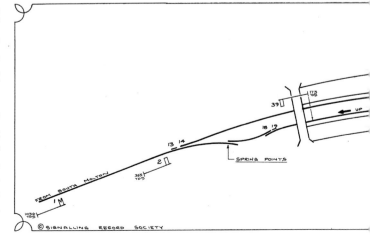

No. 6364 about to depart Filleigh for Barnstaple in the early 1960s, showing the platform-mounted, wooden-posted bracket Down Starting signal (No. 3), along with the subsidiary arms permitting access to the goods loop, which was signalled for bi-directional working, and the goods yard. The Up Starting signal can also just be seen by the bridge beyond the end of the train, which had been moved to the Down side for sighting purposes in 1936. *James G. Tawse*

and 34, being furthest from the box, were worked by electric point motors (with hand generators).

The Up Home and Up Starting signals were moved from the Up side to the Down side of the line on 29th and 30th January 1936 respectively. On 4th June 1936, the Up home was moved 12 feet out and the Down Starting signal renewed but repositioned nearer the track; it was also increased in height by 6 feet. All this work appears

to have been in preparation for the extensive track improvements carried out in 1937. On 21st March 1937, various signals were renewed as part of these overall line improvements.

On 7th May 1937, a Down platform was added and, on 15th December 1937, the Up and Down platform loops came into use. The layout here was unusual in that there was a second, goods only loop to the west of the station. The main running line had a line parallel

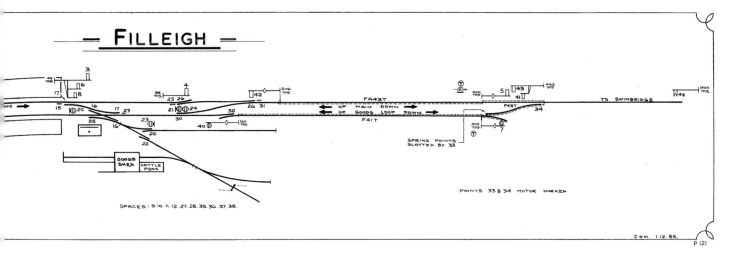

— FILLEIGH —

SPACES: 9. 10. 11. 12. 27. 28. 35. 36. 37. 38.

POINTS 33 & 34 MOTOR WORKED

SPRING POINTS SLOTTED BY 33

TO SWIMBRIDGE

Although not of the highest quality, this westwards view at Filleigh does clearly show the double-compound point providing access to the bi-directional goods loop (which commenced beyond the far end of the Up loop), the only such point on the D&SR line. A clearer view of the signal in the foreground can be found on page 372. *Jim Elson collection*

auxiliary token machine recovered at the same time, with points No's 33 and 34 at the Barnstaple end of the Up and Down goods loop being spiked, clipped and padlocked. At this date, the Down bracket signal on the platform (No's 3, 6 and 8) was reduced to just a Down Starting signal (No. 3) and the Goods Loop Advanced Starting signal, operated by lever No. 7, made redundant and taken out of use. Further rationalisation took place in September 1964, with the Down platform loop line being taken out of use, along with the goods yard sidings. The box closed on 6th September 1964, thus creating a single line section from South Molton through to Swimbridge for the remaining two years of the line's life.

SWIMBRIDGE

Swimbridge Signal Box was of a non-standard design, brick-built with a gabled slated roof and located at 204 miles, 2 chains. Its date of opening has not been established but it was certainly in place at the date of the 1880s 2-chain survey and the 1888 edition 25 inch Ordnance Survey. The circa 1904 photograph of the station in Volume 1 (*page 132*) shows the box shortly after being extended to accept

to it which was also bi-directional and could be accessed in the Down direction by the double compound point at the station throat in front of the signal box. Up passenger trains would avoid the goods section of the loop and enter the platform loop from the main running line at the crossover just outside of the station throat (between 88 and 160 yards from the signal box), opposite the goods yard. The goods loop extended west, towards Barnstaple, such that the entrance to the loop for Up goods trains was 463 yards from the signal box. The goods loop signals at both ends of the loop were siding signals, that is red signal arms with a white metal circle on them.

In December 1946 it was reported that the facing connection to the goods loop was temporarily out of use and the Up Distant signal was disconnected but it has not been established why this occurred.

The goods loop was taken out of use on 20th December 1961 and the

The Down Starting signal at Swimbridge was adjacent to the road over bridge and was unusual in being a wooden GWR arm mounted on a pre-cast concrete post. Such posts were not common on the GWR system but some could be found each side of Machynlleth on the Cambrian main line. The signal, seen here on the last day, 1st October 1966, may have been a replacement following the derailment here that will be referred to in Volume 3. Note also the catch points sign. *Michael L. Roach*

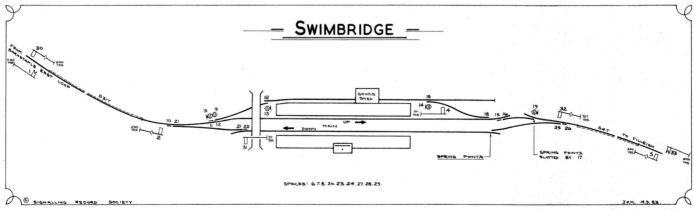

An Up train bearing the 'B' train indicator arrives at Swimbridge circa the early 1950s. On the left on the Down platform is the unique Swimbridge Signal Box, which did not conform to a GWR type and in earlier years boasted B&ER style bargeboards. Was it perhaps the only surviving example (barring the base of the first Wiveliscombe box) of one of the original signal boxes on the line? *R.J. Sellick, courtesy the National Railway Museum*

a larger frame, when it had Bristol & Exeter Railway-style bargeboards to the gable ends. There is a temptation to speculate therefore, that the box was built by the B&ER either for the opening of the line or soon after but there is currently no evidence to support this.

As mentioned above, the box was extended in 1904 to accept a twenty-one lever frame, having become a staff station when the electric train staff was introduced in 1893. There was a further extension to the frame from 4th April 1937, when the box was fitted with a VT 5-bar frame with 4 inch centres and thirty-three levers. The loop was then lengthened and signals altered from 20th June 1937, at which point the electric train token system became operational.

The single line section was extended to South Molton from 6th September 1964, when Filleigh Signal Box closed. The only siding was taken out of use and levers bolted in September 1964, the rails being recovered on 18th November 1964, leaving just the passing loop. The box officially closed with the line on 3rd October 1966.

BARNSTAPLE EAST LOOP

Opened on 1st July 1905 as Barnstaple East Junction Signal Box, when the East Loop was brought in to use, it was renamed Barnstaple East Loop Signal Box from 11th March 1950 (when the loop was out of use). It was a GWR Type 28B box, measuring 17 feet by 10 feet and elevated to 5 feet, located at 207 miles and 24 chains. It had a stud locking frame and thirteen levers.

The Distant signals for the junction were fixed at danger from 19th August 1908. It is worth mentioning here that, in the early days, the Distant signals had red arms with a white chevron, yellow distant signals not being introduced until the late 1920s.

As mentioned previously, there was electric train staff operation from Swimbridge to Barnstaple GWR from 1893 but after East Junction box was established, the electric train staff section ended there when it was open, the section between East Junction and Barnstaple GWR being operated by train staff and ticket. When

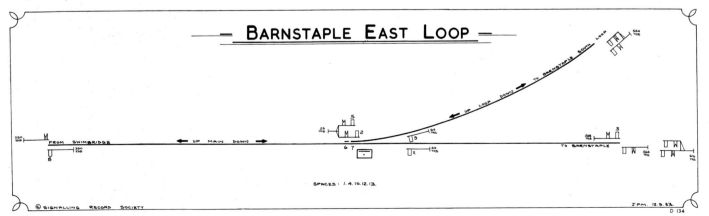

This rather cruel enlargement from a circa late 1920s view of a train leaving Barnstaple GWR (see Vol. 1, page 155) provides our only glimpse to date of Barnstaple East Junction Signal Box. It faced the junction from the north, the East Loop curving away to the left and the photograph was clearly taken outside of the summer months, when the loop was out of use, as the bracket signal has all its arms removed.
Arthur Halls, courtesy National Railway Museum

the line upgraded to electric train token in 1937, the arrangements were similar in that the section, outside of the summer months (the only time East Junction was open), between Swimbridge and Barnstaple GWR was operated by key token. In the summer, the key token section ended at East Junction and train staff and ticket was retained from East Junction to Barnstaple GWR. East Junction to South Junction was staff and ticket until 1960, when there was an electric train token section from Swimbridge to Barnstaple Junction.

The signal box was only opened during the summer months (broadly, early July to late September) each year. It is understood that during the rest of the year, the signal arms were removed. From 4th September 1939, the East Loop was locked out of use, a situation which persisted until June 1960, when Victoria Road station closed. In the late 1950s, the East Loop Starting signal (No. 9) had a white iron cross (X) fixed to it signifying its non-operational status. Following the closure of Victoria Road in 1960, the East Loop became operational again and Taunton trains then ran direct into Barnstaple Junction station. Barnstaple East Loop Signal Box was closed on 12th June 1960, at the time Victoria Road closed to passenger services, although photographic evidence indicates that the box was stripped of its equipment and left in a run down state (possibly having been damaged by fire) ahead of the official closure date.

BARNSTAPLE SOUTH LOOP

Barnstaple South Junction Signal Box box was also opened on 1st July 1905, when the East Loop was brought in to use, which with the West Loop thus created a triangle. It was a GWR Type 28B, measuring 17 feet by 10 feet and elevated to 5 feet, so was identical to the cabin at East Junction and as with that box, it was renamed on 11th March 1950, becoming Barnstaple South Loop Signal Box. It had a stud locking frame with thirteen levers, and train staff and ticket was the method of train control throughout its life for the

A poor quality but again rare view of Barnstaple South Junction Signal Box, looking north in GWR days circa 1930, after the painting of Distant arms in yellow with black chevrons; these were also fixed Distants. The line to Barnstaple GWR station curves round to the left, with the D&SR route in to the station running across the background. *Jim Elson collection*

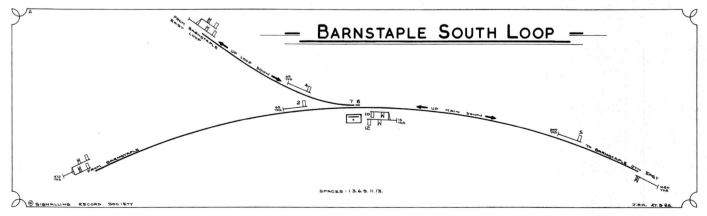

— BARNSTAPLE SOUTH LOOP —

East Junction/South Junction, Barnstaple GWR/South Junction and South Junction/ Barnstaple Junction sections. The Distant signals were fixed at danger from 19th August 1908.

As with East box, the South box was also only open during the summer months from 1905 to 4th September 1939 and the route was secured for trains to run only from Barnstaple GWR to Barnstaple Junction SR in the winter months. Again, like at East Junction, signal arms were removed when not in use. The box was reduced to ground frame status (for access to Victoria Road goods) from 12th June 1960, when the East Loop reopened, with the points being switched for direct running for all passenger services between Swimbridge and Barnstaple Junction after Victoria Road closed to passengers. The former line to Victoria Road was converted to siding status to serve the Victoria Road goods depot. The box (as a ground frame) closed on 3rd October 1966, the day the line closed and the route from Barnstaple Junction to Victoria Road was then given siding status throughout its length until final closure of the goods yard in 1970.

BARNSTAPLE GWR (VICTORIA ROAD FROM 11TH MARCH 1950)

The original box was in operation from 1873 until circa 1910, by which time the new box had been built and become operational. The second box was a GWR Type 3, measuring 17 feet by 10 feet and an operating floor height of 8 feet. It had a VT 3-bar frame with 4 inch centres and thirty-six levers, which was installed in 1910; the original box is believed to have had forty-two levers. The electric train staff was used to Swimbridge from 1893 but train staff and ticket was operated to East Junction in the summer months only following the opening of that box in 1905. This system was replaced by electric train token in 1937. Train staff and ticket were required for the East Loop to South Junction section in the summer months when the South Junction box was open and to Barnstaple Junction (East) box (later Barnstaple Junction 'A') during the rest of the year; this also applied after Barnstaple South Junction Box was moth-balled in 1939. When Victoria Road closed in 1960, electric train token commenced operation for the section between Barnstaple Junction

A fine study of the Siding signals for leaving the middle siding, towards the shed line (right) or running line (left), mounted on a wooden post bracket. On the right is another Siding signal, No. 17, for leaving the back road and note, too, the lattice post Starting signal on the left for departures from the main platform. This circa mid-1920s photograph also provides more detail of the engine shed complex. The turntable was sited to the right of the shed, with a kick-back siding serving the wooden coal stage on the right. The brick building between the stage and the shed is likely to have housed a sand drying plant, with attendant small furnace and chimney. Set at an angle to the shed itself, it does not feature on large scale maps of the site or any known plans and had been demolished by the mid 1930s. The offices and locomen's mess room is hidden by the water tower. *E. Wallis Collection, courtesy Kevin Robertson*

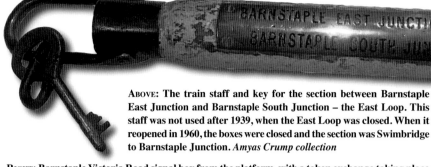

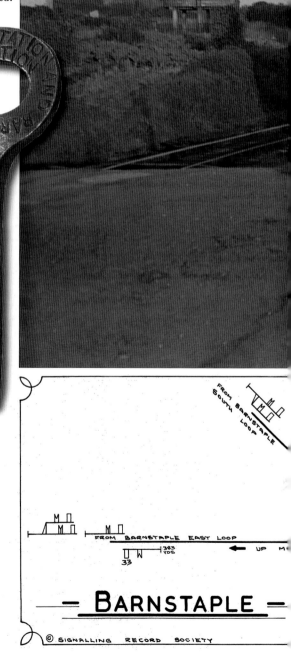

ABOVE: The train staff and key for the section between Barnstaple East Junction and Barnstaple South Junction – the East Loop. This staff was not used after 1939, when the East Loop was closed. When it reopened in 1960, the boxes were closed and the section was Swimbridge to Barnstaple Junction. *Amyas Crump collection*

RIGHT: Barnstaple Victoria Road signal box from the platform, with a token exchange taking place between the signalman and the driver of an unidentified Class '43XX' 2-6-0, in what looks to be a rather posed view for the benefit of the photographer. The picture is undated but is likely to have been taken in the early 1950s, possibly shortly after closure of the engine shed in January 1951 but before the track was lifted in July 1953. The water tower had been demolished in GWR days, probably in the early 1930s as it had gone by 1935, and the sand drying plant possibly at the same time, although a remnant of it can be seen still standing between the two Siding signals. However, the loss of these two structures now provided a glimpse here of the wooden offices and mess room lean-to built against the south wall of the shed. The wooden coaling stage had also been dismantled. The bracket Siding signal seen in the previous picture had been replaced by the twin ground disc signal in the right foreground, whilst the brick-built hut on the right edge of the picture was the yard staff and shunters' cabin. The signal box appears to be still in GWR colours and there is a view too of the concrete water tank in the left background which held the station's water supply. *Roger J. Sellick, courtesy the National Railway Museum*

INSET RIGHT: A close up of the key for the West Loop, inscribed Barnstaple GWR Station and Barnstaple South Station. *Amyas Crump collection*

and Swimbridge. When the chord line (later the West Loop) to Barnstaple Junction was first opened in 1887, train services were instructed by the service time table to '*stop dead at the GW signal box to admit the Exchange of the Train Staff and Ticket ...*' before entering the station.

Most of the signals in the station area were of the square-post type. However, the main platform Starting signal was on a lattice post, similar to that at Milverton. In the 1920s, there were a number of siding signals: one to leave the shed road, No. 20, one to leave the back road, No. 17, and a bracket signal to leave the middle siding to access the shed line or running line. These carried red arms with a white ring. Latterly, only two of these Siding signals remained, the bracket signal in the middle siding being replaced by two discs (No's 19 and 21).

The engine shed sidings were removed on 26th July 1953, this being the only significant rationalisation at the station before it closed to passenger traffic. Point No. 15 was retained as a trap. The fixed Distant arms on the Victoria Road bracket signal (below No's 32 and 34) for the branch to South Junction were out of use and marked with metal crosses to signify this just before closure of the station. The signal box closed with the removal of passenger services from the station on 12th June 1960. Following this, Victoria Road was relegated to a decade-long role as a goods depot at the end of a long siding from Barnstaple Junction, worked on the 'one engine in steam' principle, for which a signal box was not required.

As a side note, it is interesting to record that although the station officially changed its name from Barnstaple GWR to Barnstaple Victoria Road on 26th September 1949, the S&T department apparently did not amend the signal box's name until 11th March 1950, the same date that East Junction and South Junction changed their names as indicated above. This delay presumably reflected the number of S&T papers and records that required amending for a simple station name change.

The box had been removed by early 1965, as it does not appear in photographs of the station taken during the visit of the Exmoor Ranger rail tour on 27th March that year (*which will feature in Vol. 3*), but the actual date of its demolition has not been established.

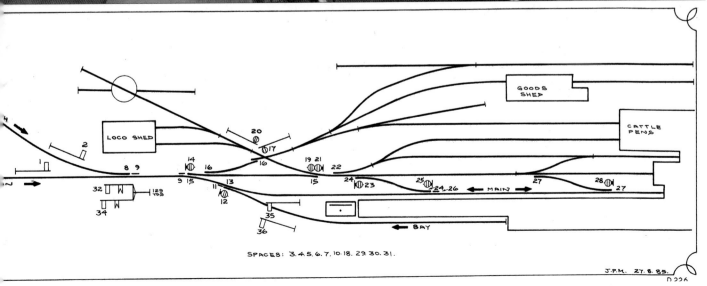

SPACES: 3. 4. 5. 6. 7. 10·18. 29. 30. 31.

J.P.M. 27. 8. 85.

D 226

LOCATION	WINTER WORKING	SUMMER WORKING
Swimbridge-Barnstaple GWR	Electric Token	
Swimbridge-Barnstaple East Junction		Electric Token
Barnstaple East Junction-Barnstaple GWR		Train Staff (red) & Ticket
Barnstaple GWR- Barnstaple Junction	Train Staff (red) & Ticket	
Barnstaple East Junction-Barnstaple South Junction		Train Staff (white) & Ticket
Barnstaple South Junction-Barnstaple Junction		Train Staff (blue) & Ticket
Barnstaple GWR-Barnstaple South Junction		Train Staff (yellow) & Ticket

THE LOOP LINE BETWEEN EAST JUNCTION AND SOUTH JUNCTION

The loop line between East Junction and South Junction, known variously as the East Curve or East Chord and latterly as the East Loop, was opened on 1st July 1905 and enabled trains to run direct from Swimbridge to Barnstaple Junction station, in theory to avoid Barnstaple GWR station and the inevitable train movements and shunting operations required there. However, the spur was never used in the early years by ordinary local train services but only for limited-stop and Ilfracombe trains (*as will be described in Vol. 3*).

The East Junction and South Junction boxes were generally closed during the winter time table (mid-September to mid-June) but re-opened for the working of through services over the East Loop in the summer months (see Appendix 15). It is understood that the loop junction signals were still connected to their relevant signal boxes but they either bore white crosses to indicate that they were not in use or, more usually, were removed as indicated in the working time table when not in use during the rest of the year.

The East Loop was taken out of use on 4th September 1939 after the end of that summer season but was not lifted. It was re-opened in June 1960 when Victoria Road closed to passenger traffic, after which all services ran directly through to Barnstaple Junction station. There is no firm evidence that the East Loop saw any use during this period, even during the years of the Second World War. There is a rumour that it was used to turn a circus train sometime in the 1950s but this is unsubstantiated and, in any case, at some point after its closure, some of the rails close to the East Loop Junction Signal Box had been lifted.

When the East Loop was re-opened in 1960, the points at East Loop Junction were clipped out of use and a length of rail on what had been the main line removed. The renamed Barnstaple East Loop Junction Signal Box was taken out of use, along with the similarly renamed Barnstaple South Loop Junction Signal Box. The latter was replaced by a ground frame that controlled access to Victoria Road goods depot, which was released when required by insertion of the token for the Swimbridge section. With a mid-section ground frame like this, a train could be shunted clear (into the West Loop to Victoria Road) and the token then placed back into the intermediate token instrument to enable the running line to be clear.

After closure of the station to passenger services, what had been the main line between East Junction and Victoria Road became redundant and was soon lifted. Although the exact date that the track was recovered has not yet been established, photographic evidence indicates that the line had gone by May 1961.

The token and staff arrangements at the Barnstaple end after the 1937 introduction of the electric token on the line are set out in the table at the top of the page.

FLORENCE SIDING

Whilst the history of Florence Siding is covered in Volume 1 (pages 21-22) and is also illustrated on the 2-chain survey (page 120), it deserves a further mention here in respect of the signalling arrangements and point work. The nature of the signals is also interesting, as the siding was open in the early years of the line when it was broad gauge.

The siding was $33^3/_4$ miles from Taunton and 130 chains east of South Molton, near where the River Mole passed under the railway, and was only in use in the period from March 1874 until the late 1890s. The *1886 Service Time Table* indicated that there was no block telegraph at the siding and there was never a signal box provided for it, the siding being operated by a ground frame.

The original intention was to open the siding for traffic on 1st February 1874 (on the basis of a letter from Richard Hassard, the D&SR engineer) but there were minor delays. However, the Florence Mining Company siding eventually became the subject of a report by the Board of Trade Inspector, Colonel Hutchinson, on 18th March 1874, just prior to its eventual opening.

Essentially, the letter read '… *the siding arrangements … are satisfactory except the signals and points are not working freely … and that the locking bars has been fixed a little too high. Upon condition that these matters are set right I can recommend the Board of Trade sanction the use of this siding junction.*' The aim was to open the siding for mineral traffic brought down by horse-drawn railway wagons from the mines up on the hill.

The siding was operated by a ground frame and the signalling and track layout is set out below. The frame comprised four levers:

• one to work both ends of the main siding (at the time of opening there was only one operational point off the D&SR, with an option for two additional points and sidings as the diagram shows)
• one to work the Home signal from the ground frame by the point into the siding

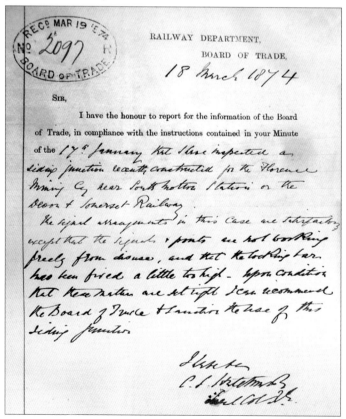

Col. Hutchinson's letter to the BoT of 18th March 1874 in regards to Florence siding. *Courtesy National Archives*

The Florence Mine broad gauge sidings, narrow gauge tramroad sidings and the transshipment wharf, as redrawn from the original plan submitted to the Board of Trade. The plan was further annotated by hand:

'The Florence Mining Co Ltd
per Sydney Hawkins
2 Suffolk Lane
Cannon St
E,C
Jan 17. 1874'

Sydney Hawkins, his brother William and George Bush, were the owners of the Florence Mining Company at this time.

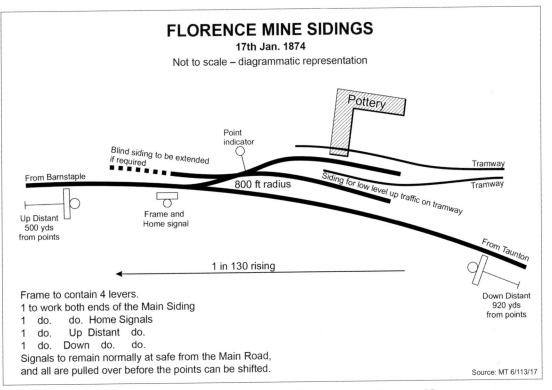

FLORENCE MINE SIDINGS
17th Jan. 1874
Not to scale – diagrammatic representation

Pottery

Point indicator

Blind siding to be extended if required

From Barnstaple

800 ft radius

Siding for low level up traffic on tramway

Tramway

Tramway

Up Distant 500 yds from points

Frame and Home signal

1 in 130 rising

From Taunton

Down Distant 920 yds from points

Frame to contain 4 levers.
1 to work both ends of the Main Siding
1 do.   do.   Home Signals
1 do.   Up Distant do.
1 do.   Down do.   do.
Signals to remain normally at safe from the Main Road, and all are pulled over before the points can be shifted.

Source: MT 6/113/17

- one to work the Up Distant 500 yards from the points
- one to work the Down Distant 920 yards from the points

The *October 1892 Service Time Table* outlined the operating procedure at the siding:

'The points at Florence siding between South Molton and Molland will be locked by a key fixed in the end of the electric train staff. The driver of any train which has to call at that place to pick up or put off trucks must on arrival hand the staff to the guard and must take care that he does not resume his journey until it has been returned to him.'

A Summary of D&SR Signal Boxes in 1937

A summary table of the signal boxes on the line in place in 1937 up to closure is set out below. The dates shown refer to when the box existing at this time dated from; most were replacements and some had been replaced more than once, whilst three were originals never replaced and one was an original that had been extended. Of the fourteen boxes (not including the main line Norton Fitzwarren), there were eight different GWR types, plus one non-standard (B&ER?).

Signal Box	Date Built	Type of Box (GWR)	Working Levers
Norton Fitzwarren	1932	31	131
Milverton	1903	7B	37
Wiveliscombe	1906	27C	24
Venn Cross	1905	7B	29
Morebath	1937	12A	31
Morebath Junction	*1884	3	23
Dulverton	1910	27C	54
East Anstey	1901	5	29
Bishops Nympton & Molland	1937	12B	30
South Molton	1901	7A	33
Filleigh	1937	12D	44
Swimbridge	**1904	Non Standard	33
East Junction	*1905	28B	13
Barnstaple GWR	1910	3	36
South Junction	*1905	28B	13

* Original boxes, never replaced
** Existing box extended rather than new box built. This was possibly the original B&ER box

Miscellaneous Signalling and Related Matters – Auxiliary Token Huts

As has been outlined above, there were two stations on the D&SR that had auxiliary token huts. This was a location, other than the relevant signal box, where an auxiliary token instrument and tokens were kept, usually a small cabin. Of the two on the D&SR, one was at the foot of the Down Starting signal at Dulverton and the other by the Down Advanced Starting signal at Filleigh. This facilitated token exchanges when the signalman was particularly busy and saved him the time it would take to walk to meet a footplate crew who were a long distance from the signal box. At Dulverton, for example, the box was at the east end of the station on the Up platform, so when a Down train was ready to proceed to East Anstey and an Up train had just arrived (and had given up possession of the token for the Dulverton to East Anstey section to the signalman), the fireman of the Down train would go to the auxiliary token hut and telephone the signalman to get permission to withdraw a token. This was only given once East Anstey box had given 'line clear' and both signalmen had depressed their plungers so the fireman could withdraw the token. He would then lift the token from the column to the centre opening, press it forward as if using an ordinary key in a lock to engage on the centre pin of the instrument and then turn it as far left as possible. Once the key was free, it could be withdrawn from the instrument. He would then inform the signalman that the token had been withdrawn, so the train could proceed. The distance between the signal box and the auxiliary hut at Dulverton was 138 yards, so a walk there and back would amount to 276 yards for the signalman and a possible time delay for the train. A similar arrangement for withdrawing the token operated at Filleigh, where the distance from the box to the hut was over 400 yards.

The Dulverton to East Anstey and Filleigh to South Molton sections each had forty tokens to allow for the number held in the auxiliary token instruments at Dulverton and Filleigh.

Mid-section ground frames (like the one introduced at South Junction) with intermediate token instruments were worked like auxiliary instruments.

Signal and Telegraph (S&T)

The main S&T base for day to day work on the D&SR was at Dulverton. The linemen would report to the inspector at Taunton (a Mr Burt until 1951 and George Hacker after that), and renewals and enhancement work were carried out by the Taunton based staff. The GWR's S&T headquarters were at Reading, to which the various local inspectors reported. The signalling personnel dealt with the mechanical side, namely points, signals, facing point locks, point rods, slide bars, signal wires, etc. The telegraph personnel attended to the telegraph and telephone equipment, and signal box instruments, including the electric staff or electric token machines.

In the early years, the 'mechanical' and 'electrical' teams were separated, combining some time in the late 1930s/early 1940s and so covering all aspects of signalling maintenance. The S&T employees at Dulverton covered the line between Dulverton and Barnstaple (two men) and Dulverton to Stoke Cannon on the Exe Valley line (a further two men). The Morebath to Norton Fitzwarren section was covered from Taunton. Towards the end of the line's life and after the Exe Valley Branch had been closed in 1963, the Dulverton men covered both sides of the D&SR from their base, operating in pairs as before. The S&T staff were also responsible for moving the tokens between boxes to balance them. It is understood from Jim Elson, who was based at Venn Cross in the late 1940s, that there were twenty tokens per section generally on the line, with forty at Dulverton and Filleigh because of their auxiliary token machines.

The Taunton S&T Department No. 3 Section Roster of maintenance for 11th April 1945 shows that, in the second week (weeks 1, 3 and 4 being spent on the Minehead Branch), work was carried out at Morebath, Venn Cross, Wiveliscombe and Milverton.

Mileposts and Gradient Posts

Mileposts were required by statute; quarter mileposts were not but, nonetheless, they were to be found throughout on the D&SR in later years. From the 1930s, the GWR started producing concrete mileposts, rather than the previously used cast iron letters on a wooden mounting, as well as concrete gradient posts, which were prevalent along the line. These were cast by the Taunton Division concrete works, which was situated just to the north-east of Taunton station and which had previously produced some experimental concrete sleepers that had been unsuccessfully trialled on the D&SR in 1917-18 (see Vol. 1, page 140).

Catch and Trap Points

For safe operation of the line given the gradients on it, a number of which began/ended in station throats, numerous catch and trap points were installed, particularly following the 1937 improvements, as is evident from some of the photographs. Catch points are sprung

LOOSE RUNAWAY CATCH POINTS OR DEAD END TRAP SIDINGS—continued.

Station or Signal Box	Up or Down Line	Where situated	If connected or worked from Box	Gradient 1 in
Milverton	Down Line ..	210 yards West of Signal Box ..	Spring points slotted.	82
Wiveliscombe	Down Loop ..	209 yards West of Signal Box ..	,,	726
Venn Cross	Up Loop ..	179 yards West of Signal Box ..	,, ...	60
,, ,, ...	Down Loop ..	130 yards East of Signal Box ..	,,	58
Morebath	Up Loop ..	176 yards East of Signal Box ..	,, ...	Level
,, ...	Down Loop ..	115 yards East of Signal Box ..	,, ...	264
Morebath Jct.	Down Barnstaple Loop.	102 yards West of Signal Box ..	Self-acting ..	100
,, ,, ...		289 yards East of Signal Box ..	,, ..	100
,, ,, ...	Up Exe Valley Loop.	71 yards Tiverton Side of Signal Box.	,, ..	100
Dulverton	Down Loop ..	212 yards West of Signal Box ..	Spring points slotted.	60
East Anstey	Down Loop ..	160 yards East of Signal Box ..	,,	330
Bishops Nympton & Molland	Up Loop	53 yards East of Signal Box ..	,,	155
South Molton	Up Loop ..	125 yards East of Signal Box ..	,,	330
,, ,, ...	Down Loop ..	116 yards East of Signal Box ..	,, ..	60
,, ,, ...	,, ,, ..	116 yards East of Signal Box ..		3 0
Filleigh	Up Loop ..	224 yards East of Signal Box ..	Self-acting ..	60
,, ...	Up and Down Goods Loop.	396 yards West of Signal Box ..	Spring points slotted.	1200
Swimbridge	Down Loop ..	204 yards East of Signal Box ..	Self-acting ..	Level
,, ...	Up Loop ..	204 yards East of Signal Box ..	Spring points slotted.	Level

Note.—Levers, Clips and Padlocks are kept in the Signal Boxes.

and are always self-acting, that is, they are not controlled by the signalman and are automatically pushed across as the train passes over them. They then spring open again, so if the train were to roll back, the point will derail the train to protect the running line. In some locations, sprung catch points may need to be additionally operated from a signal box and in these instances, an arrangement known as a 'slotted joint' was provided. Trap points are controlled by the signalman and were usually installed to stop movements over-running or passing signals; they are also locked to the signals. The extract above, from the *Appendix to the GWR Service Time Table 1947*, lists the location of catch and trap points on the D&SR.

Train Operation over Facing Points and Inclines

In the early days of GWR train operation up to the 1880s, and as will be seen from the early track diagrams, the GWR did not have facing points into sidings, as it was a Board of Trade requirement not to have them. However, facing points at junctions, single line loops and termini were allowed. In such circumstances where there were a number of facing points on the D&SR – Milverton and Venn Cross for example – restrictions applied. In the *GWR Service Time Table 1900*, trains or engines were not permitted to run past any facing point on the D&SR at a speed greater than 15mph (this was increased from the 10mph shown in 1891).

Also, when running down all inclines, speeds were not to exceed 40mph (30mph in 1891) for passenger trains and 15mph for goods trains. Furthermore, the guard in charge of every train when shunting vehicles on or near an incline was strictly ordered not to allow the engine to be uncoupled until he had securely put on the brakes and safely spragged the last vehicle, and he was not to commence his journey without a supply of sprags in his van for this purpose. Great care was also to be taken to remove the sprags before starting the goods train on its way. A sprag was a length of hardwood (usually square and about one foot in length) that could be inserted between the wagon's spoked wheels to impede movement of the wheel when the train was stationary. They were sometimes tapered at one end to facilitate insertion between the spokes and examples feature in at least two of the photographs within these pages.

THE ECONOMIC SYSTEM OF MAINTENANCE AND THE MOTOR TROLLEY ECONOMIC SYSTEM OF MAINTENANCE

The economic system of maintenance was introduced on the line on 30th September 1912. The motor trolley economic system of maintenance was subsequently introduced from 18th September 1933.

The ganger's job was to make daily examinations of the length of track in his charge and with his men carry out necessary repairs. In the days before the economic system of maintenance there would be two flagmen, one at each end of the gang for protection, and a number of gangs would be responsible for specific lengths of track. The economic system of maintenance was so called because it introduced financial savings, primarily by removing the flag men and enabling gangs to cover longer sections of track. In addition, with the development of occupation control instruments, the ganger's section could overlap token sections. These two matters led to a saving of manpower and less potential disruption to the trains on the line.

Access to a GWR volume formerly held by the Chief Engineer's Office at Paddington and entitled *The GWR Economic System of Maintenance*, outlines the position for the D&SR, amongst other lines. It mapped the route covered and the allocation of the new telephone huts. The stretch of line between Dulverton and Barnstaple was the subject of a financial costing in 1912.

The two pages dealing with the D&SR line are shown below. The first, numbered 147, shows the spacing of the telephone huts, which were between 53 chains and a maximum of 67 chains apart, linked to the ETS section and the number of men in the gang (usually a ganger plus four men). Even at the maximum 67 chains – 1,474 yards or 0.84 of a mile – the ganger never had far to walk to the nearest telephone. There is a summary of the length of lines to be maintained (28 miles 75$^3/_4$ chains in total including sidings; 23 miles 65 chains of route mileage). The number of daily trains (regular, occasional and maximum between Dulverton and South Molton, and South Molton and Barnstaple) was also stated. The second page showed that twenty-six huts were provided with telephones and occupation key instruments, along with

DELIVERY OF AN ABTUS BABE

Amyas Crump has seen a supplier copy of an invoice which indicated a delivery to Mr H.A. Alexander, Engineering Department of South Moulton [sic] Station, GWR, shipped on 5th September 1933: one Abtus Babe No. 36-D Motor Inspection Car, with 16 inch all steel diameter wheels and GWR lamp brackets. It was supplied with a sealed tool box containing amongst other items, one pair of pliers, a rope starter, a spare set of four brake blocks, an engine instruction book and an instruction book for the car. Delivery was via GWR goods (there was no mention of purchase price).

147

Barnstaple Branch between Dulverton + Barnstaple

Worked by Electric Train Staff.

Permanent Way.-	m.	c.
00 B.H. –		11
95 B.H. –		9½
92 B.H. –	1.	26½
68d B.H. –	8.	17
01 B.H. –		59¾
76 B.H. –	1.	12½
86a B.H. –	13.	36½
	25.	12 3/24

Maximum Gradient 1 in 58

Minimum Curve Radius 12 chs.

Converted to the Motor Trolley system of maintenance on 18th Sept 1933.

No. of Trains.

Between 6.0 am and 5.30 pm			Per day of 24 hours		
Regular	Occasional	Maximum	Regular	Occasional	Maximum
(a) 16	6	22	23	10	33
(b) 20	4	24	25	8	33

No Sunday Trains.

(a) Between Barnstaple and South Molton.
(b) Between South Molton and Dulverton.

Length.	Three lines.	Double.	Single.	S.R.M.	Sidings.	Total.
m. c.	m. c.	m. c.	m. c.	m. c.	m. c.	m. c.
23 65	. 15	. 77¾	22. 52½	25. 12¾	3. 63	28. 75¾

148

No. of Huts provided with Telephones and Occupation Key Instruments.	26
No. of Telephones at Stations + Signal Boxes	7
Total	33

Estimated cost of Installation.-	£	s.	d.
33 Telephones + Occupation Key Instruments &c.	520.	0.	0
26 Telephone Huts.	91.	0.	0
5 Velocipede Car Huts	16.	0.	0
5 Velocipede Cars fitted with low gear	37.	10.	0
4 Mechanical Trollies fitted with low gear + arrangement for disconnecting handle.	45.	0.	0
5 Watches.	10	0.	0
5 Suits of Oilskins for Gangers.	3.	15.	0
Total.	722.	5.	0

Under Standard Rules this Branch was maintained by:-

	Total No. of men.	Wages per annum.	No. of men per mile.
3 Gangs of 5 men ea. / 2 . 6 . / 1 . 7 .	34	1684. 16. 0	1.17
Under new System.-			
3 Gangs of 5 men ea. / 1 Gang of 6 / 1 . 7 .	28	1383. 4. 0	.97
Gross saving in men + wages per ann.	6	301. 12. 0	.20

The Gangers are provided with watches and examine their own lengths daily on Velocipede Inspection Cars. Mechanical Trollies provided for 4 Gangs.

Economic System brought into operation on 30th Sept. 1912

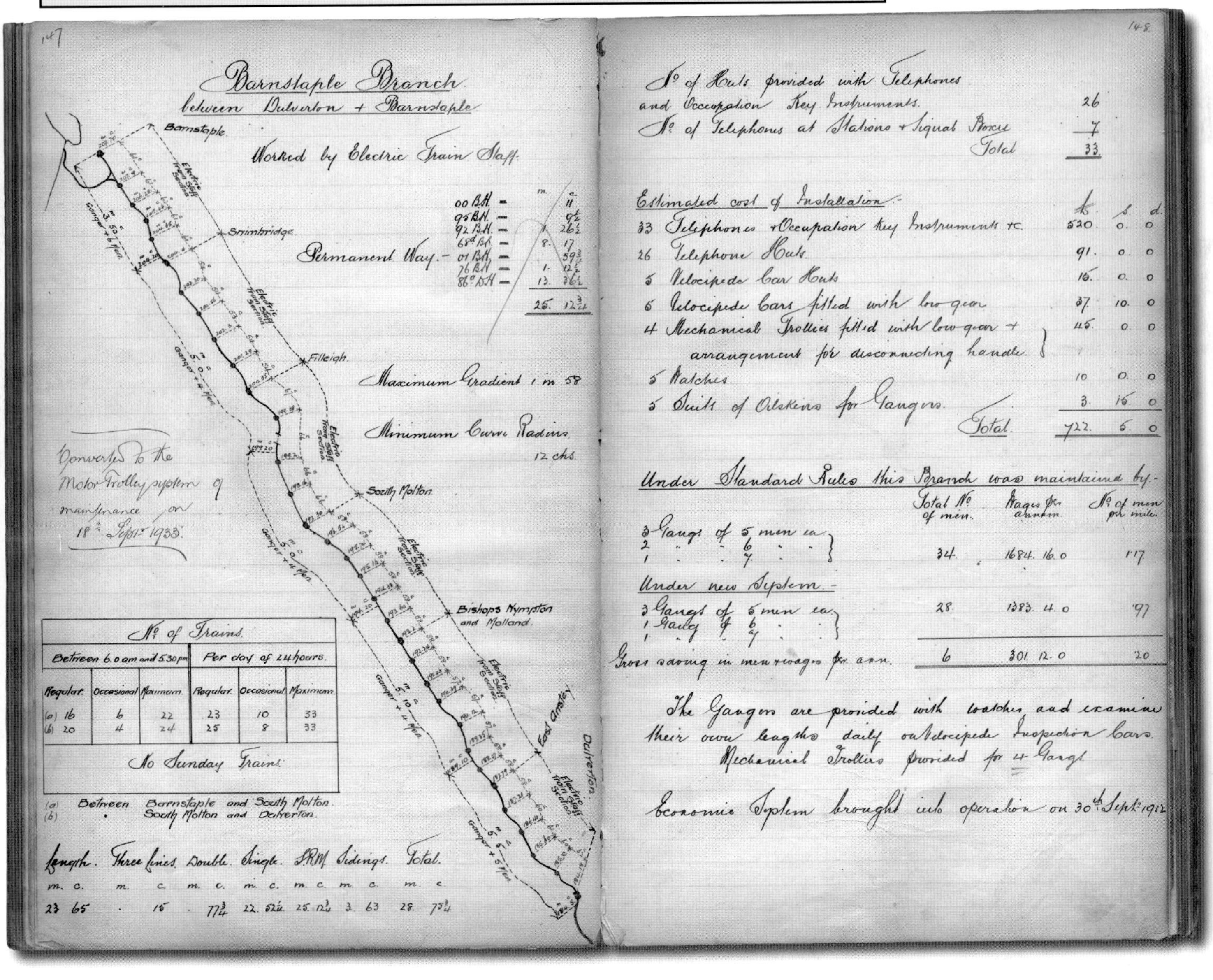

seven additional telephones for stations and signal boxes specific for this use; the cost of installation amounted to £611. Five car huts (cost £15) were also provided for each ganger's section, along with five velocipede cars (cost £37 10s) and four mechanical trollies (cost £45). The total cost of all matters was £722 5s.

It was reported that the mechanical trollies had low gearing and arrangements for disconnecting the handle. With gradients of up to 1 in 58 on the line, the low gearing was certainly an advantage. The page was also annotated to show that the section had been converted to the motor trolley system of maintenance.

The table towards the foot of the second page (numbered 148) shows that there was a saving of six men (twenty-eight in the gang doing the work previously required from thirty-four men) at an annual cost of £301 12s. This would result in 'pay-back' of the investment in just less than two and a half years. Also, the number of men per mile was effectively reduced from 1.17 to 0.97 per mile. One of the obvious savings made with the introduction of occupation instruments was the removal of the flagman, two of whom were required for each gang working on a single line, one at the front and one at the rear.

A footnote stated that: '*The Gangers are provided with watches and examine their own lengths* [about 5 miles each] *daily on Velocipede Inspection cars. Mechanical Trollies provided for 4 gangs.*'

In the Up direction towards Taunton, the Dulverton gang worked the section between Morebath Junction and Bampton, as well as the main line. Beyond Morebath Junction to Morebath there were no key boxes. Between Venn Cross and Wiveliscombe there were four or five key boxes and set down points for the trollies. Between Wiveliscombe and Milverton there were three.

Under the economic system of maintenance, a lone ganger would usually travel the line by means of a three-wheeled velocipede. Four-wheeled trollies were also provided but these were normally used for transporting the gang and any materials required; these vehicles were often hand or pump operated. In carrying out these tasks, a section of line had to be protected (as described below) so that trains could not enter the section whilst the gang was at work.

THE GANGER'S TROLLEY

The ganger's trolley, sometimes with a trailer attached to it, could carry all of the equipment required as well as the men themselves. The trolleys were each fitted with sanding apparatus, a fire extinguisher, a klaxon horn and two red lamps (one each at front and rear) for when in tunnels, and there were also motorised versions. A trolley could be placed on or removed from the line by two or three men, being equipped with a portable turntable and a light ramp. A ganger's inspection velocipede could be removed from the line quite easily by one man.

The essential work of the gang and access to their relevant section,

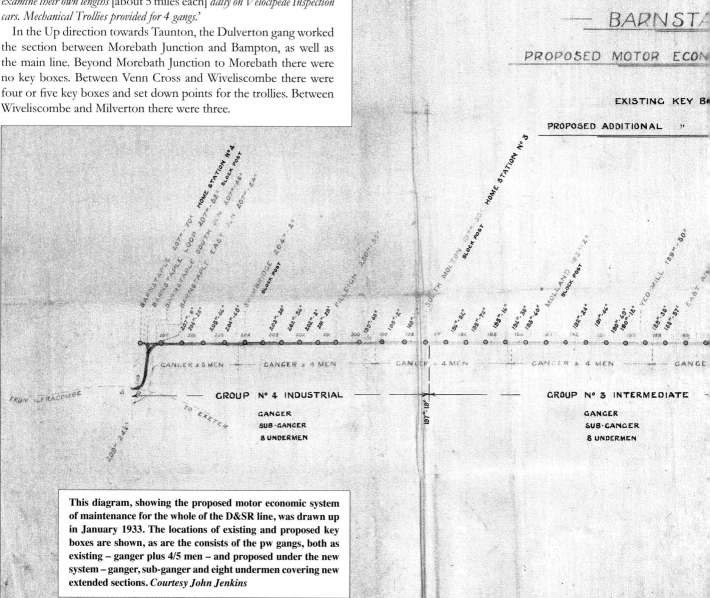

This diagram, showing the proposed motor economic system of maintenance for the whole of the D&SR line, was drawn up in January 1933. The locations of existing and proposed key boxes are shown, as are the consists of the pw gangs, both as existing – ganger plus 4/5 men – and proposed under the new system – ganger, sub-ganger and eight undermen covering new extended sections. *Courtesy John Jenkins*

whether by motor trolley or velocipede, had to fit in with the running of the train services and cause minimal disruption to them. Gangers were only able to enter a section in this manner with the permission of the signalman and so they too had their own safety system. This was akin to the ETS/ETT for access to a section of line requiring maintenance, which is why the telephone huts and key instruments were required.

THE GANGER, PLATELAYERS AND THE USE OF THE GANGER'S OCCUPATION KEY (GOK)

The ganger was the man in charge of the platelayers and their duties were many and varied. They looked after the rails, such as oiling fishplates, checking points and tightening nuts, as well as the sleepers, ballast and boundary fences, cutting back vegetation, cleaning ditches and clearing snow. In addition, they had a watching brief on the condition of station and halt platforms, public access roads and paths. As the platelayers usually worked on or near the running lines, they always had to be alert to approaching trains, which had to whistle on their approach to the work site, to notify the work force. The gang then stood well back from the passing train.

For heavier work and when the work site was a significant distance from the station area, the platelayers used a trolley. This was a rail mounted, heavy metal-framed, low-slung, four-wheeled vehicle, sometimes motorised (petrol driven), which could carry tools, sleepers, chairs, bolts, fence posts, wire and related equipment, in fact just about everything required to maintain the permanent way. The non-motorised trolleys would be propelled by two men. Given that the trolley would need to occupy a section of line, it was treated like it was a train. Thus, on a single line, the use of the trolley would block it in both directions, so the timing of access to the relevant section had to be respectful of the time table and minimise disruption. The trolley was relatively easy to manhandle and was required to be taken off the track once the gang had arrived at their work destination – or more appropriately at the nearest run-off location specifically created for this purpose, the run off being a set of rails perpendicular to the track.

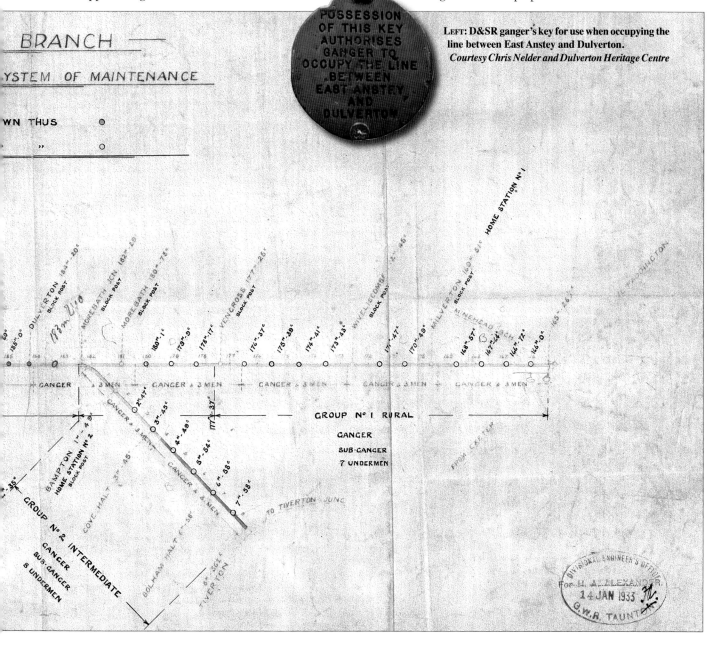

LEFT: D&SR ganger's key for use when occupying the line between East Anstey and Dulverton.
Courtesy Chris Nelder and Dulverton Heritage Centre

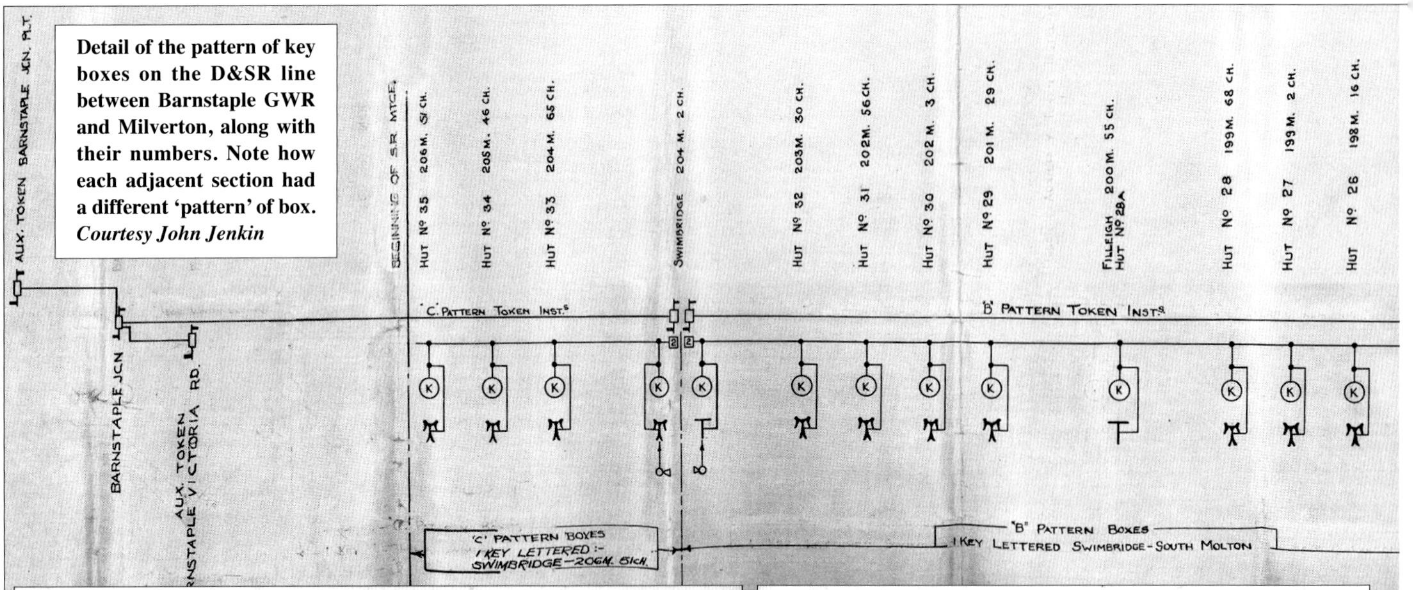

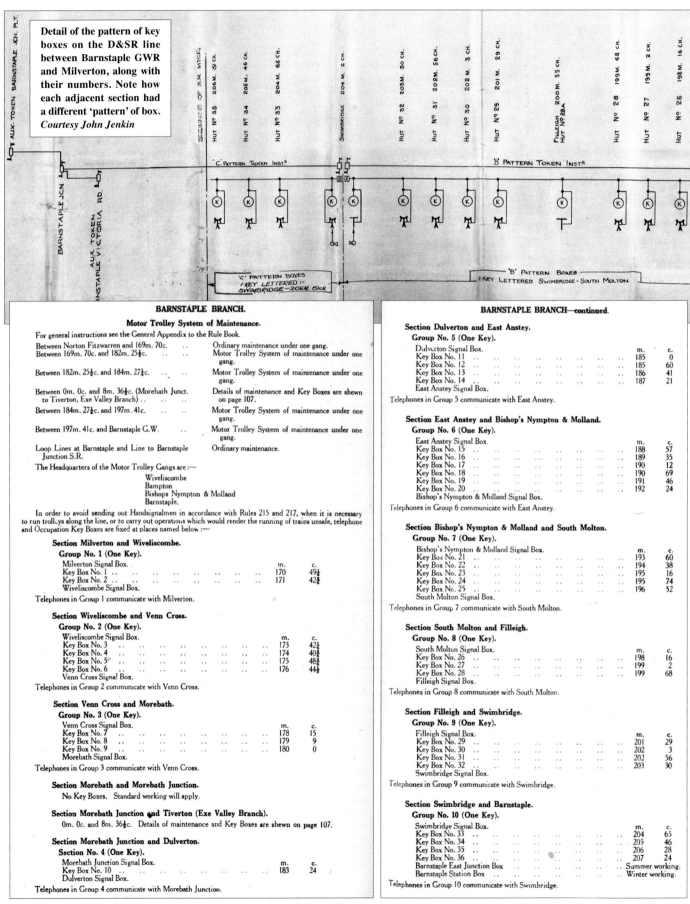

Detail of the pattern of key boxes on the D&SR line between Barnstaple GWR and Milverton, along with their numbers. Note how each adjacent section had a different 'pattern' of box. ***Courtesy John Jenkin***

BARNSTAPLE BRANCH.

Motor Trolley System of Maintenance.

For general instructions see the General Appendix to the Rule Book.

Between Norton Fitzwarren and 169m. 70c. ..	Ordinary maintenance under one gang.
Between 169m. 70c. and 182m. 25¼c.	Motor Trolley System of maintenance under one gang.
Between 182m. 25¼c. and 184m. 27¼c.	Motor Trolley System of maintenance under one gang.
Between 0m. 0c. and 8m. 36½c. (Morebath Junct. to Tiverton, Exe Valley Branch)	Details of maintenance and Key Boxes are shewn on page 107.
Between 184m. 27¼c. and 197m. 41c.	Motor Trolley System of maintenance under one gang.
Between 197m. 41c. and Barnstaple G.W. ..	Motor Trolley System of maintenance under one gang.
Loop Lines at Barnstaple and Line to Barnstaple Junction S.R.	Ordinary maintenance.

The Headquarters of the Motor Trolley Gangs are:—

Wiveliscombe
Bampton
Bishops Nympton & Molland
Barnstaple.

In order to avoid sending out Handsignalmen in accordance with Rules 215 and 217, when it is necessary to run trolleys along the line, or to carry out operations which would render the running of trains unsafe, telephone and Occupation Key Boxes are fixed at places named below:—

Section Milverton and Wiveliscombe.

Group No. 1 (One Key).

	m.	c.
Milverton Signal Box.		
Key Box No. 1 ..	170	49¼
Key Box No. 2 ..	171	42¾
Wiveliscombe Signal Box.		

Telephones in Group 1 communicate with Milverton.

Section Wiveliscombe and Venn Cross.

Group No. 2 (One Key).

	m.	c.
Wiveliscombe Signal Box.		
Key Box No. 3 ..	173	42¼
Key Box No. 4 ..	174	40¾
Key Box No. 5 ..	175	48¾
Key Box No. 6 ..	176	44½
Venn Cross Signal Box.		

Telephones in Group 2 communicate with Venn Cross.

Section Venn Cross and Morebath.

Group No. 3 (One Key).

	m.	c.
Venn Cross Signal Box.		
Key Box No. 7 ..	178	15
Key Box No. 8 ..	179	9
Key Box No. 9 ..	180	0
Morebath Signal Box.		

Telephones in Group 3 communicate with Venn Cross.

Section Morebath and Morebath Junction.

No Key Boxes. Standard working will apply.

Section Morebath Junction and Tiverton (Exe Valley Branch).

0m. 0c. and 8m. 36½c. Details of maintenance and Key Boxes are shewn on page 107.

Section Morebath Junction and Dulverton.

Section No. 4 (One Key).

	m.	c.
Morebath Junction Signal Box.		
Key Box No. 10 ..	183	24
Dulverton Signal Box.		

Telephones in Group 4 communicate with Morebath Junction.

BARNSTAPLE BRANCH—continued.

Section Dulverton and East Anstey.

Group No. 5 (One Key).

	m.	c.
Dulverton Signal Box.		
Key Box No. 11 ..	185	0
Key Box No. 12 ..	185	60
Key Box No. 13 ..	186	41
Key Box No. 14 ..	187	21
East Anstey Signal Box.		

Telephones in Group 5 communicate with East Anstey.

Section East Anstey and Bishop's Nympton & Molland.

Group No. 6 (One Key).

	m.	c.
East Anstey Signal Box.		
Key Box No. 15 ..	188	57
Key Box No. 16 ..	189	35
Key Box No. 17 ..	190	12
Key Box No. 18 ..	190	69
Key Box No. 19 ..	191	46
Key Box No. 20 ..	192	24
Bishop's Nympton & Molland Signal Box.		

Telephones in Group 6 communicate with East Anstey.

Section Bishop's Nympton & Molland and South Molton.

Group No. 7 (One Key).

	m.	c.
Bishop's Nympton & Molland Signal Box.		
Key Box No. 21 ..	193	60
Key Box No. 22 ..	194	38
Key Box No. 23 ..	195	16
Key Box No. 24 ..	195	74
Key Box No. 25 ..	196	52
South Molton Signal Box.		

Telephones in Group 7 communicate with South Molton.

Section South Molton and Filleigh.

Group No. 8 (One Key).

	m.	c.
South Molton Signal Box.		
Key Box No. 26 ..	198	16
Key Box No. 27 ..	199	2
Key Box No. 28 ..	199	68
Filleigh Signal Box.		

Telephones in Group 8 communicate with South Molton.

Section Filleigh and Swimbridge.

Group No. 9 (One Key).

	m.	c.
Filleigh Signal Box.		
Key Box No. 29 ..	201	29
Key Box No. 30 ..	202	3
Key Box No. 31 ..	202	56
Key Box No. 32 ..	203	30
Swimbridge Signal Box.		

Telephones in Group 9 communicate with Swimbridge.

Section Swimbridge and Barnstaple.

Group No. 10 (One Key).

	m.	c.
Swimbridge Signal Box.		
Key Box No. 33 ..	204	65
Key Box No. 34 ..	205	46
Key Box No. 35 ..	206	28
Key Box No. 36 ..	207	24
Barnstaple East Junction Box ..	Summer working.	
Barnstaple Station Box ..	Winter working.	

Telephones in Group 10 communicate with Swimbridge.

The motor trolley system of maintenance for the branch as set out in the *GWR Appendix to No 5 Section of the Service Time Tables, Exeter Division (February 1947, and until further notice)*. It listed the type of maintenance along with the location of all occupation key boxes from Milverton westwards.

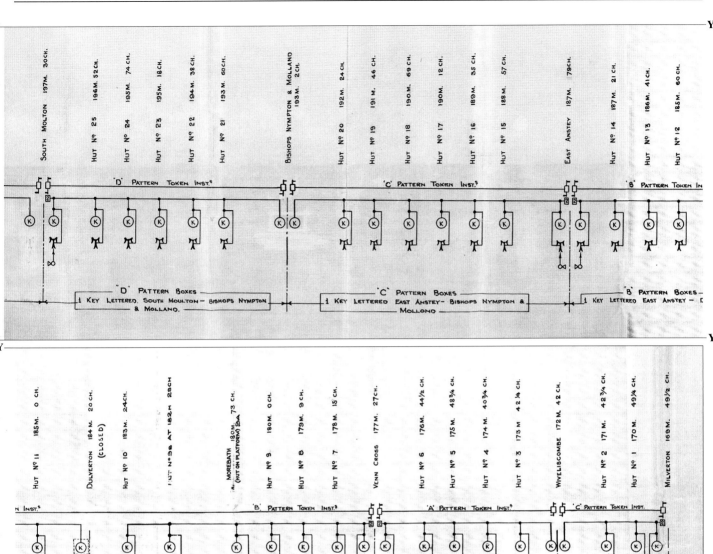

Access to the section of line to be worked on would be the responsibility of the signalman and the ganger's foreman and the Gangers' Occupation Key (GOK) would, like the ETT, play a key safety role. The GOK was a large brass key usually with relevant signal box names inscribed on it, as shown in the accompanying illustration. However, it was possible to have two non-overlapping occupation key sections within one ETT section.

Although the occupation key system was similar to ETT it was more complicated in operation. There were two instruments needed for the system to work; the ganger's key instruments and the control instrument. The GOK would be locked into a key instrument at one signal box, there being only one such key. In order for this to be taken out and given to the ganger, the signalman at the departure box had to firstly contact the signalman at the next block section, usually by telephone. The first signalman would ask the second to hold down the plunger on the ETT instrument. This would unlock a slide in the control instrument in the first signal box, enabling that signalman to pull out both sets of slides as far as they would go, thereby unlocking

the key instrument but locking the control slide. The occupation key could then be removed by the first signalman and given to the ganger. The drawing out of the control slide took the train token circuit out of use. As a consequence, no train could enter the section until the ganger reached the next box (or an intermediate location, as described below) and the key replaced in the instrument, with the second signalman then calling the first by telephone to confirm that the key had been replaced. Then the slides in the control instrument of the first box could be replaced and the token instruments became operational again. When the occupation key was in the ganger's possession, the token circuit was disabled and he could carry out any necessary track work without the need to protect the site with flagmen and detonators, as no train could enter the section. Each GOK would be of differing configuration to prevent replacement into the wrong instrument on return.

If the gang were required to stop in a section, the ganger would need to make use of the occupational key instruments in the sections between signal boxes to release the section for trains to pass. These occupation key instruments were usually located about three-quarters

Looking slightly incongruous, a ganger's motor trolley coasts down the bank in to Wiveliscombe circa 1963, in a view which also shows good detail of the water tower and the horse loading dock; the latter appears not to have seen any use for some time and the siding was removed in 1964. *Peter Barnfield*

of a mile to one mile apart (*see map overleaf for accurate distances on the Dulverton to Barnstaple section of the D&SR*) and were contained in large white wooden boxes usually fixed to or near telegraph poles. They contained the key instrument and a telephone which connected to the adjacent signal boxes. On arrival at the instrument, the ganger would insert the GOK in order to unlock the token instruments. He would then ring the first signal box to confirm his action – 'line clear', he had reached his destination and the trolley was off the track – and location, so that the signalman and train crew would know where the workmen were. Inserting the key in the instrument and turning it would lock it in. This then released the slides in the control instrument in the first box, which were then pushed back in by the first signalman. The token instruments were then tested to be working satisfactorily. If that was the case, trains could then pass through the section in the normal manner with the ETT.

When the platelayers' work was finished at the site and before putting the trolley back on the running line, the ganger would go back to the instrument to retrieve the GOK. He would ring the first signal box and the signalman would then in turn ring the second box signalman, to ask him to hold down the plunger on the token instrument. The first signalman would then pull the control slide and press the button above it to release the occupation key instrument in the relevant section at the lineside, allowing the ganger to remove the GOK and take it with him. The section was then locked out so the gang and their trolley could proceed along the section. Once the gang had returned to base (signal box one or two), the clearance procedure for opening the section had to be followed, with the GOK returned to the occupational key instrument in the signal box of the adjacent section.

SIGNALS - A GENERAL REVIEW

Most signals on the line throughout its life were of the typical GWR wooden square-post lower quadrant type, with wooden painted signal arms. However, the Intermediate Down Starting signal at Milverton and the Starting signal at Barnstaple Victoria Road were on lattice posts; the dates of their erection are unknown but both were certainly in place by the 1920s. It is understood that they were provided at times when timber was in short supply and when the debate over concrete signals, occasionally used by the GWR, was still raging. The lattice signals were similar in style to those used on the L&SWR, produced by Stevens & Sons of London and Glasgow. The signal at Milverton was initially sited on the wrong side of the line but was moved to the Down side at an unknown date and both survived until closure.

In the latter days of the line, commencing around 1958, tubular steel, round-post lower quadrant signals with pressed steel arms began to appear, as is noted in various of the sections above.

A number of Distant signals on the branch were fixed but some were able to be worked by the signalman, contrary to normal GWR single line practice. This was made possible in the 1930s by the installation of Whitaker automatic token exchange apparatus and the relaying of loop points with 'long lead' turnouts to facilitate faster running. Both of these improvements meant that token exchange could take place at speeds up to 40mph, rather that the usual 10mph demanded of a manual exchange between fireman and signalman.

Although not strictly on the D&SR, the Down Starting signal at Norton Fitzwarren, which dated from the 1920s was interesting and is thus also illustrated here. There was also the unusual centrally-pivoted, non-standard spectacle, Down Home signal at Venn Cross, which was illustrated in Chapter 7.

A study of the Norton Fitzwarren bracket Down Starting signal prior to the 1930s quadrupling of the line. The branch signal arms are the two lower ones at platform level, with Barnstaple to the left and Minehead to the right, affording equal priority to both routes. The main line arm has a lower co-acting signal and all of the arms are centrally pivoted, with the post located between the running lines. The token pick-up apparatus is visible to the left of the Down line by the signal box and the signalman's bike. The collection apparatus is on the opposite side of the line, near what was the stationmaster's house; this was demolished when the line was quadrupled. *E. Wallis Collection, courtesy Kevin Robertson*

ABOVE LEFT: **The approach to the Taw Bridge, looking north in the mid 1920s from just outside of Barnstaple Junction, on the chord line to Barnstaple GWR. The ex-L&SWR signals shown are the Advanced Starting signal on a wooden post on the left and the lattice post Outer Home signal on the right.**

ABOVE RIGHT: **The rear of Advanced Starting signal, looking towards Barnstaple Junction station, which can just be made out in the right distance.**
Both E. Wallis Collection, courtesy Kevin Robertson

In later years (post 1920s), the Outer Home signal into Barnstaple Junction A signal box (which was renamed Barnstaple Junction East in BR days), on the east side of the Taw Bridge, was in Southern territory, so it was an upper quadrant bracket signal with lattice posts in typical Southern region style. It is not known whether it replaced an L&SWR lower quadrant bracket from earlier years. However, photographic evidence shows two L&SWR lower quadrant signals virtually next to each other just outside of Barnstaple Junction, on the west side of the bridge on the branch to Barnstaple GWR, so the simple single arm L&SWR Home signal may have been sufficient at the time. One of these signals was lattice, the other square-post of wooden construction.

As seen in the Barnstaple Victoria Road section, the goods yard had a number of GWR lower quadrant semaphore Shunting or Siding signals in the 1920s. There was a bracket signal by the middle siding, the left arm for movements on to the running line and the right arm for entrance into the locomotive shed. There was an additional Shunt signal at the throat of the back road siding (No. 17 on the signal box diagram).

EXPERIMENTATION IN THE 1930S

There was growing pressure on the GWR in the 1930s to speed up the working of some of the longer single lines it owned, including the Taunton to Barnstaple and Minehead branches. The pressure for higher speeds on the former was partially brought about by competition from the SR in serving Barnstaple and Ilfracombe.

This led to the fitting of the Whitaker token exchange apparatus pick up and collection posts throughout the length of the line and certain locomotives, as described below. This apparatus, provided by the Railway Signal Company of Fazakerley, in Liverpool, had been used with some success on the Midland & Great Northern Joint Railway and the Somerset & Dorset Joint Railway. However, as the D&SR line did not have a dedicated set of locomotives, as was to an extent the case on those lines, the fitting of such apparatus could have been expensive but, under New Works Order No. 9/842 of 23rd June 1933, eight locomotives of the '45XX' Class were fitted. The following is a list of the engines that were out-shopped with the equipment and the dates that it was fitted:

No's 4581, 5503, 5537, 5542, 5543 on 11th July 1933

No. 5521 on 12th July 1933

No's 5551, 5571 on 13th July 1933;

Additionally, under New Works Order No. 9/1355 of 1934, further locomotives were fitted:

No. 5501 on 18th June 1934

No's 5502, 5525 on 22nd June 1934

No. 5505 on 26th June 1934

No. 5522 on 29th June 1934

No. 5569 on 7th July 1934

The main purpose of the apparatus was for use in the summer time table but it would seem that, initially, it did not work as well as was expected. Also at this time, the GWR was looking to use its new express diesel railcars on the D&SR and there was little possibility of fixing the Whitaker apparatus to these units. Accordingly, these two factors led to a reappraisal of the installation of token exchangers throughout the line to Barnstaple. On 17th May 1936, a joint report was made to the general manager on the feasibility of a Centralised Traffic Control (CTC) installation. This would have resulted in signalling the whole of the Barnstaple line from a single central switch panel located at Dulverton. The CTC would control loop points and the running signals, and release ground frames for local shunting movements. The scheme was costed at £79,000, including £3,000 for the installation of additional catch points and some sleeper replacement. These new (wooden) sleepers would have been needed to replace long lengths of the line which had recently been re-laid with steel sleepers, which could not have been retained if full track circuiting was to be installed. In the end, cost considerations ruled the CTC system out of contention.

The GWR officers then considered a second alternative, namely the introduction throughout the Barnstaple and Minehead lines of a token-less lock and block system. A lot of planning and drawing work was done, along with some preparation for installation. However, a demonstration at Reading of the proposed system, set up for inspecting officers of the Ministry of Transport on 19th October 1936, resulted in the project being aborted. The officers were not in favour of the basic proposals on safety grounds, as a driver might have been able to start a train despite a red signal. As a consequence, the officers insisted on a number of expensive changes, such as co-acting detonators at the section signals, and this led to the experiment being abandoned as uneconomic.

RIGHT: The CTC planning paper for Dulverton, dated 7th March 1938.

BELOW LEFT: The CTC panel for Barnstaple.

BELOW RIGHT: The panel for Dulverton and Morebath Junction.

All Mike Christensen collection

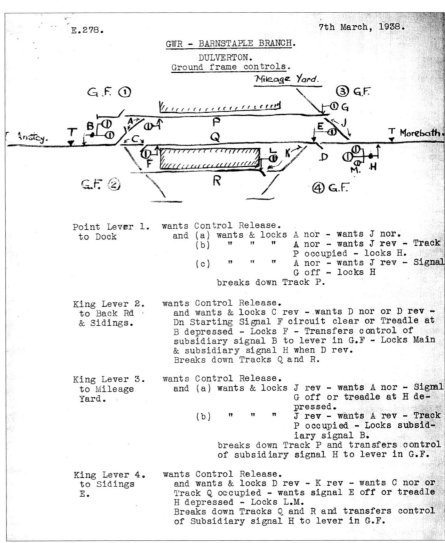

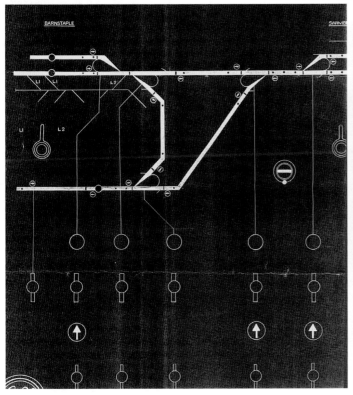

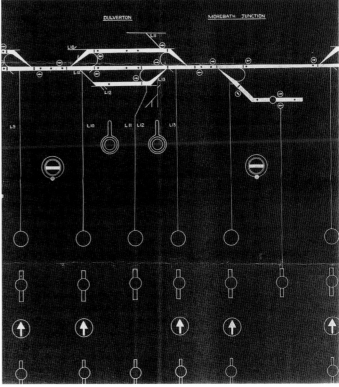

This all led towards the 1937 changes carried out on the D&SR, whereby the line from Norton Fitzwarren to Milverton was doubled (opened on 7th February) and the rest of the single line returned to the use of token exchangers, with focus and energy being applied to making the system work. One change was to the design of the hoop on the token pouch; the traditional shape was circular but it was changed to one with a straight bar across the top, which could then attach to the 'wishbone' style arms that extended out of the pouch. This was to overcome a previous operational problem, in that if the locomotive was rocking from side to side, a successful exchange could still be effected. With the new system and apparatus, exchange of tokens could technically happen at speeds of up to 40mph.

On 1st May 1938, a notice was issued jointly by R.W. Higgins, the Divisional Superintendent, and A.W.H. Christison, the Locomotive Superintendent, showing that installation of the apparatus had been completed at all through stations on both the Barnstaple and Minehead branches.

This resulted to a change to the *1938 Summer Time Table* to show a reduction in running times, including non-stop trains (*to be discussed in Vol. 3*). At this point, the heavier tender engines used on the Barnstaple and Minehead branches were beginning to be fitted with the exchange apparatus. These included 'Bulldogs' No's 3443 *Chaffinch* and 4117, 'Mogul' No. 6364, and then others such as No. 7304 and, subsequently, No. 7314. Although the costs of installation remained an issue, Collett Class '22XX' 0-6-0s No's 2211, 2212, 2213 and 2214 were also so fitted in 1940.

Detail of Whitaker token catching apparatus mounted on a locomotive tender, showing the 'jaws'. *Roger Carpenter collection*

WHITAKER APPARATUS

As mentioned above, Whitaker apparatus was adopted on the line from 1938, the whole purpose being to facilitate faster running, with token exchange happening at up to 40mph rather than manual exchanges at the reduced speeds of 5 to 10mph. The system required a special catcher on the left side of the locomotive, such as a 'Prairie' tank, or on the tender in the case of a 'Mogul' or Collett 0-6-0. There were specific rail-side posts with receiving and delivery equipment on the top. Alfred Whitaker had developed the apparatus whilst Locomotive Superintendent of the Somerset & Dorset Joint Railway, and it had been trialled on that line and used successfully since about 1905.

The GWR's policy was to set the rail-side apparatus at a distance from the platforms. This was so the locomotive did not have to run through the platform with the catcher jaws out or to avoid the possibility of a pouch from a missed exchange bouncing along and injuring passengers. The distance of the apparatus from the signal box meant a walk for the signalman. He was then supposed to return to his box after setting the token apparatus to pull off the Distant signal, as this was not to be done before the token had been set up, and then come back to collect the incoming token from its pouch after the train had passed; a lot of walking for the signalman unless he could delegate the task to a junior porter. The pouch was made of leather, with a small hoop at the top to facilitate its pick up/collection. They were complicated and expensive to make, and had a short service-life due to wear and tear or loss.

The token receiving and delivery apparatus was set on a cast-iron post located near the running line. Where the lineside equipment was for jointly receiving and delivering the token, the receiving jaws were set as the top arm. Below this was the

ELECTRIC TOKEN EXCHANGING APPARATUS

Signal Box	Direction	Position of — Setting Down Post	Position of — Picking Up Post
Milverton	Up	,, ,, ,,	90 yards Taunton side of Signal Box (Setting down only)
,,	Down	,, ,, ,,	90 yards Taunton side of Signal Box (Picking up only)
Wiveliscombe	Up	,, ,, ,,	168 yards Taunton side of Signal Box
,,	Down	,, ,, ,,	75 ,, ,, ,, ,, ,,
Venn Cross	Up	,, ,, ,,	115 yards Barnstaple side of Signal Box
,,	Down	,, ,, ,,	120 ,, ,, ,, ,, ,,
Morebath	Up	,, ,, ,,	111 ,, ,, ,, ,, ,,
,,	Down	,, ,, ,,	120 ,, ,, ,, ,, ,,
Morebath Jn.	*Up	,, ,, ,,	9 yards Taunton side of Signal Box
,, ,,	*Down	,, ,, ,,	16 ,, ,, ,, ,, ,,
,, ,,	†Up	Opposite Signal Box	Opposite Signal Box
,, ,,	†Down	,, ,, ,,	,, ,, ,,
Dulverton	*Up	Automatic Token Exchange	65 yards Taunton side of Signal Box
,, ,,	*Down	,, ,, ,,	157 ,, ,, ,, ,, ,,
,, ,,	†Up	Taunton end of Platform	Taunton end of Platform
,, ,,	†Down	,, ,, ,,	,, ,, ,,
East Anstey	Up	Automatic Token Exchange	76 yards Barnstaple side of Signal Box
,,	Down	,, ,, ,,	79 ,, ,, ,, ,, ,,
Bishops Nympton & Molland	Up	,, ,, ,,	76 yards Taunton side of Signal Box
	Down	,, ,, ,,	76 ,, ,, ,, ,, ,,
South Molton	Up	,, ,, ,,	152 ,, ,, ,, ,, ,,
,,	Down	,, ,, ,,	150 ,, ,, ,, ,, ,,
Filleigh	Up	,, ,, ,,	59 yards Barnstaple side of Signal Box
,,	Down	,, ,, ,,	64 ,, ,, ,, ,, ,,
Swimbridge	Up	,, ,, ,,	176 yards Taunton side of Signal Box
,,	Down	,, ,, ,,	145 ,, ,, ,, ,, ,,
Bampton	Up		Exeter end of Platform
Tiverton	Down	Bampton side of Signal Box	Exeter end of Signal Box
Stoke Canon Jn.	Down	Opposite Signal Box	
,,	Up		Opposite Signal Box
Newton Abbot East	Up	Opposite Signal Box for Down Through, Main and Relief Lines	
Goodrington	Up	North side of Signal Box	
,,	Down		Opposite Signal Box.

*For Barnstaple Branch Trains.   † For Exe Valley Branch Trains.

ABOVE: The location of automatic token exchange apparatus on the D&SR, from the *GWR General Rule Book*.

RIGHT: The token for the Dulverton-East Anstey section in its leather pouch. Note the slightly bent hoop, so designed to facilitate receiving and delivery from the ground mounted token apparatus. *Amyas Crump collection*

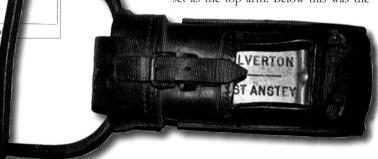

ABOVE: A view of the double track section on the approach to Milverton station, taken after closure with condemned wagons stored alongside the Down platform. In the left foreground is the Down line delivery apparatus, whilst the Up line set-down/receiving apparatus can be seen on the right at. *G.H. Tilt, courtesy Mike Christensen*

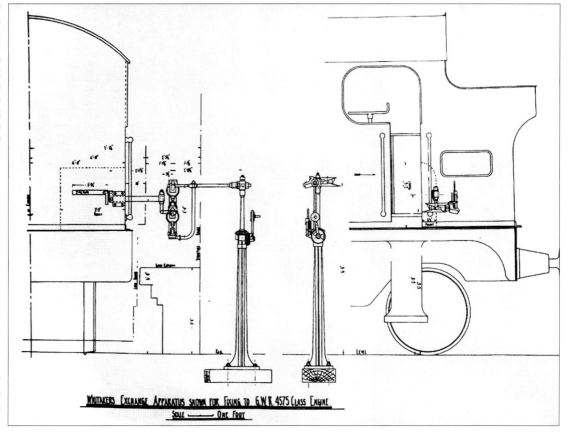

WHITAKERS EXCHANGE APPARATUS SHOWN FOR FIXING TO G.W.R. 4575 CLASS ENGINE

SCALE ——— ONE FOOT

RIGHT: Diagram of Whitaker token exchange apparatus from the front and the side. *Courtesy Mike Christensen*

Right: Token apparatus fixed to the side of 'Prairie' tank No. 5537. This was one of the first batch of locomotives to be fitted with it, on 11th July 1933. *R. Buckley*

Below: A close up of one of the automatic token exchange posts at Wiveliscombe. The receiving 'jaws' are mounted at the top, above the delivery 'ears' which are below. *G.H. Tilt, courtesy Mike Christensen*

Below this was the horizontal arm, on which were mounted spring loaded 'ears' that held the outgoing token pouch for the forward section, until the moment of exchange. When not in use for token exchange, the receiving and delivery apparatus was kept with the arms parallel to the running line (and padlocked in that position when the signalman was off duty). To set the arm at right angles to the track ready for an exchange, the signalman lifted the catch mounted on the post and swung the balance lever carrying the counterweight upwards and over the centre; the weight then fell slightly down and held the jaws in position until the moment of exchange. This setting of the apparatus was facilitated by a pair of bevel gear wheels and a weighted lever. The impact of the incoming pouch hitting the receiving jaws was sufficient to bring the balance weight back over the top of dead centre and the weight itself then operated to swing the exchanging arm, jaws and receiving pouch back parallel to the running line.

At Milverton on the double track section to the east of the station, full receiving and delivering apparatus was not required on both sides of the line. Accordingly, the line-side equipment delivered on the Down line, ahead of the platform, and received on the Up line.

In order to make the exchange, the token carried on the footplate would be placed on the delivery clip, which was mounted immediately behind the receiver jaw, with the metal hoop at the top. The jaws fitted to the locomotives were cast originally in brass or gun-metal and later aluminium alloy and comprised three spring-controlled fingers, with a rubber buffer at the inner end of the fork, together with a 4 inch by $1^1/2$ inch soft rubber pad on the underside and to the rear of the jaw, to cushion the blow

A Down train hauled by No. 6390 about to pass over the points at Morebath Junction on 30th August 1961. The fireman is leaning on the cabside watching the token exchange, which appears to have just taken place, whilst an interested passenger also watches from the first window of the front carriage.
Michael J. Fox, courtesy Rail Archive Stephenson

from the pouch as it swung back once collected. The receiver on the ground (the top arm) was similarly structured.

As a train passed the ground apparatus (receiving arm), the jaws located on the top arm would collect the token from the locomotive or tender, by hooking on to the metal hoop at the top of the pouch. At the same time, the jaws on the locomotive's apparatus would grab the metal hoop of the token for the next section, which had been placed on the lower arm (the delivery arm) of the ground apparatus by the signalman.

Finally, the maximum speeds that were relevant from 1939 (as laid out in the service time table), after the line had been upgraded with longer loops and greater radius points, and the provision of Whitaker Apparatus, are shown in Appendix 9.

OTHER TOKEN EXCHANGE APPARATUS

Where an exchange was to be undertaken but without use of Whitaker apparatus, the signalman would often attach the token to a metal hooped-frame. Initially, these were with a leather pouch at the base to house the key but, subsequently, a metal housing was developed to provide extra support to mitigate damage to the token itself. These large hooped token carriers also had ground-mounted exchangers, being of a simpler design than those required for fast exchange. The photographs on the following two pages illustrate earlier and later methods of picking up and setting down the hooped token carrier.

LEFT: The token for an Exe Valley line train, for the first section of its journey from Dulverton to Morebath Junction (along the D&SR) in its hoop.
Amyas Crump collection

BELOW: A painted but worn aluminium electric train token for the Dulverton to East Anstey section. *Author*

A token exchange at Dulverton in the 1920s, showing the old style, ground-mounted exchange post on the Down line. Close study reveals that the staff hoop (with the staff attached) is hanging from the setting down arm, having just been deposited by the fireman of the Down train. The signalman waits, standing clear to recover the staff from the setting down 'horn'. Note the 'SPEED NOT TO EXCEED 15 MILES PER HOUR' notice at the top of the post. An Exe Valley line train waits in the bay on the left. *E. Wallis Collection, courtesy Kevin Robertson*

ABOVE: A view of the Exe Valley token exchange apparatus at Morebath Junction in use. The token is fixed at the base of the hoop, the shape of which made it easy for the fireman to collect. The rear of the delivery apparatus was spring-loaded and opened in the direction of travel of the train, thus releasing the token hoop. The rails at right angles to the running line behind were for placing the ganger's pw trolley on the track, which was housed in shed in the right foreground.
Courtesy Tiverton Museum

ABOVE RIGHT: The Exe Valley line token catcher at Dulverton. The hook was used by the fireman to place the hoop and token on just ahead of the train arriving in the platform. In the background is the Up line Whitaker ground apparatus for the D&SR.
Hugh Davies collection

RIGHT: Diagram of ETT picking up and setting down posts, from *GWR Regulations for Train Signalling on Double and Single Lines* (1936).

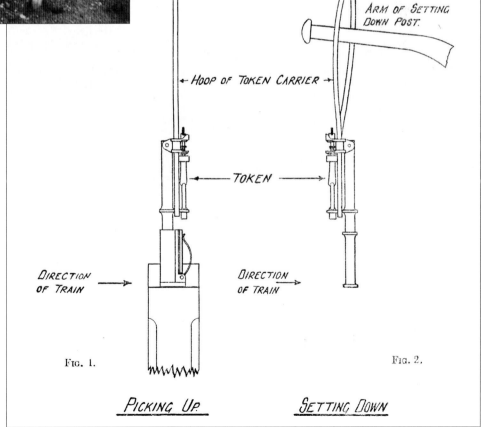

SIGNALMAN'S PAY AND SIGNAL BOX CLASSIFICATION ON THE D&SR

In 1922, a new system of classifying signal boxes was introduced. Previously, the GWR had classified lines according to the traffic handled and graded signal boxes on those lines accordingly. The new system graded boxes on work performed, marks being give for each operation performed by the signalman. For example, one mark was given for pulling or pushing a lever, or for opening or closing gates, whilst half a mark was awarded for pressing a release plunger and so on. As an aside, it was a system where it was clearly in the signalmen's interest to be as 'busy' as possible, and this sometimes led to slight abuse of the system.

The table below summarises the classification of the station signal boxes on the line along with the average number of marks per hour in both 1923 and 1925, showing how some of the boxes had been deemed to be busier than two years earlier.

The bottom table shows the grading bands and the relevant pay scales. This grading lasted for fifty years.

SIGNAL BOX LEVERS – COLOUR CODES	
SIGNAL	OPERATING COLOUR
Distant Signal*	Yellow*
Stop Signal	Red
Ground Signal	Red
Calling-on Signal	Red
Points	Black
Facing Point Lock	Blue
Detonators	Black and White chevrons, pointing up the lever for Up line detonators and down the lever for Down line detonators

* Prior to the change in the colour of the Distant signal arm from red to yellow in the 1920s the Distant lever arm was green.

SIGNAL BOX	1923		1925	
	CLASS	AV. MARKS	CLASS	AV. MARKS
Milverton	5	44	5	59
Wiveliscombe	5	54	4	72
Venn Cross	5	45	5	69
Morebath	5	36	5	36
Dulverton	4	206	3	206
East Anstey	5	41	5	55
Bishops Nympton & Molland	5	48	5	48
South Molton	5	40	5	70
Filleigh	5	37	5	37
Swimbridge	5	40	5	40
Barnstaple	4	109	4	109
East Junction	Summer posts			
South Junction	Summer posts			

SIGNALMAN'S PAY IN 1922		
CLASS	AV. NO. OF MARKS	STANDARD PAY RATE PER WEEK
Special	375 upwards	75/-
1	300-374	70/-
2	225-299	65/-
3	150-224	60/-
4	75-149	55/-
5	30-74	50/-
6	1-29	48/-

Signal box key and brass plates believed to be from Swimbridge box. The top number determined the signal or point that the lever controlled, whilst the lower numbers were the interlocked levers which needed to be pulled first. The right-hand plate No. 18 covered the goods loop headshunt point at the Up end of the platform, No. 16 was the trap point at the exit to the loop and No's 11 and 12 operated the Up facing points into the goods loop. No. 9 operated the shunt signal by point No. 12. *Author*

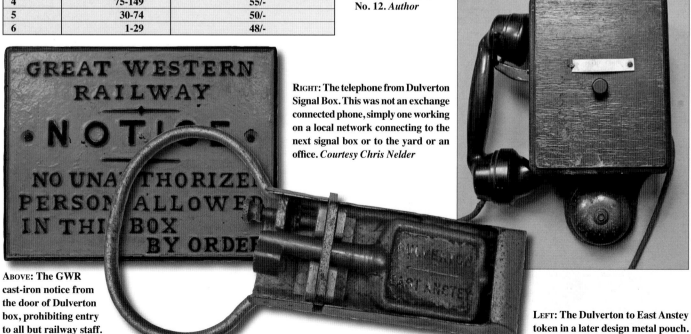

ABOVE: The GWR cast-iron notice from the door of Dulverton box, prohibiting entry to all but railway staff. *Courtesy Chris Nelder*

RIGHT: The telephone from Dulverton Signal Box. This was not an exchange connected phone, simply one working on a local network connecting to the next signal box or to the yard or an office. *Courtesy Chris Nelder*

LEFT: The Dulverton to East Anstey token in a later design metal pouch. *Mike Christensen collection*

COMMUNICATION ON THE LINE

Little has been established on telephone communication between stations. Some of the telegraph poles between stations show a maximum of nine wires. The token and ganger's keys would each have one wire (with earth return), which would leave seven wires for telephone lines (the seventh may have been for the ganger's telephone). The token line was usually the 'saddle' wire on top of the poles, so that no other sagging wire could make contact with it. The pole arms were located on the Up (London) side of the post, with each telephone circuit on adjacent wires on the arm and these crossed every quarter of a mile to reduce cross-talk from the other circuits.

Taunton was directly connected to Dulverton, the office telephone number being 174, the signal box being 175. The other stations were connected by switch to Barnstaple and there were individual circuits between neighbouring signal boxes.

RELEVANT LOCATION	NUMBER
Barnstaple office	199
East Junction box	195
Barnstaple goods	198
Barnstaple loco	197
Barnstaple Parcels	200
Barnstaple South box	196
Bishops Nympton box..	191
East Anstey box	190
Filleigh office	193
South Molton box..	192
Swimbridge box	194
Milverton box..	169
Morebath box..	172
Morebath Junction box.	173
Norton box	140
Venn Cross box	171
Wiveliscombe box..	170

The following telephone numbers were allocated to stations, signal boxes, goods yards and receiving offices in 1911. These were all 2-button telephones:

STATION	SERIAL NO.
Milverton..	1593
Wiveliscombe..	1594
Venn Cross	1595
Morebath..	1596
Morebath Junction Signal Box	1597
Dulverton.	1598
East Anstey.	1599
Bishops Nympton & Molland	1600
South Molton..	1601
Filleigh	1602
Swimbridge	1603
Barnstaple East Junction	1604
Barnstaple South Junction	1605
Barnstaple Victoria Road Station . ..	1608
Barnstaple Junction	1606
Engine shed.	1607

The station telephone numbers in 1930 were noted as follows; these are believed to be the General Post Office (GPO) telephone numbers, not the internal railway ones:

STATION	TELEPHONE NO.
Wiveliscombe..	Wiveliscombe 22
Venn Cross	Venn Cross 1
Morebath	Bampton 39
Dulverton.	Dulverton 27
South Molton..	South Molton 18

At this time there was no telephone at Milverton, East Anstey, Bishops Nympton & Molland or Swimbridge. Blue enamelled signs advised the general public that they could make calls from stations which had telephones.

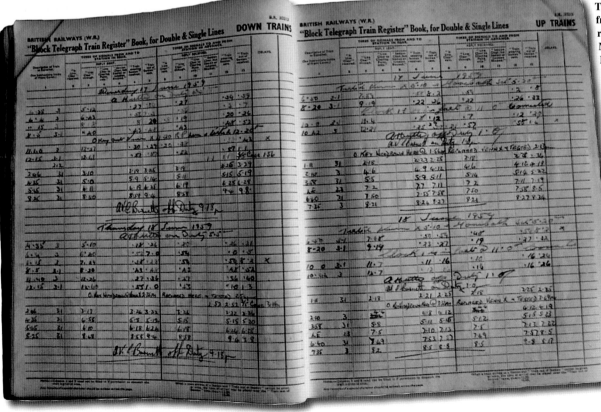

Two sample pages from the train registers for Morebath Signal Box, of which the books for 13th March 1959 to 29th October 1959 and 30th October 1959 to 21st June 1960 are known to survive. They are discussed in more detail overleaf and these pages are for Down and Up trains on 17th June 1959. *Charlie Fennemore collection*

Morebath Signal Box Train Registers 1959-60

The main regular signalmen at Morebath at this time were Messrs A.V.C. Burnett, A. Hutton and D.E. Lock. There was a regular checking of the accuracy of the signal box clock at 11.00am, adjustment being made when necessary. The ganger would occupy the section of the line on a regular basis to carry out his duties (bell code 2-1-2). The Down pick-up goods to Dulverton would on occasion shunt the yard and recess there to allow other (passenger) trains to continue. This was not a daily occurrence in this period. No Up goods was indicated as shunting the yard, which is not surprising given its location on the Down side. It therefore must be presumed that any goods outward wagons were attached to a Down goods, for working back east later on. There were from time to time additional Down through goods laid on and the engine would often return later in the day 'light' (LE bell code 2-3), or with only a brake van attached (EBV bell code 1-1-3). There would be the occasional Sunday working, such as a Down and Up ballast, for example. The signal box would have to open specifically for this and be staffed by one of the regular signalmen. One such example was on 7th June 1959, with a permanent way train (bell code 3) which came into the section at 9.17am and cleared at 9.22am. This worked back getting 'line clear' at 12.39pm. Also, on Thursday 21st April 1960, the register is annotated with 'C Spl', bell code 3. Although this was not given a livestock bell code it is believed to be a special for cattle. The Down working was at 1.47pm (train entering section) and the return working was 7.34pm (ditto). Tuesday 22nd December had a ballast train (bell code 3) recorded as getting line clear from Venn Cross at 9.37am and with bell code 2-2-3 was required to stop in the section, which it did and the line clear from Morebath Junction box was received at 10.12am. On Saturday 7th November 1959, there was a 3-1 Special passenger that passed through the Morebath section at around 11.13pm. There was an empty coaching stock return (bell code 2-2-1) passing through at circa 12.14am. This meant signalman Burnett signed off at 12.32am on 10th November, after signing on at noon on 9th! His signature that night compared to his normal signing indicates he was not best pleased with this timing. Indeed, on Monday 9th November, he signed on at 5.05am to start the morning shifts that week, not much of a break for him but it showed the dedication which was required for the job.

On ordinary weekday/Saturday mornings, the signalman would clock on around 5.05am (in good time ahead of the 4.35am off Taunton, the Down Bristol goods) and work until 1.00pm for the first shift. The second shift was from 1.00pm until 9.20/9.40 pm (flexible times), depending on what time the 7.35pm Up Bristol goods passed though, after which the signalman would carry out certain duties in the box before departing home. If signalman A worked the first shift in week 1, they would change over for week 2 (the free Sunday giving the opportunity to do this), with signalman B working the early shift in week 2. The first shift signalman would normally deal with four Down goods (the last of which might lay up in the yard) and three Down passenger trains. This would be counter-balanced by three Up passenger trains and one Up goods. The 12.25pm ex-Taunton passenger would often pass through the Morebath section during the shift change-over. The second shift signalman would handle three Up goods and three Up passenger, along with three Down passenger trains. If the 11.40 ex-Taunton Down goods was detained in the yard, this would usually follow the 12.25pm ex-Taunton passenger once it had cleared the section to Morebath Junction (usually around 1.15pm)

Summer Saturdays were more intense. Taking 25th July 1959 by way of example, there were fifteen Down trains (five fast passenger

services, bell code 4; eight ordinary passenger trains, bell code 3-1; and two goods, bell code 3). In the Up direction there were also fifteen trains (three fast passenger, bell code 4; ten ordinary passenger, bell code 3-1; one goods, bell code 3; and one EBV, bell code 2-3 – this being *in lieu* of the Up Bristol goods that night). With extended hours the signalmen's shifts were broadly as follows. A.V.C. Burnett on duty at 4.30am, off duty at 12 noon. A. Hutton on at noon and clocked off that night at 10.46pm – a 10 hour 46 minute shift. However, weekdays did not always have reliable shift times. On Tuesday 26th April 1960, the Up Bristol goods was running exceptionally late. The 7.35pm ex-Barnstaple Victoria Road normally passed Morebath at 8.30/9pm but on this night it entered the section at about 11.15pm and was out of the Venn Cross section at 11.30pm. This meant Mr Hutton, who was signalman on duty then, did his shift from 1pm to 11.40pm a total of 10 hours and 40 minutes. In the last three hours and 40 minutes, only one Up and one Down passenger train passed through his section, along with a light engine at circa 9.45pm and of course the Bristol goods.

There was the occasional hiccup. For example, on Wednesday 20th April 1960 D.E. Lock noted '*Sheep reported on the line by the down distant 6.55am*'. The 6.15am ex-Taunton goods ran through soon after (getting 'line clear' at 7.02am from Venn Cross and entering the section at 7.14am), no doubt having been warned by the Venn Cross signalman of the presence of the livestock and to proceed with caution. The register also records a trolley at 7.37am and this may have been despatched after the goods to remove the sheep and repair any fencing. On Friday 3rd June 1960, Mr Burnett recorded '*unable to pull point No. 10 rectified @ 7.30pm*'. This meant that the 3.58pm ex-Barnstaple was noted as '*away from wrong road*' – No. 10 was a trap point on the Up loop (*see page 419*) – so the Up train had a rare opportunity to use the Down line. Friday 25th March 1960 recorded '*BV*' with bell code 4 down at around 5.17pm. There was a return working at 10.18pm (bell code 3-1). It is speculation but this may have been a breakdown train, perhaps dealing with the derailment of 'Mogul' No. 6323 at Dulverton on an Up goods. Both the Up passenger trains from Barnstaple (the 3.58pm and 6.40pm) were delayed (passing through at around 6.33pm, over 1 hour 15 minutes later than normal, and 8.14pm, about 15 minutes later than normal, respectively). The 7.35pm Up Bristol goods went through at about 11.07pm, giving another late night to Mr Burnett who was on duty from 1.00pm to 11.30pm.

Monday 16th May 1960 saw some trolley activity (bell code 2-1-2), as summarised from the register below. This was in the Up direction and the times from and to Morebath Junction Signal Box, the block post in the rear, are recorded:

Description of train as signalled	Line clear through	Section clear but section or junction blocked	Train entering section received	Train out of section sent
TR 2-1-2		8.22	8.22	8.32
8.20am ex-Taunton 3-1	9.15		9.22	9.26
TR 2-1-2		10.31	10.31	10.39
10am ex-Taunton 3-1	11.09		11.11	11.15
TR 2-1-2		11.15	11.15	11.43
10.25 ex-Taunton 3 (goods)	12.14		12.19	12.24

This summary gives a flavour of what passed along the line in the late 1950s from the signalman's perspective. Paassenger and goods services from 1871 to 1966 will be comprehensively reviewed in Volume 3.

APPENDIX 8
BARNSTAPLE BRANCH GRADIENT PROFILE

The gradient profile for the D&SR line or Barnstaple Branch is presented on the end papers, whilst the *1893 Service Time Table* summarised the inclines on the route succinctly in a table that is reconstituted below.

STATION TO STATION	GRADIENT	RISE/FALL
Norton Fitzwarren-Milverton	1 in 66	Rise
Milverton-Wiveliscombe	1 in 60	Rise
Wiveliscombe-Venn Cross	1 in 58.1	Rise
Venn Cross-Morebath	1 in 60	Fall
Morebath-Morebath Junction	1 in 100	Rise
Morebath Junction-Dulverton	1 in 58	Fall
Dulverton-East Anstey	1 in 58.1	Rise
East Anstey-Molland	1 mile 1 in 58.5	Fall
East Anstey-Molland	3/4 mile 1 in 70	Fall
East Anstey-Molland	1/2 mile 1 in 184	Fall
Molland-South Molton	1 in 66	Fall
South Molton-Filleigh	1 in 60	Rise
Filleigh-Swimbridge	1 in 60	Fall
Swimbridge-Barnstaple GWR	1 in 60	Fall
Barnstaple GWR*-Barnstaple L&SWR*	1 in 70	Fall
* Barnstaple Junction Railway		

As a result of the gradient profile of the line, there were many special instructions and speed restrictions applying to it.

In the *1886 Service Time Table* there was a stipulation that no train or engine must run past any facing point at a greater speed than 10mph. When running down inclines the speed must not exceed 30mph for passenger trains and 15mph for goods trains. The guard in charge of every train when he may have had the occasion to shunt vehicles on or near an incline was strictly ordered not to allow the engine to be uncoupled until he had securely put on the brake and safely spragged the last vehicle, and he was not to commence his journey without a supply of sprags in his van for this purpose. Great care had to be taken to remove the sprag from the wheel before starting. The speed of all trains passing over Castle Hill Viaduct and the Tone Viaduct was not to exceed 15mph. Furthermore, all trains not advertised to stop at staff stations and junctions had to stop dead at those stations to admit the exchange of the train tickets and staff [*i.e.* token]. Catch points were situated at this time at East Anstey, on the Up line 178 yards west of East Anstey Signal Box.

APPENDIX 9
MAXIMUM SPEEDS OF TRAINS THROUGH JUNCTIONS ETC

The following summary has been extracted and retabulated from the *1939 Service Time Table* but it broadly reflects the limits in place for the remainder of the life of the line.

The speed of Up and Down trains anywhere on the Barnstaple Branch was not to exceed 60mph and was then further restricted to the lower speeds as shown in the table, right. Also, the speed of trains was not to exceed 40mph when exchanging tokens by the automatic apparatus.

LOCATION	INSTRUCTION	MPH
Norton Fitzwarren	Through connections between main line and branch	40
MP169 and Milverton Stn	All Up and Down trains	55
Milverton to River Tone viaduct 175 miles and 76ch	All Down trains	45
Milverton to River Tone viaduct 175 miles and 76ch	All Up trains over junction to double line	40
Wiveliscombe to Milverton double line junction	All Up trains	45
Wiveliscombe	All Up trains entering or leaving station loop	15
Venn Cross and Wiveliscombe	All Up trains between Tone viaduct and Wiveliscombe	45
	All Up and Down trains over Tone viaduct 175 miles and 76ch and 176 miles 7ch	*25
Tone viaduct and Venn Cross	All Up and Down trains	55
Venn Cross	All Up trains entering or leaving station loop	40
Morebath	All Up trains entering or leaving station loop	40
Morebath Junction	All Down trains between station and 182 miles 50ch	40
Morebath Junction	All Up trains entering or leaving station loop	40
Morebath Junction and Dulverton	All Down trains between 182 miles and 50ch and Dulverton Station	50
	All Up trains between Dulverton and Morebath Junction	50
Dulverton 183 miles 53ch	All Up and Down trains over River Exe Bridge	*25
Dulverton	All Up and Down trains through station loop	40
Dulverton	All Up trains entering bay line Down side	5
Dulverton and East Anstey	All Up and Down trains between 184 1/4 mp and 185mp	50
	All Up and Down trains between 185 mp and East Anstey station	55
East Anstey	All Up trains entering or leaving station loop	40
Bishops Nympton & Molland	All Up and Down trains entering or leaving station loop	40
South Molton	All Up and Down trains entering or leaving station loop	40
South Molton and Filleigh	All Up and Down trains between 198 1/2 mp and Castle Hill viaduct	50
	All Up and Down trains over Castle Hill viaduct 199 miles 72ch and 200 miles 9ch	*25
Filleigh	All Up and Down trains entering or leaving station loop	40
Filleigh and Swimbridge	All Up and Down trains between 203 1/2 mp and Swimbridge station	50
Swimbridge	All Up trains entering or leaving station loop	40
Barnstaple	All Up and Down trains between East and South Junction boxes over direct loop	15
Barnstaple GW and South Junctn	All Up and Down trains over loop	10
Barnstaple South Junction and River Taw bridge 209 miles 5ch	All Up and Down trains	40
River Taw bridge 209 miles 5ch and Southern Railway Junction Station	All Up and Down trains	30
* note those speeds are reduced to 15 miles per hour for engines of 2-6-0 'M' Class only		

APPENDIX 10
SUMMARY OF TRAFFIC DEALT WITH AT STATIONS – PASSENGERS

PASSENGER TRAFFIC TOTALS 1903-1938

Year	Payroll cost £ (& staff no's)		Total Receipts £	Tickets issued (season tickets)		Passenger receipts £	Parcel no's	Parcels receipts £	Total passenger & parcels receipts £
1903	4,559	(90)	69,099	152,374	(A)	17,214	108,017	10,688	27,902
1913	4,849	(69)	76,352	132,416	(A)	17,735	129,751	9,717	27,452
1923	12,865	(81)	126,357	143,863	(353)	29,042	127,178	10,849	39,891
1924	12,115	(81)	124,030	134,126	(286)	28,111	A	10,243	38,354
1925	12,534	(81)	129,652	132,261	(270)	27,832	A	9,867	37,699
1926	11,617	(84)	124,357	114,329	(243)	26,679	A	11,949	38,628
1927	12,316	(83)	130,507	112,855	(235)	26,193	A	11,447	37,640
1928	12,499	(86)	133,842	112,844	(270)	25,706	A	11,250	36,956
1929	13,345	(87)	135,770	107,783	(288)	24,884	123,962	10,899	35,783
1930	13,225	(89)	128,634	96,752	(347)	23,279	123,790	10,697	33,976
1931	13,160	(90)	120,476	91,132	(325)	20,987	121,370	9,451	30,438
1932	12,652	(88)	107,000	85,995	(311)	19,266	118,820	8,202	27,468
1933	13,374	(87)	103,830	81,124	(381)	18,566	128,137	8,004	26,570
1934	13,575	(87)	106,376	78,653	(366)	17,865	129,236	8,026	25,891
1935	15,203	(92)	109,930	77,903	(365)	17,926	131,913	5,125	23,051
1936	15,123	(94)	113,303	74,559	(419)	17,979	135,025	4,978	22,957
1937	15,957	(93)	108,317	72,883	(570)	18,642	132,229	4,484	23,126
1938	15,613	(92)	101,628	66,419	(565)	17,742	127,569	4,086	21,828

A – Not recorded

REVIEW OF THE PERIOD 1923-1938

The table above shows the passenger traffic, parcels and staff totals for the whole of the D&SR line for the period 1923 to 1938, with 1903 and 1913 added for comparison.

In 1936, ninety-four staff were employed at a total cost of £15,123. However, the wages cost for 1937, when staff totalled ninety-three, was the highest at £15,957, with employees earning an average of £171. The differential from 1903, when wages totalled £4,559, to 1923 when the figure had increased to £12, 865 but with fewer staff (ninety as against eighty-one) was over 300%. Wages in 1903 were about 6.5% of total receipts, increasing to about 10% in the period 1923 to 1930, at which point total receipts started to decline from their peak in 1929 at £135,770, such that in 1938 wages were around 15% of total receipts.

Total receipts climbed from £69,099 to a 1929 peak of £135,770, broadly declining then to £101,628 in 1938.

Tickets peaked at 152,374 issued in 1903 and there was then a steady decline from this figure over the period reviewed (with occasional up-turns) to 66,419 in 1938, a dramatic decline influenced first by the increase in motor bus competition and then the rise of the motor car. This of course did not include through traffic starting off the branch.

Passenger and parcels receipts in 1903 were 40% of the total revenue but by 1938 this had declined to 21.6%, so goods revenues were providing a significant contribution to the line. The highest passenger revenues of £39,891 were in 1923.

REVIEW OF THE PERIOD 1939-1959

In this period, intermediate stations had the years 1940, 1945, 1950, 1955 and 1958 recorded, whilst for Dulverton, South Molton and Barnstaple it was all years.

Staff numbers at most stations remained consistent throughout this period, the run down of the line having not yet begun. However, some station staff, such as those at East Anstey and Swimbridge, were consolidated into the Barnstaple numbers, so the total at that station reached fifty-eight. Payroll costs at Barnstaple peaked at £14,212 for forty-three employees in 1949, the last year for which records are available. All reporting at Barnstaple Victoria Road was transferred to the Southern Region with effect from 1st February 1958.

What is apparent is the substantial increase in wages from 1940 to 1945 and beyond, with a number of stations showing 25-75% increases in the war period. Taking Dulverton by way of example, in 1939 thirteen staff were paid £2,109 but, by 1945, the same number were paid £3,270 (a 55% increase) and £4,113 by 1949 – a 95% increase in the ten years during and after the war.

Ticket sales substantially increased at all stations during the 1940-1945 period, with 1944 the year that most stations recorded their highest passenger numbers: Dulverton 28,296, South Molton 16,100 and Barnstaple 19,548. Most stations then showed a dramatic decline over the next fifteen years: Dulverton 15,314 tickets issued in 1959, South Molton 4,450 in 1959 and Barnstaple 12,925 in 1957. However Barnstaple's numbers had improved from a post-war low of 9,301 in 1951, whilst tickets issued at Milverton and Wiveliscombe showed an upturn towards the end of the 1950s. It might be speculated that the car was having a more dramatic impact on passengers travelling the line but perhaps the up-turn reflected a movement of workers travelling to Taunton on a regular basis.

Passenger and parcels receipts not surprisingly mirrored ticket sales. However, Venn Cross dealt with £1,128 and 1,171 worth of parcels in 1950 and 1951 respectively, these two years providing an isolated peak of receipts there. Parcels receipts at Victoria Road in 1952 peaked at £7,183 which despite a reduction in ticket sales and their revenue, gave that station its best year with passenger and parcels receipts totalling £15,938. In this year, 82,236 parcels were forwarded and 54,441 received (136,677 in total).

Milk traffic was also recorded for some stations in some years, the amounts being included in miscellaneous forwarded in the parcels numbers in the overall summaries. Extracts are isolated here for Wiveliscombe and Dulverton (non-railborne figures are ignored).

WIVELISCOMBE

YEAR	GALLONS	CANS	£
1947	2,750	411	42
1948	8,748	1,202	A
1949	9,511	1,324	A
1950	11,478	1,475	A
1951	9,921	1,435	A
1952	2,279	336	A

A – Not recorded

DULVERTON

YEAR	GALLONS	CANS	CASES	£
1947	4,237	569	0	78
1948	13,021	1,541	0	191
1949	12,494	1,396	0	171
1950	12,050	1,395	0	197
1951	15,789	1,753	0	306
1952	16,226	1,877	0	356
1953	21,017	2,333	5	481
1954	9,147	1,050	4	225

APPENDIX 11
SUMMARY OF TRAFFIC DEALT WITH AT STATIONS – GOODS

GOODS TRAFFIC TOTALS 1903-1938											
Year	Coal/Coke charged/ forwarded (tons)	Other minerals (tons)	General merchandise forwarded (tons)	Coal/Coke charged/ received (tons)	Other minerals received (tons)	General merchandise received (tons)	Coal/Coke not charged forwarded/ received (tons)	Total goods tonnage	Total receipts (excl. not charged) £	Livestock wagons forwarded/ received	Total carted tonnage (incl. total goods tonnage)
1903	49	2,651	16,509	6,817	16,647	39,431	9,657	91,761	41,197	2,588	13,174
1913	73	2,651	17,603	7,436	17,337	43,418	10,693	99,211	48,900	2,952	15,176
1923	45	681	14,653	3,691	18,194	46,768	16,317	100,349	86,468	2,585	14,711
1924	112	726	13,850	3,826	21,936	51,687	17,320	109,457	85,676	2,944	15,429
1925	87	809	15,437	3,483	28,603	53,519	16,267	118,205	91,953	3,004	15,978
1926	135	1,633	14,410	3,169	22,586	51,371	12,187	105,491	85,729	3,034	14,910
1927	122	2,079	14,579	2,899	22,608	51,369	18,099	111,755	92,867	3,062	16,016
1928	160	1,326	17,742	3,027	18,333	53,813	16,225	110,626	96,886	3,216	16,259
1929	154	2,469	18,353	2,705	16,100	57,067	18,860	115,708	99,987	3,220	17,598
1930	131	2,400	13,771	2,643	19,159	54,023	18,913	111,040	94,658	3,342	16,459
1931	105	837	10,942	2,682	17,638	56,119	18,766	107,089	90,038	3,013	15,697
1932	114	1,463	9,679	3,095	13,442	51,636	17,471	96,900	79,532	2,184	15,287
1933	43	2,064	10,789	3,157	13,605	50,553	14,838	95,049	77,260	1,614	24,134
1934	41	2,123	9,454	2,837	12,404	54,800	14,331	95,990	80,485	1,557	27,476
1935	107	2,393	10,427	3,254	11,686	60,338	15,236	103,441	86,879	1,836	34,920
1936	96	1,908	11,097	3,187	10,961	62,977	15,913	106,139	90,346	1,849	42,144
1937	73	2,136	10,597	2,853	8,679	58,007	17,032	99,377	85,191	1,436	41,559
1938	28	2,036	8,907	2,554	8,204	52,050	16,159	89,938	79,800	1,053	37,268

REVIEW OF THE PERIOD 1923-1938

A review of goods traffic on the D&SR for the period 1923 to 1938, with 1903 and 1913 added for comparison, shows that total tonnage increased from 91,761 in 1903 to a peak of 115,708 in 1929, then broadly declining to 89,938 in 1938. The greater proportion was general merchandise coming in, followed by coal and other minerals (in). General merchandise was the significant export with other minerals (not coal) trailing substantially below. Livestock wagons forwarded and received peaked in 1930 at 3,342 but by 1938 were only 1,053.

Of the individual stations, South Molton dealt with the largest goods tonnages, peaking in 1925 at 22,246 tons, being followed by Dulverton (18,998 tons in 1929) and Wiveliscombe (15,704 tons in 1903). More information is available in the tables in the individual station sections in chapters 6, 7 and 8.

REVIEW OF THE PERIOD 1939-1959

Numbers have been summarised separately for this period, partly because most of the intermediate stations have only the 1940 and 1945 numbers recorded for this period but also because from 1947 most had their figures zoned with the larger stations at each end of the line or on the Exe Valley Branch. Stations to Morebath were zoned with Taunton, Dulverton and East Anstey were zoned at Tiverton, and Bishops Nympton & Molland, Filleigh and Swimbridge were all zoned with Barnstaple. Dulverton, South Molton and Barnstaple, the main stations on the D&SR, had all their years recorded.

At Dulverton during this period, total tonnage peaked at 16,339 in 1944. The war years unsurprisingly produced a surge in traffic all along the line and Dulverton showed tonnages well in excess of 10,000 tons for the duration but then showed an almost immediate fall in 1947 to their lowest level of 9,064 tons. General merchandise forwarded was the greatest tonnage, peaking at 9,673 tons in 1944, with coal/coke received next at 4,053 tons in that year. The third

highest was general merchandise again, albeit at only 3,596 tons in 1946. Livestock wagons were down on those conveyed in the 1920s and early 1930s but exceeded 146 wagons for all of the years between 1939 and 1946.

At South Molton, total tonnage peaked at 29,580 in 1949, despite the 1947 and 1948 totals being only 11,081 and 14,171 tons respectively. The bulk of this high tonnage, which was also repeated in 1950 and 1951, was general merchandise received (11,876 tons in 1949), followed by coal/coke received (8,791 tons). General merchandise forwarded was 4,275 tons, an amount otherwise only surpassed in the 1942-1946 period. Minerals received were over 1,700 tons for all years but was at 4,194 tons in 1949. Livestock wagons were recorded at 626 in 1950, which numbers held up reasonably well, being over 350 for every year in the 1940 to 1954 period, with the exception of 1947 which had a low of 115 wagons.

At Barnstaple, goods tonnage peaked during the Second World War again, in 1944, with total goods amounting to 72,822 tons. General merchandise received at 49,553 formed the bulk of this, whilst general merchandise forwarded comprised 18,077 tons of the total. Other minerals received exceeded the tonnage of coal/coke received, at 2,685 and 1,690 tons respectively. From 1st November 1950, the Barnstaple Junction numbers were also included, so these are ignored in this comparison as they show a disproportionate result. However, it should be mentioned that in common with the rest of the line, the total Barnstaple goods tonnage trend was downwards. General merchandise received was still the largest category, being around 60% of the total for most years. The coal/coke tonnage was usually between 25% and 30% of the total. Livestock wagons forwarded and received peaked at 1,228 in 1950 (ignoring the Barnstaple Junction inclusive numbers), albeit showing little change from the figure of 1,185 dealt with in 1946.

APPENDIX 12
STATEMENTS OF TRAFFIC 1876 AND 1877

STATEMENT OF TRAFFIC 1876

Passengers	Tickets				Goods – tons; Cattle – heads; Receipts – £					
Stations	Singles	Returns	Total	Receipts	Coal & Coke	Minerals	Carted	Not Carted	Cattle	Gross Receipts
Milverton	6,416	6,769	13,185	927	1,894	2,997	307	1,947	4,402	1,688
Wiveliscombe	8,809	7,723	16,532	1,694	2,943	3,437	901	5,062	2,564	4,433
Venn Cross	1,554	2,376	3,930	290	80	320	76	1,235	656	558
Morebath	2,751	1,998	4,749	659	1,279	587	384	1,876	1,140	1,634
East Anstey	2,127	2,493	4,620	394	181	2,101	184	1,670	4,400	1,143
Dulverton	4,877	2,470	7,347	1,533	1,438	1,442	726	2,307	4,089	2,798
Molland	2,891	5,098	7,989	489	129	2,283	247	898	4,445	1,068
South Molton	10,820	9,469	20,289	2,278	2,480	9,221	1,896	4,301	7,809	6,769
Castle Hill*	3,548	3,423	6,971	532	576	2,736	114	740	1,253	844
Swimbridge	3,495	4,434	7,929	335	4	1,423	341	1,322	294	938
Barnstaple	22,153	6,745	28,898	6,349	636	2,953	3,492	8,042	1,385	7,553
Total	69,441	52,998	122,439	15,480	11,640	29,500	8,668	29,400	32,437	29,426

STATEMENT OF TRAFFIC 1877

Passengers	Tickets				Goods – tons; Cattle – heads; Receipts – £					
Stations	Singles	Returns	Total	Receipts	Coal & Coke	Minerals	Carted	Not Carted	Cattle	Gross Receipts
Milverton	6,684	6,615	13,299	873	2,545	3,036	240	2,127	3,390	1,715
Wiveliscombe	8,977	7,505	16,482	1,599	4,230	2,408	865	4,556	3,558	4,220
Venn Cross	1,356	2,119	3,475	251	105	293	57	985	407	4,451
Morebath	3,106	2,030	5,136	684	1,687	739	372	1,764	1,655	1,587
East Anstey	2,204	2,604	4,808	414	127	1,426	183	1,757	1,851	1,066
Dulverton	5,132	2,807	7,939	1,438	1,456	2,052	753	1,940	5,124	2,819
Molland	2,513	5,224	7,737	494	155	1850	256	830	4,581	1,053
South Molton	11,924	9,616	21,540	2,365	2,930	6,290	1,907	4,688	10,797	6,633
Castle Hill	3,735	3,707	7,442	602	1,391	1,455	118	610	977	753
Swimbridge	3,357	4,286	7,643	319	0	307	370	1,097	747	997
Barnstaple	31,219	6,298	37,517	6,389	1,204	2,101	2,937	8,231	6,967	7,631
Total	80,207	52,811	133,018	15,428	15,830	21,957	8,058	28,585	40,054	28,919

Note: These tables are reproduced from records held at the National Archives. The stations are listed as shown here, with East Anstey and Dulverton in the wrong geographical order.
*Castle Hill was renamed Filleigh 1st January 1881

APPENDIX 13
A DESCRIPTION OF THE LINE FROM 1892

In the 1892 edition of *Thorough Guides, North Devon and Cornwall*, the reader is taken on a descriptive journey from London (Paddington) to Minehead, Barnstaple and Ilfracombe by the Great Western Railway. The extract covering the Taunton to Barnstaple line is set out here:

'*Taunton to Barnstaple &c. Taunton to Dulverton, 21m; South Molton 34m; Barnstaple 44¹/2m.*

– Dulverton Station (by road) to Simonsbath, 16m; Lynmouth, 25¹/2m.

– South Molton (by road) to North Molton, 3¹/2m; Simonsbath, 10m; Lynton 20m.

This branch, the Devon and Somerset, leaves the main line at the same point as the Minehead branch, Norton Fitzwarren, and a few miles further reaches the southern slopes of Exmoor, which it skirts nearly all the rest of the way to Barnstaple, without anywhere encroaching on the uncultivated part of the moor. Pedestrians wishing to cross Exmoor may with advantage leave the train at Dulverton for Exford, Winsford, Porlock, Simonsbath and Lynton, or at South Molton, for Simonsbath and Lynton only.

The views obtained from the line are at first extensive and richly Devonian in character, though the County of Devon is not finally entered till Dulverton station has been passed [the guide acknowledges that Venn Cross and Morebath stations are in Devon, Dulverton in Somerset]. *The views extend from the Quantock Hills in the north to the Black Downs, which lie on the confines of Somerset and Devon in the south. Conspicuous on the latter is the Wellington Monument, which crowns a spur of the range a few miles from the town of Wellington. The scenery is particularly pleasing in the neighbourhood of Wiveliscombe (9m), where the line makes a long sweep to the right and back again, entering a little way further the Venn Cross Tunnel. Hence nearly all the way to Barnstaple it follows a long shallow depression in the hills, affording no distant views except an occasional glimpse of moorland to the north and rich woodland to the south, from points where it crosses the various streams issuing from Exmoor. Chief amongst these are the Exe and the Barle both of which are crossed just short of Dulverton station.*

For the next dozen miles there is nothing to note until at thirty four miles from Taunton we reach South Molton a little market town (³/4 mile south of the station) on the right bank of the Mole, one of the Exmoor feeders of the Taw. The next station is Castle Hill, in approaching which we cross by viaduct the park of Earl Fortescue, with little Bray, a tributary of the Taw, below. In seven miles further, through pretty but in unremarkable country, we reach Barnstaple.'

APPENDIX 14
A JOURNEY ALONG THE LINE IN 1958

I am grateful to Mr James G. Tawse for permission to use his notes and photographs in respect of a journey he made from Taunton to Barnstaple on Saturday 15th February 1958. This was part of a weekend rail tour of Devon and Somerset, and the whole trip was summarised in *Steam Days* No. 24. The table attached is James's manual record of the run taken from his guard's book-style log.

Having got up early, James first travelled on the 7.24am Taunton to Minehead train and then back to Taunton in time to board the 10.15am train to Barnstaple Junction. 'Mogul' Class '43XX' 2-6-0 No. 6364 was at the head of a three-coach load, consisting of a 1931-built two-coach branch set (the usual 'B-Set') and an additional Composite Corridor Brake. As one of his objectives was to take photographs, James found a compartment to himself in the non-corridor stock, which enabled him to move across the compartment to view either side of the line without bothering other passengers. Having settled into his seat and with the first part of the journey out of the way, his first impressions were of the engine working hard after Wiveliscombe as it climbed to the first summit at Venn Cross. Thereafter it followed a sawtooth-like profile as the line crossed the valleys of several rivers

working time table were not always the same as those shown in the public time table. It was widespread (but not consistent) practice to show public times at intermediate stations either one or two minutes earlier than the working times, with standing instructions that in such cases *'Trains must leave at the advertised times whenever practicable'*. The Western Region applied the practice almost universally, unfortunately resulting in imprecise working and sometimes confusing the staff. On this particular run, public times were half a minute or one minute earlier, except for the two minutes at Dulverton. Thus the porter may well have been protesting that the train was leaving early against public time at 11.24am.

By this time the scenery, which had been rewarding all along, became dramatic as the train emerged from Castle Hill Tunnel, through a wooded cutting and on to Castle Hill Viaduct. Although there was a 15mph restriction over the viaduct, James's records show that they had gained more time, maybe by taking liberties with the speed restrictions at various locations. The train left Filleigh (the next station after the viaduct) two minutes early on public time, although James is doubtful anyone missed it!

MILES	STATION OR LOCATION	BOOKED AM (A/D)	ACTUAL AM	MINS LATE	EXPLANATION	GAINS (ENGINE/STATIONS)
0	Taunton	10.15(d)	10.16 (d)	1	Guard talking with porter	
2	Norton Fitzwarren	10.19/10.20	10.20.5/10.21	1.5	0.5 min signal; light engine crossing	0.5 (s)
6.5	Milverton	10.27.5/10.28.5	10.28/10.28.5			0.5(e)/0.5(s)
9.4	Wiveliscombe	10.34.5/10.36	10.35/10.36	0.5	0.5 min engine	0.5 (s)
14.2	Venn Cross	10.46/10.47	10.46/10.46.5			0.5 (s)
17.8	Morebath	10.52/10.53	10X51.5/10.52		x freight	0.5 (s)
19.2	Morebath Junction		10.55.5/10.56	0.5	Waiting for signalman to exchange token	
19.3	Morebath Jnc Halt	10.57/10.57.5	10.56.5/10.57	1		
21.1	Dulverton	11X01/11.05	11X01.5/11.04		Home signal; crossing train entering (passenger)	1.5 (e)
24.8	East Anstey	11.13/11.14	11.12/11.13			
26.5	Yeo Mill Halt	11.17.5/11.18.5	11.16.5/11.17			0.5 (s)
29.9	Bishops Nympton & M.	11X24/11.25	11X22/11.23		X freight. See also note below *	0.5 (e)
34.2	South Molton	11.32/11.34	11.29.5/11.32.5	1	Some effort to hold train for right time	0.5 (e)
37.5	Filleigh	11.42/11.43	11.39/11.40			1.5 (e)
40.9	Swimbridge	11.49/11.50	11.45.5/11.48	1.5	Some effort to hold train for right time	0.5 (e)
44.7/0	Barnstaple VR	11.56/12.05pm	11.54/12.01			2 (s)
1.8	Barnstaple Jnc	12.10 (a)	12.06 (a)			

*After departure the porter gave a hand signal for the train to stop but it did not. The guard merely waved cheerfully!

TRAIN CONSIST: COACH TYPE	NUMBER	TONS
Brake composite (BC)-B Set	W6372W	30.5
Brake composite (BC)-B Set	W6371W	30.5
Brake composite corridor (BCK)	W6579W	31

running down from Exmoor. East Anstey marked the second major summit at 700 feet.

There was little of operating note in the early stages of the run, save for the crossing of a short goods train at Morebath, with classmate No. 6398 in charge.

At Dulverton, the 10.00am Barnstaple Junction to Taunton service crossed James's Down train and a Class '45XX' 2-6-2T was simmering on the connecting Exe Valley train in the bay platform. Another goods crossed at Bishops Nympton & Molland station (most likely the 9.55am from Victoria Road to Taunton). At this point time was being gained on the schedule. As the train pulled away the porter waved up as if to stop it but the guard misinterpreted the signal and merely waved cheerfully back as they headed west.

As James explained, the station departure times shown in the

No. 6398 runs into Morebath's Up loop with a Taunton-bound goods, crossing with the Down train carrying the photographer on 15th February 1958. *James G. Tawse*

APPENDIX 15: GWR NOTICE 9TH JULY 1920, REOPENING OF BARNSTAPLE EAST LOOP

Notice No. 113.

PRIVATE, AND NOT FOR PUBLICATION.

GREAT WESTERN RAILWAY.

EXETER DISTRICT.

(For the use of the Company's Servants only.)

NOTICE TO ENGINEMEN AND ALL CONCERNED.

FRIDAY, JULY 9th, 1920.

RE-OPENING OF THE DIRECT JUNCTION LOOP LINE AND EAST AND SOUTH JUNCTION SIGNAL BOXES AT BARNSTAPLE.

The direct Junction Loop Line between the Great Western and London and South Western Lines at Barnstaple will be re-opened on Friday, July 9th, the East and South Junction Boxes at Barnstaple, and the Signals for these Boxes will again be brought into use.

PLAN OF LOOP.

Trains from Taunton to Ilfracombe which pass over the Loop must have the Coaches formed in the following order:—Engine, Coaches for Ilfracombe, Coaches for Barnstaple.

Trains to Ilfracombe will run to the Home Signal or clear of the points as required at the Barnstaple South Junction Box. Station Master, Barnstaple, will arrange for an Engine, accompanied by a Traffic Department man, to be waiting at the South Junction Down Home Signal. On arrival of the Train, the Traffic Department man will divide it, and send the Ilfracombe portion forward, after attaching the side and tail lamps. He will then place a tail lamp on the Barnstaple portion, and accompany it as Guard to the Station.

Trains from, Ilfracombe and Barnstaple to Taunton will be dealt with in like manner, The Engine and Coaches from Ilfracombe will run to the East Junction Loop Home Signal, and the Coaches from Barnstaple Station will be attached to the Coaches from Ilfracombe as shewn in the Exeter District Coach Working Programme, after which the Train will proceed to Taunton.

Trains from Taunton which run direct into Barnstaple Station must be formed at Taunton in the following manner:—Engine, Barnstaple Coaches, Ilfracombe Coaches (if any) ; and the method of working will be as at present.

Station Master, Taunton, to instruct his Staff, when the Barnstaple Branch Trains are being dealt with at Taunton, that the Passengers and Luggage for Stations on the L. & S.W.R. System must be placed in the proper portion of the Trains, and to thoroughly examine the Trains, in order to ascertain that the Passengers are in their proper compartments.

The Station Masters at Norton Fitzwarren and on the Barnstaple Branch must also pay particular attention to this and see that everything possible is done to place the Passengers and stow the Luggage in the proper portions of the Train, and if a vehicle is attached *en route* Barnstaple must at once be advised.

On FRIDAY, JULY 9th, 1920,

Between 6·0 a.m. and 12·0 noon, the East and South Junction Boxes at Barnstaple will be re-opened.

The Telegraphic arrangements will be as follows :—

Electric Train Staff Block System and Telephone Circuit between East Junction and Swimbridge.

Single Line Disc Block and Bell communication between Barnstaple G.W. Station Box and East Junction.

Single Line Disc Block and Bell communication between Barnstaple East and South Junction Boxes.

Preece's 3-Wire Single Line Block communication between Barnstaple G.W. Station Box and South Junction Box.

Preece's 3-Wire Single Line Block communication between South Junction and Barnstaple L. & S.W. Box.

Telephonic communication between G.W. Station Box, East and South Junction Boxes, Booking Office and Goods Office.

Telephonic communication at the South Junction Box on the Barnstaple G.W. Parcels Office—Barnstaple L. & S.W. Booking Office circuit.

Single Needle speaking communication at East Junction Box on the Taunton-Barnstaple circuit.

The Electric Train Staff Exchanging Apparatus will be brought into use at the East Junction Box, and taken out of use at the Station Box.

An Engine to be available during the morning of July 9th, to test the road as required by the Permanent Way Department.

On and from FRIDAY, JULY 9th,

The Train Staff Sections and the Working will be as under:—

Electric Staff System	} Between Swimbridge and the Barnstaple East Junction Box.
Train Staff and Ticket System	} Between East Junction Box and Barnstaple Station Box.
Train Staff and Ticket System	} Between Barnstaple Station Box and South Junction Box.
Train Staff and Ticket System	} Between South Junction Box and the L. & S.W. Junction Box.
Train Staff and Ticket System	} Between East Junction and South Junction Boxes only.

2

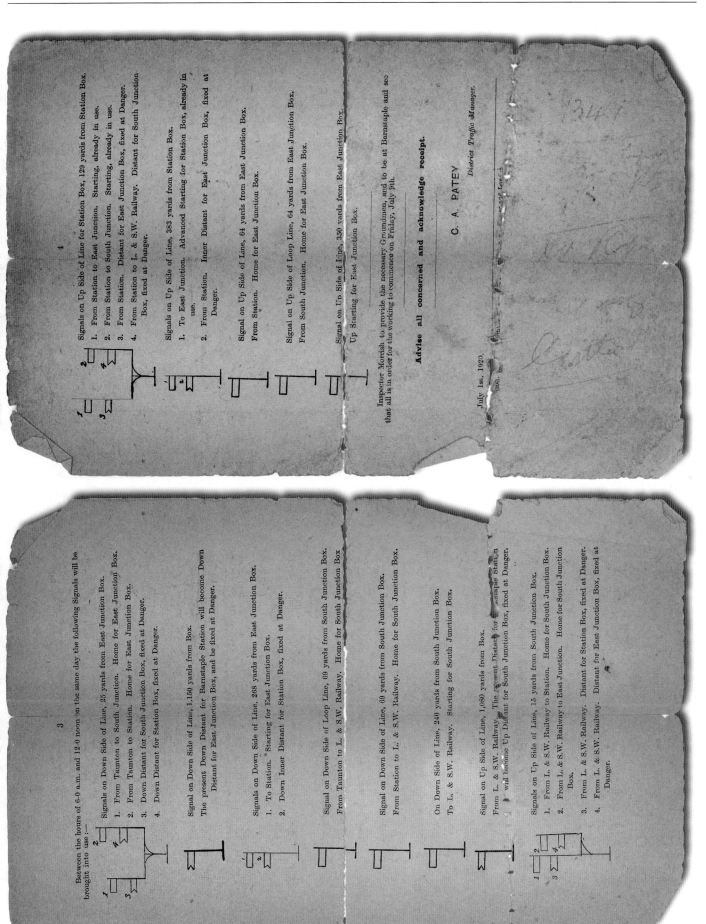

4

Signals on Up Side of Line for Station Box, 129 yards from Station Box.
1. From Station to East Junction. Starting, already in use.
2. From Station to South Junction. Starting, already in use.
3. From Station. Distant for East Junction Box, fixed at Danger.
4. From Station to L. & S.W. Railway. Distant for South Junction Box, fixed at Danger.

Signals on Up Side of Line, 383 yards from Station Box.
1. To East Junction. Advanced Starting for Station Box, already in use.
2. From Station. Inner Distant for East Junction Box, fixed at Danger.

Signal on Up Side of Line, 64 yards from East Junction Box.
From Station. Home for East Junction Box.

Signal on Up Side of Loop Line, 64 yards from East Junction Box.
From South Junction. Home for East Junction Box.

Signal on Up Side of Line, 350 yards from East Junction Box.
Up Starting for East Junction Box.

Advise all concerned and acknowledge receipt.

C. A. PATEY
District Traffic Manager,

July 1st, 1920.

(500).

Inspector Morrish to provide the necessary Groundmen, and to be at Barnstaple and see that all is in order for the working to commence on Friday, July 9th.

3

Between the hours of 6-0 a.m. and 12-0 noon on the same day the following Signals will be brought into use :—

Signals on Down Side of Line, 25 yards from East Junction Box.
1. From Taunton to South Junction. Home for East Junction Box.
2. From Taunton to Station. Home for East Junction Box.
3. Down Distant for South Junction Box, fixed at Danger.
4. Down Distant for Station Box, fixed at Danger.

Signal on Down Side of Line, 1,150 yards from Box.
The present Down Distant for Barnstaple Station will become Down Distant for East Junction Box, and be fixed at Danger.

Signals on Down Side of Line, 268 yards from East Junction Box.
1. To Station. Starting for East Junction Box.
2. Down Inner Distant for Station Box, fixed at Danger.

Signal on Down Side of Loop Line, 69 yards from South Junction Box.
From Taunton to L. & S.W. Railway. Home for South Junction Box.

Signal on Down Side of Line, 69 yards from South Junction Box.
From Station to L. & S.W. Railway. Home for South Junction Box.

On Down Side of Line, 240 yards from South Junction Box.
To L. & S.W. Railway. Starting for South Junction Box.

Signal on Up Side of Line, 1,080 yards from Box.
From L. & S.W. Railway. The present Distant for ...staple Station will become Up Distant for South Junction Box, fixed at Danger.

Signals on Up Side of Line, 15 yards from South Junction Box.
1. From L. & S.W. Railway to Station. Home for South Junction Box.
2. From L. & S.W. Railway to East Junction. Home for South Junction Box.
3. From L. & S.W. Railway. Distant for Station Box, fixed at Danger.
4. From L. & S.W. Railway. Distant for East Junction Box, fixed at Danger.

No. 1466 waits in the Exe Valley bay at Dulverton for a connecting Taunton to Barnstaple line train in the early 1960s. The Collett 0-4-2T was allocated to Exeter shed from April 1961 to withdrawal in December 1963. The box vans visible alongside the Up platform indicate that some shunting is under way, probably a pick-up goods collecting some wagons for Taunton or dropping a couple off in the Up yard. On the right there is a good view of the 6-ton yard crane and the coal yard beyond. *Courtesy The Lens of Sutton Association*

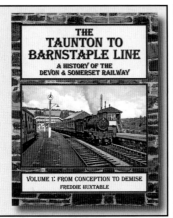

THE
TAUNTON TO BARNSTAPLE LINE
A HISTORY OF THE
DEVON & SOMERSET RAILWAY

VOLUME 1:
FROM CONCEPTION TO DEMISE

FREDDIE HUXTABLE

232 pages, gloss art paper
colour laminated board covers
ISBN 9781911038 15 3
Price £25 (+ £4 p&p)

CONTENTS – VOLUME 3
WORKING THE LINE

CONTENTS – VOLUME 1
FROM CONCEPTION TO DEMISE